The Common Ground
A PLACE FOR NATURE IN BRITAIN'S FUTURE?

RICHARD MABEY

The Common Ground

A PLACE FOR NATURE IN BRITAIN'S FUTURE?

HUTCHINSON

London Melbourne Sydney Auckland Johannesburg

in association with the
Nature Conservancy Council

Hutchinson & Co. (Publishers) Ltd

An imprint of the Hutchinson Publishing Group

3 Fitzroy Square, London W1P 6JD

Hutchinson Group (Australia) Pty Ltd
30–32 Cremorne Street, Richmond South, Victoria 3121
PO Box 151, Broadway, New South Wales 2007

Hutchinson Group (NZ) Ltd
32–34 View Road, PO Box 40–086, Glenfield, Auckland 10

Hutchinson Group (SA) (Pty) Ltd
PO Box 337, Bergvlei 2012, South Africa

First published 1980

© Richard Mabey 1980

Set in Palatino by Input Typesetting Ltd

Printed and bound in Great Britain by
William Clowes (Beccles) Limited, Beccles and London

British CIP Data
Mabey, Richard
  The common ground.
  1. Nature conservation – Great Britain
  I. Title II. Nature Conservancy Council
  639'.9'0941   QH77.G7

ISBN 0 09 139170 9

Contents

Illustrations

Plates

COLOUR

(*between pages 48 and 49*)
Lady orchid
Natural images
Buttercup meadows

(*between pages 80 and 81*)
Pollards
Tree lungwort lichen
Bluebells under old hornbeam coppice
House martins
Baby seal
Common buzzard

(*between pages 144 and 145*)
Corncrake in meadow
Swans in the Ouse Washes
Woodwalton Fen
Blue-tailed damselfly
Langstone Harbour in 'false colour'
Cornflower

(*between pages 208 and 209*)
Large blue butterfly
Southern heathlands
Pine marten

8

In the text

ILLUSTRATION ACKNOWLEDGEMENTS

Illustrations are reproduced by courtesy of the following:

Between pages 48 and 49: lady orchid – John Mason/NCC; Chequered Skipper sign – John Mason/NCC; a place in town – *Daily Telegraph*; flower o' the corn – London Transport; osprey sign – *Daily Telegraph*; buttercup meadows – Derek Ratcliffe/NCC.

Between pages 80 and 81: pollard willow poster – ©1979 Pentamedia BV, Flerdaan 41, Naarden, Holland; tree lungwort lichen – Heather Angel; bluebells – Richard Mabey; house martins – Joe Van Wormer/Bruce Coleman Ltd; baby seal – Alan McGregor; common buzzard – Alan McGregor.

Between pages 144 and 145: corncrake – Alan McGregor; swans in the Ouse Washes – John Mason/NCC; Woodwalton Fen – John Mason/NCC; blue-tailed damselfly – John Mason/NCC; Langstone Harbour – © University of Cambridge; cornflower – Christopher Grey-Wilson.

Between pages 208 and 209: large blue butterfly – David G. Measures; nightjar – Frank V. Blackburn; Studland and Godlingston Heaths – J. Rees Cox/NCC; pine marten – R. Balharry/The Natural History Photographic Agency.

Between pages 240 and 241: field cow-wheat – Kenneth J. Adams, from *The Flora of Essex* by Stanley Jermyn, published by the Essex Naturalists' Trust Ltd; Ynyslas dunes and board-walk – Robin Bovey/NCC; viper's-bugloss, village pond, dead elms and black poplars, and Wylye churchyard – Richard Mabey.

Between pages 112 and 113: hen harriers feeding – Donald Watson, from *The Hen Harrier* by Donald Watson, published by T. & A. D. Poyser Ltd, original drawing lent by Bill Jackson; collared dove – Dennis Green/RSPB; Cetti's warbler – M. D. England/Ardea, London; still life with lichens – David Richardson, from *The Vanishing Lichens* by David Richardson, published by David & Charles Ltd; surveying meadows – Jean Ross; oak standards – W. H. Palmer, from *Hayley Wood* by Oliver Rackham, published by the Cambridgeshire and Isle of Ely Naturalists' Trust Ltd; Scottish pinewoods – Derek Ratcliffe/NCC; pollard oak in Moccas Park – J. Cooter; deer parks: Moccas Park – J. Cooter; Bradgate Park – David T. Grewcock; ant-hills – Peter Wakely/NCC.

Between pages 192 and 193: waste ground under Spaghetti Junction – Peter Wakely, from *The Endless Village* by W. G. Teagle, published by the NCC (West Midlands Region); agricultural landscapes – from *New Agricultural Landscapes* published by the Countryside Commission; harvesting reeds – Eastern Counties Newspapers Ltd; Minsmere car park – Jeremy Sorensen; avocet – Michael W. Richards/RSPB; osprey – Eric Hosking/RSPB; ducks over the Thames – Pamela Harrison, FRPS; otter – from the film *Tarka the Otter*, the Rank Organisation; greater horseshoe bat – Eric Hosking; Woodchester Mansion – Peter Wakely/NCC, (photo montage by Peter Dorp); ecological industry – Tom Taylor; timber trees at Ham Street Woods – NCC (South-East Region).

In text: elm leaves – Dr R. H. Richens, reproduced from Dr Richens' *Studies on Ulmus: VII Essex Elms*; plan of Hatfield Forest – Oliver Rackham, from *Trees and Woodland in the British Landscape* by Oliver Rackham, published by J. M. Dent & Sons Ltd; Dorset maps: heathland – from a paper by N. R. Webb and L. E. Haskins, *An Ecological Survey of Heathland in the Poole Basin, Dorset, England*, first published in Biological Conservation, 17(4), June 1980; chalk downland – condensed and simplified from A. Carys Jones, *The Conservation of Chalk Downland in Dorset*, published by Dorset County Planning Department, 1973; Broads diagram – from *The Future of Broadland*, published by the NCC; Castor Hanglands – from NCC document.

Foreword by the Chairman of the Nature Conservancy Council, Fred Holliday

> Oh wad some pow'r the giftie gie us
> To see oursels as others see us.

These oft-quoted words by Robert Burns are an especially appropriate introduction to this book. It was written at the instigation of the Nature Conservancy Council; we felt it important that people should know more about nature conservation, warts and all, so that public debate of the issues that arise increasingly often could be on a more fully informed basis. But those deeply engaged in the day-to-day operations of an agency are unable to take the same detached view of its ideals and affairs as a well-informed 'outsider'.

We approached Richard Mabey and were delighted that he accepted the suggestion. But it is his book. He has visited many of our offices and nature reserves and had discussions with many of our staff, but he was free to make his own judgements on what he included and concluded, and it is written in his own style and from his own viewpoint.

The Common Ground is, then, *not* an expression of the views and policies of the Nature Conservancy Council; but it is a book that I commend for its grasp of the problems, its insight into the important issues and, perhaps most importantly, its feel for the subject. The author so well conveys the inspiration and pleasure that so many concerned with nature conservation find in it and the commitment they give to it.

Laws are necessary in all aspects of our complex modern life. They can be designed to compel, to set standards and to give powers to those whose duty it is to act on our behalf. We have all such types of laws for nature conservation in Britain but, without wide understanding of and support for its objectives, legislation is severely restricted in what it can achieve. Richard Mabey recognizes that, to be effective, nature conservation policy must call upon a wide range of approaches and methods – that it entails conserving species and their habitats, but also influencing people's attitudes and actions and capturing their interest and imagination.

The Nature Conservancy Council is the official agency set up by Parliament 'for the purposes of nature conservation and fostering the understanding thereof'. I stress the word 'foster', because it has never been the intention that nature conservation should be done by the NCC alone. It involves a partnership with all sorts of men and women acting both individually and through organizations. The more there are who understand and care about the subject and its problems, the more fruitful will that partnership be and to the greater benefit of all of us. This book should help in achieving that goal.

Fred Holliday

Preface and Acknowledgements

When the Nature Conservancy Council suggested to me in the summer of 1977 that I might write, with their support, a book to 'widen the public debate on nature conservation', they generously insisted that their association with the book would in no way imply any restrictions on the expression of my own opinions. It would, I think, have been a sign of an ominously closed mind if the experience of working on this book had not caused me to change some of these opinions; indeed, though a few have hardened, others have been reversed. But my *viewpoint* – that of a concerned member of the public – has necessarily remained the same, and if there is a single perspective running through this book it is that of the ordinary 'consumer' of wildlife, which seems to me the viewpoint most commonly overlooked. I hope I have steered clear of offering didactic 'solutions' to the problems facing conservation at present: what 'the debate' needs is an inquisitive and open-minded discussion between all parties, not a laying down of the law. So whilst I have tried to represent fairly the viewpoints of those many parties who have an interest in the natural world – landowners, foresters, scientists, committed naturalists – and have concentrated on trying to make current scientific thinking about conservation more accessible to a wider audience, I have also felt it important – I hope not presumptuously – to try and present the *public's* view of conservation to the professionals.

But I think I can say that, thanks to the NCC and the many others who helped me with this book, I have become a rather better informed member of the public! During the intensive period of research work on the book in 1978 I was privileged to be given free access to many internal NCC documents, and to visit sites that I might never otherwise have seen. So my acknowledgment to the many helpers listed below – who gave me so much of their time and experience, talked to me at great length, read and commented on sections of the manuscript, provided photographs, guided me on field expeditions, ferried me about and, with their families, frequently fed and accommodated me – is not just an appreciation of the immense contribution they have made to the book, but a personal expression of thanks for making my research work such a pleasant and rewarding experience. If not all the places I visited or the stories I was told have found their way into the final text, they all played their part in shaping it.

(The list below gives the organizations to which those named were attached at the time I met them.)

In the NCC itself, my thanks to Professor Fred Holliday, the Chairman, and Bob Boote, the Director General, and to

John and Phil Arnott
George Barker
Tim Bines
Nettie Bonnar
Ian Bonner
Robin Bovey
Morton Boyd
Roger Bray
Tony Cadwalladr
Neill Campbell
Ian Carr
Arnold Cooke
Rees Cox
Peter Walters Davies
Peter Davis
Eve Dennis
Edward Devereux
Pat Doody
Mike D'Oyly
Brian Ducker
John Duffield
Lynne Farrell
Ian Findlay
Helga Frankland
Chris Fuller
Peter Gay

Martin George
Russell Gomm
David Goode
Andrew Graham
Robin Hamilton
Roy Harris
David Harvey
Philip Horton
Michael Hudson
Eddie Idle
Don Jefferies
Alexander Kerr
Noel King
Michael Labern
Art Lance
Stuart Lane
Derek Langslow
Joanna Martin
Gordon Mason
John Mason
Maurice Massey
Michael Matthew
John Maylam
Bill McKenzie
Roger Mitchell
Norman Moore

John Morley
Peter Mountford
Martin Musgrave
Chris Newbold
Peter Nicholson
Brian O'Connor
George Peterken
Tom Pritchard
Colin Ranson
Derek Ratcliffe
Michael Rawes
Jean Ross
Philip Rothwell
Malcolm Rush
Michael Schofield
Peter Schofield

Dick Seamons
Keith Selmes
John Shackles
Chris Shaw
Bridget Smith
Alan Stubbs
John Thompson
Marion Thomson
Ian Tillotson
Colin Tubbs
Michael Tuck
Peter Wakely
Derek Wells
Rob Williams
David Withrington

From the Institute of Terrestrial Ecology: Max Hooper, Franklyn Perring, Jeremy Thomas, Michael Way and Terry Wells.

From the Royal Society for the Protection of Birds, who gave their whole-hearted support to the book from the very beginning: Ian Prestt, the Director, and John Crudass, Chief Reserves Officer; Colin Bibby, Nicholas Hammond and Gerald Searle; and wardens Clifford Carson in the Ouse Washes, Tony Pickup at Dungeness, and Jeremy Sorensen at Minsmere.

From the Nature Conservation Trusts: C. R. Cuthbert from the Gloucestershire Trust; Elizabeth Eyden from Somerset; Edgar Milne-Redhead and Evangeline Dickson from Suffolk.

The County Planning Departments of Norfolk and Hertfordshire also gave me every assistance, and I should like to thank R. I. Maxwell, J. R. Matthews and P. N. G. Hardy in Norfolk, and David Overton, Mike Crafer and Peter Lawrence in Hertfordshire.

Many friends and helpers were unstinting with their advice and hospitality: Eddie Anderson, Tim Appleton, warden at Rutland Water, Nigel Ashby, Mr and Mrs Ash of the West Wales Farm Park, Professor Tony Bradshaw of the Department of Botany, Liverpool University, David and Janet Cobham, Arthur Childs at Melbury Park, Lyndis Cole of Land Use Consultants, Richard Cooper of the Suffolk Trust for Conservation Volunteers, Philip Coxon, Gigi Crompton, Alan Cummins, David Dymond, Basil Garnons-Williams, Mr and Mrs Hack of the Rake

Factory at Whelnetham, Rachel Hamilton, James Hart, warden of the Bradfield Woods, Nick and Chris Hepher, John James of the Woodland Trust, Peter Lambley of Norwich Castle Museum, Mr and Mrs Martin of Rookery Farm, Suffolk, Mr and Mrs Oddie of Clattinger Farm, Wiltshire, Wendy Pettigrew of the National Conservation Corps, Jeffery Preece and Harry Lees at Hams Hall, Oliver Rackham, Dr R. H. Richens, Francis Rose, Elizabeth Roy, J. T. R. Sharrock, Marion Sherratt, Charles Sinker, the Hon. A. D. Tryon of the Great Bustard Trust, and Justin Ward.

At Hutchinson, thanks to Terence Blacker, and Carol O'Brien, and to Joanna Sutherland for performing the onerous business of organizing the illustrations so efficiently.

Particular thanks to Robin McIntosh, my personal assistant, who helped with some of the research and deciphered and typed many successive drafts of the manuscript; to Francesca Greenoak, who at every stage of the research and writing was, as usual, a pillar of wisdom and support; and finally to Philip Oswald, the NCC's Head of Publicity who, with Peter Gay, first suggested the idea of the book, and throughout its progress helped me keep my sense of perspective, fed me with encouragement, inspiration and a continuous flow of ideas and information, arranged many of my field trips (and was even able to make time from his own very busy life to accompany me on some of them) and endured my moods and blocks with patience and understanding.

None of these people has any responsibility for any errors, misrepresentations or omissions in the text, or any of the opinions expressed in it, which are mine alone. I suspect that some of my views will not be shared by the people who have given so generously of their time and experience over the last two years, but I know they will appreciate that a book on a subject so intrinsically complex and emotionally potent must, in the end, be a personal statement. At its roots, nature conservation seems to me to be a human celebration of the diversity of life, and perhaps a recognition of our own diversity is the first step we have to take towards this.

RICHARD MABEY, Berkhamsted, 1979.

PART ONE
Perspectives

PROLOGUE

I often pulled my hat over my eyes to watch the rising of the lark, or to see the hawk hang in the summer sky and the kite take its circles round the wood. I often lingered a minute on the woodland stile to hear the woodpigeons clapping their wings among the dark oaks. I hunted curious flowers in rapture and muttered thoughts in their praise. I loved the pasture with its rushes and thistles and sheep-tracks. I adored the wild, marshy fen with its solitary heronshaw sweeing along in its melancholy sky. I wandered the heath in raptures among the rabbit burrows and golden-blossomed furze. I dropt down on a thymy mole-hill or mossy eminence to survey the summer land-scape. . . . I marked the various colours in flat, spreading fields, check-ered into closes of different-tinctured grain like the colours of a map; the copper-tinted clover in blossom; the sun-tanned green of the ripen-ing hay; the lighter charlock and the sunset imitation of the scarlet headaches; the blue corn-bottles crowding their splendid colours in large sheets over the land and troubling the cornfields with destroying beauty; the different greens of the woodland trees, the dark óak, the paler ash, the mellow lime, the white poplars peeping above the rest like leafy steeples, the grey willow shining in the sun, as if the morning mist still lingered on its cool green. . . . I observed all this with the same raptures as I have done since. But I knew nothing of poetry. It was felt and not uttered.

JOHN CLARE, from *The Autobiography*[1]

It is ironic that, of all the descriptions and celebrations that have come down to us from the English countryside's supposed golden past, it is the works of John Clare that we are turning to more and more for some kind of solace in its troubled present. Clare was a self-taught farm labourer, not a scientist or cam-paigning politician. He was writing nearly 150 years ago – cer-tainly a time of great agricultural upheaval, but hardly bothered by the kind of land-use conflicts we face today. Yet his writings touch with uncanny accuracy our own affections and worries.

There is the detail of the landscape: the heron in a fenland sky, the gorse in blossom on the heath. There is the image of a pattern of agriculture still of a piece with the natural world. And there is that underlying sense of poignancy and loss, not just of a particular countryside, but of a spontaneous, unfettered experience of it that seems – almost by the act of recollection – to belong irretrievably in the past.

Clare lived through the statutory enclosure of his native village. He witnessed the end of Helpston's open-field system, the fencing and ploughing of the common fens and pastures of Emmonsales Heath, and the break-up of a pattern of life that had survived relatively intact since the establishment of the manorial system 800 years before. Out of that traumatic experience came what is perhaps the most powerful of all his poems, the elegy for his lost homeland which he called 'Remembrances'. It still reads like a battle hymn. One by one the casualties are listed: 'Langley bush . . . old eastwell's boiling spring . . . pleasant Swordy well'. And bitterly, sharply, the culprit – 'the axe of spoiler and self interest' – is identified:

> And crossberry way and old round oaks narrow lane
> With its hollow trees like pulpits I shall never see again
> Inclosure like a buonaparte let not a thing remain
> It levelled every bush and tree and levelled every hill
> And hung the moles for traitors – though the brook is running still
> It runs a naked stream and chill

It is in this poem, perhaps more than any other, that we can trace the source of our sympathy with Clare. It is not just that what is under attack seems to be precisely the same now as it was then. I think that what we recognize more is the sense of affront, of an invasion of personal territory by forces beyond our control. Clare was describing a transformation in the fabric of rural England in terms of the destruction of specific features by identified agents. Yet they are not just particularized, they are *personalized*. Those were *his* trees, *his* brooks, *his* moles – not by virtue of ownership, but of *familiarity*. And it is this that joins us across a century and a half, for with losses that close to the heart it makes not a jot of difference if the cause is an enclosing landlord or a new motorway.

It is as well to make it clear at the outset that my own commitment to nature conservation originates – as I suspect it does for most people – in just such a sense of personal loss. In the last twenty-five years I have seen my own countryside transformed in ways that follow almost exactly those witnessed by Clare, and have found my own responses to these changes echoing his. The stretch of the Chilterns in which I grew up, my 'home range', was (though I did not realize it at the time) a compact medieval relic, a square mile of ancient woods, hedges and pastures flanking the sides of a shallow river valley. The stream was a winterbourne, a 'woe-water', supposed to flow in full spate only in times of war or trouble. When I was a teenager the valley was threatened with what was to become a familiar shadow across Britain's countryside: the prospect of a six-lane motorway along one of its sides. As it happened, the road was postponed, resurrected, postponed again, and still has not materialized. Yet in the twenty years that have passed since it was first mooted, the landscape it would have crossed has changed in ways almost as drastic as if it had been covered by tarmac. Not far short of half the hedges have been grubbed out. A thirty-acre primrose copse was cleared for wheat with such speed that I wondered if my memory of playing in it as a child was a fantasy. The woe-water, ironically, vanished underground, and the hollow oaks and ashes that lined it (which had once had three species of owl nesting in them) were felled one by one. One spring I found the steep pastures where I used to pick mushrooms covered with unfamiliar white granules, and within a few years not only the mushrooms had vanished but the cowslips as well.

As I grew up I learnt all the received justifications for this: world starvation, a national economic recession, an expanding population. Yet all I saw then was the rich landowners getting richer, the poorer farmers having to sell up, and a stabilizing population whose national obsession seemed to be finding ways of eating less. I understand the real force behind some of these pressures now (and the private interests concealed in others). Yet I find it no easier to accept the way they so often casually ride over the interests not just of different individuals but of whole communities. And though we are now beginning to realize the wider importance of the natural world – even the small fragments remaining on these islands – I do not feel that this makes the *personal* case for nature conservation any less important. There are, after all, many millions of people who have such a case.

The greatest shock in the present transformation is that it has come about not so much from an invasion by urban sprawl or industrial development, but from insidious and often unobserved changes in the internal workings of the countryside itself. We were not prepared for this. The attacks upon the countryside that accelerated in the expansionist years after the Second World War had made the conflict seem a very clear and traditional one. It was the green fields of St George's England versus the dragons of Mammon and industry: open-cast mining, oil refineries, nuclear power stations, new airports. Seeing the fields apparently changing colour of their own accord produced a considerable sense of confusion not only about the morality of conservation but about the particular objectives towards which it was directed. It was one thing to question the need for new motorways when oil looked like running out by the end of the century; but quite another to press for what seemed like obstructions to the production of more food for a hungry world or to ways of easing the labour of men who worked the land. If we wanted to keep our wildlife, would we have to begin regarding it as another article of trade between countryside and consumer – perhaps even begin *paying* for it, as we did for bread and beer and newsprint? When it was put that baldly it seemed an alien and offensive suggestion, an infringement of a natural right that would be on a par with having to pay for air or sunshine. It also seemed, in some less definable way, to debase one of the intrinsic values of nature, which is – and it is not a truism to say so – its *naturalness*.

Nature has always had this double meaning for us, being a matter of style as much as of content, a way of being as much as a collection of particular living things. For much of our history the two had run parallel, and the 'natural things' – the bluebells and the butterflies – had appeared 'naturally', without effort or planning. That was part of their appeal. But the radical changes brought about by the new agriculture made us sharply aware that what we had regarded as a natural landscape was a much more complex product of growth and husbandry. The turf of the southern chalk downs, which W. H. Hudson christened 'the living garment', turned out to be the product of intensive sheep-grazing. A good deal of it had once been under the plough and before that the site of Celtic forts and townships. The wild sweeps of moorland in the Scottish Highlands had been created by a massive programme of forest clearance. The

Norfolk Broads were the flooded remains of medieval open-cast peat-mines. Heaths and reedbeds would cease to exist if they were not deliberately cut or burnt. Even the new protectiveness itself seems to compromise the natural world with a slight hint of preciousness. Could we really use the word 'natural' about orchids which depended on artificial pollination for their survival, or butterflies that had to be bred in tented enclosures?

These new realizations raised many fundamental questions. If part of what we valued about nature was its wildness and spontaneity, was deliberate nature conservation a contradiction in terms? Was the familiar picture of British wildlife we had inherited, and which was captured so perfectly by Clare, already an anachronism, on a par with the perennial nostalgia for some pastoral Golden Age? Had the time come for us, as products of late-twentieth-century industrialization, to 'grow out' of the natural world? We could always save its bits and pieces in zoos and botanic gardens if we wished. If we preferred to be thoroughly modern we could even make them out of plastic, as was seriously suggested in a report produced by a senior official in the Department of the Environment:

The city of the future must be clean and green, safe and sound. . . . I suggest that a landscape architect visits Kew Gardens and selects typical specimens of endangered species, e.g. elm and beech with prevalent urban species, e.g. the London plane. Casts could then be taken of the selected specimens – trunks and boughs would be moulded glass-reinforced plastic. Foliage would be polythene. The tree would be bonfire and vandal proof. Foliage would be self-extinguishing.[2]

This line of argument leads us, quite clearly, into a dead-end. Seeing the structures that traditionally supported our wildlife slipping away – apparently for the very best of reasons – we have been casting about for some new, *contemporary* role for our wildlife, perhaps even for a new wildlife. We have looked at the possibilities of an urbanized nature, a fascinating world of opportunist organisms in its own right, but one which contains very few of the plants and animals we are most familiar with. We are thinking about creating entirely new 'natural' landscapes in the corners left over by intensive agriculture. We have invented the notion of the 'living museum', which, whilst it would not literally contain plastic trees, nevertheless suggests the depressing idea that our remaining wildlife might become a collection of living fossils. We have become aware that the survival of the network of wildlife on the planet may be inextricably connected with our own survival, and we argue this very persuasively, though we know it is an intellectual defence, a kind of 'nature in the head'. And none of these alternatives comes anywhere near to making up for what we are losing. The dispiriting procession of transient, unfamiliar, distant experiences they offer makes us realize that what we want from conservation is not a museum of nature, a remote collection of undifferentiaed wild 'things', but the community of distinct, familiar forms that is part of our cultural history.

And this brings us back full circle to Clare. Clare was not concerned about the maintenance of a viable breeding population of moles, or the extinction of *Quercus robur*, but about the brutal appropriation of living things that were not just part of his private experience but of the community in which he lived. And, unlike us, he was close enough to what was happening not be fooled by promises that it was all for his own good. He took for granted what we are only just beginning to appreciate, that conservation is concerned ultimately with *relationships*, between man and nature, and man and man.

The one occasion in recent years when this has been made abundantly clear was the drama over the proposed seal-cull in the Orkneys in the autumn of 1978. For a long time small numbers of seals have been killed each autumn by local fishermen, but in 1977 the Department of Agriculture and Fisheries for Scotland (DAFS) had begun a six-year programme designed to reduce the number of grey seals in Scottish waters (about half the world's population) by a quarter, because they were believed to be making serious inroads into local cod and salmon stocks.[3] Against a background of seal slaughter in many parts of the world, the level of the new culling programme triggered off international opposition and national outrage. Greenpeace's famous converted trawler, *Rainbow Warrior*, entered the fray – acting in a sense as the public's 'presence' – and positioned itself between the Norwegian marksmen and the seals. A broadly-based consortium of voluntary conservation bodies challenged the scientific basis of the culling programme, and in particular the assumption that fish taken by seals would otherwise be caught. The consortium also criticized the failure to provide an adequate model of the complex relationship between seals, prey species and the many other predators that were taking economically valuable fish (notably the factory trawlers operating just outside the fishing limits), and suggested that the DAFS might be using the seals as a scapegoat for bad fisheries management. In the face of this evident public concern the Secretary of State for Scotland cancelled the proposed cull whilst more solid evidence about the relationship between seals and fish stocks was obtained.

By the time this book is published some of this evidence may be available. Yet it is unlikely to make very much difference to public feelings about culling, for at its root the conflict has very little to do with whether or not seals cause damage to fisheries, but concerns the status they have in our culture. It is the killing itself, not its level, that is at issue. It was quite clear during the confrontation of 1978 that for most of the British public the seal has become a totem – just as, by many of the local fishermen, it is looked on as a pest. Who is to say who has the prior claim? And that is, very precisely, the *practical* problem as well as a rhetorical question. It cannot be answered by ecologists and agriculturalists alone, nor by attempting to reduce what are essentially moral problems to scientific ones.

We will find the same difficulties echoed in every issue discussed in this book. On the surface the problems of conservation present themselves as practical ones: how to manage woods so that they produce timber at the same time as sustaining wildlife, which areas of countryside are best used as farmland and which as nature reserves. Yet underneath there are more fundamental and less easily resolved conflicts of values – about who can legitimately be said to 'own' natural resources, about the rights of humans and animals, about the relative importance of present livelihoods and past traditions – conflicts which involve deeply held personal beliefs and meanings.

In the context of these conflicts, this book could be looked on as the natural world's 'case for the defence'. I have explored the issues at both levels, practical and ethical, but always the argument ends with questions of value and meaning which, like all such questions, can only be answered in a social context by a continuing *cultural* debate. We are likely to find that what begins in personal affections and commitment will ultimately have to be expressed in personal initiatives; but in the meantime we have to work our way through that cultural argument, and begin by asking whether our relationships with the natural world have indeed moved into a new phase.

TAKING STOCK

It is a good deal easier to justify nature conservation on a global scale than in the context of a small, over-populated, and no longer very prosperous offshore island. I think the comparatively modern idea that we inhabit a 'biosphere' in which all the earth's life forms are inextricably connected is now widely understood and accepted. What is still at issue, of course, is how much buffeting it can take before it begins to slide into a state of irreversible decline – and whether, should this happen, technological man would necessarily go down with it.

The International Union for Conservation of Nature (IUCN), in a *A World Conservation Strategy*, has given uncompromising answers to both these questions. The life system of the Earth, it argues, has survived by the devices of variety and adaptation, by always providing more eggs than there were baskets. In an early draft of this paper it outlined the argument:

Before the advent of humans the world was covered with a tapestry of communities of plants and animals, forest, tundra, grassland, desert, whose boundaries shifted as geological and climatic processes shaped the face of the earth. These changes, as they affect ecosystems, were and are the driving force of evolution; and the result has been the continual appearance of new types of plant and animal and the extinction of others.[4]

Then man arrived on the scene and, evolving himself, has become both part of the tapestry and its major source of change – both nature and culture. He has intervened in the environment on such an unprecedented scale that the ordinary processes of adaptation cannot keep pace. In 1978 the Worldwatch Institute published a paper entitled *Disappearing Species – The Social Challenge*, which predicted that hundreds of thousands of plant and animal species, chiefly in the tropics, would be driven into extinction before the end of the century if the rate of what is ironically known as 'development' is not checked. In the rain forests – probably the single most threatened habitat on earth – the rate of extinction may already be one species per day.

But does this matter? What if we are dependent on the ecosystem for much of our food and raw materials, and for the genetic stockpile out of which future economic plants and animals may be developed? It does not appear to have been too seriously dented by past extinctions. It still generates oxygen and fixes the energy of the sun. It is still sufficiently well-balanced to prevent the world being overrun by insects or smothered under the undecayed remains of dead organisms. And though its 'tapestry' is beginning to look decidedly tattered it still embraces more than 2 million species of plants and animals. So why bother about nature conservation? Another extract from IUCN's draft gives as concise an answer as we are likely to find:

It can be argued that there is nothing new in the present situation. Evolution and extinction have always taken place. What if humanity is now the agent? Why should we intervene? The reason is clear. It is within the power of people, as intelligent beings, to modify their ways to avoid the unnecessary destruction of variety, and it is in their interests to do so.

And those interests can be economic, spiritual, emotional, moral, or as ephemeral and personal as hobbies. Eric Eckholm, author of the Worldwatch paper, expressed precisely the same idea when he said that 'biological impoverishment and human impoverishment are inextricably linked'.[5]

The particular importance of the IUCN document is that it is the first major international policy statement to affirm the *human* importance of nature conservation. Conservation is often justified as being a scientifically objective process, or 'done for the sake of the wildlife itself' – both arguments looking to the natural world for some kind of escape from the human. It is a need we have all experienced at times, to use conservation as a penance, a way of making amends for the damage we have already done to the natural world; or as a way of recapturing some simpler, less tarnished reality. There is a place for objectivity, too, if we are even to begin to understand how the natural world works. But these perspectives are not themselves objective, 'given' facts about the world. They are the results of decisions and value judgements we have made about the relationships we want with nature. So I think it is vital – for the sake of credibility, if nothing else – that we recognize at the outset that deliberately intervening, or refraining from intervening, or adopting any conscious, positive strategy towards the natural world, is a human *choice*, whether it is made for reasons of economic self-interest, scientific inquisitiveness, faith or pure sentimentality. (There is an obvious analogy with social welfare policies here. Nature conservation is based, in effect, on the assumption that it is in the interests of the whole living community that the health, vitality and variety of its individual members is maintained, and insulated as much as possible from impoverishment and depletion.)

Lewis Thomas, in one of the essays in *The Lives of a Cell*, has described how in this century we have been through at least two revolutions in thought about our relationship to nature. The oldest and most comfortable idea was that the earth was man's personal property, to be consumed or ripped apart as we wished. Then came the Ecological Enlightenment, when we recognized that we were part of that system, as dependent on the health of the rest as trees or tadpoles. Now, whilst still believing in the new wisdom, we have realized that, like it or not, we *are* in charge:

It is a despairing prospect. Here we are, practically speaking twenty-first century mankind, filled to exuberance with our new understanding of kinship to all the family of life, and here we are, still nineteenth-century man walking boot-shod over the open face of nature, subjugating and civilising it. And we cannot stop this controlling, unless we vanish under the hill ourselves. . . . The truth is we have become more deeply involved than we ever dreamed. The fact that we sit around as we do, worrying seriously about how best to preserve the life of the earth, is itself the sharpest measure of our involvement. It is not human arrogance that has taken us in this direction, but the most natural of natural events. We developed this way, we grew this way, we are this kind of species . . . perhaps in the best of all possible worlds, functioning as a nervous system for the whole being.[6]

The essay from which the extract is taken is entitled 'Natural Man', and later in it Lewis Thomas suggests explicitly that the ultimate objective for nature conservation is the conservation of man – or at least a particular kind of man. We shall have to look again at another idea that is beginning to surface here, namely that conservation may be looked at as much in terms of styles of human behaviour as in the maintenance of species.

But for the moment we must try and answer the original question implied by *A World Conservation Strategy*. Can we, in Britain, make any contribution towards minimizing that

'unnecessary destruction of variety'? We inhabit a small portion
of the earth's surface, with a relatively impoverished flora and
fauna. If we include everything from our seventy-odd species
of mammal to our 20,000 insects, we have in Britain about
60,000 of the earth's 2 million named species. Most of these are
more common somewhere else in the world, and the very small
number which occur only in Britain are most of them closely
related to more widespread species. We could scarcely fill a
page with the list of our wild organisms that are economically
important. Perhaps, in Britain at least, the touchstones of global
rarity and absolute extinction may not be the most relevant or
useful guidelines.

EXTINCTION: DEATH BY NATURAL CAUSES?

In 1977 the Society for the Promotion of Nature Conservation
published a British Red Data Book on vascular plants.[7] This,
basically, is a catalogue of our scarcest species, the 321 that
occur in fifteen or less ten-kilometre squares. But the authors,
Franklyn Perring and Lynne Farrell, went one stage further
than the simple noting of rarity, and tried to assess how endangered these rare plants were. They devised a 'threat number',
with plants scoring points according to their scarcity, rate of
decline, attractiveness and accessibility (the last two categories
giving a rough guide to their vulnerability to collecting).

Eight plants reached a score of thirteen points: Plymouth
pear, fen ragwort, downy woundwort, and five annuals, including corncockle, which was once abundant enough to be cited in
the first blacklist of agricultural weeds, published in 1523. The
most endangered of all was probably the starfruit, a diminutive
water-plantain that grows on the muddy fringes of acid ponds.
Between 1970 and 1978 it was only reliably recorded at one
locality in Surrey, and with most of its old haunts being drained
or filled in it will almost certainly become extinct as a British
species.

Yet starfruit is not rare on the continent, nor are our seven
other outstandingly endangered species. Only eight out of the
whole 321 British Red Data Book species are included in the
'endangered' or 'vulnerable' categories in the IUCN European
lists. Nine others are regarded as rare or vulnerable in Europe,
but not in Britain. The only other British species to get any kind
of mention in these lists are the highly localized 'endemics',

which occur only in Britain and have probably never occurred anywhere else. Our rarest plant, internationally, a whitebeam *Sorbus leyana*, is one of these, with a world population of about a dozen trees.

Sorbus leyana was discovered by, and named after, the Reverend Augustin Ley, who found the shrub growing on a remote limestone crag in Breconshire in the 1890s. He had previously discovered another rare endemic whitebeam, *S. minima*, in nearby Crickhowell. Ley named this one himself, but *S. leyana* was coined in his honour by Alfred Wilmott, who in turn had yet another endemic in the Avon Gorge, *S. wilmottiana*, named after him . . . . The genus, you will gather by now, is very prone to throw up idiosyncratic local species. There are no less than thirteen of these endemic whitebeams currently growing in Britain.

Someone has calculated that only one-tenth of all the life forms that have ever existed on earth are alive at present, and no doubt obscurely different *Sorbi* have gone the round of evolution and extinction in isolated western valleys for hundreds of thousands of years. And it would probably make little difference to the scheme of things if *S. leyana* were to join the ranks of the dead. But what would it do to us? We continue to mourn the dodo, and all the other casualties of our ancestors' ignorance, in the full knowledge that extinction has been a fact of life since its beginnings. It is not the extinction alone that is the problem, but our knowledge of it. In *Pilgrim at Tinker Creek* (see page 46), Annie Dillard tells the story of the Eskimo hunter who asked a local missionary, 'If I did not know about God and sin, would I go to hell?' 'No,' replied the priest, 'not if you did not know.' 'Then why', asked the Eskimo, 'did you tell me?'[8]

Over the last 100 years we have been told very clearly about the meaning of a species, that it is the successful outcome of millions of years of natural trial and error, unique and irreplaceable. Knowing this, we have to decide whether we can accept the responsibility of being conscious, passive witnesses – or, even worse, accomplices – in the erasure of even one more from the earth. Knowledge makes extinction a moral problem as well as a material one. With *S. leyana* it may not be material at all, and the ecosystem might scarcely stir if we sat back and allowed it to vanish. But what most certainly would start to crumble would be the whole philosophical argument on which conservation is based, for if we are to admit that any one species is not important enough to try and save, to intervene on behalf of, how do we argue for the next? How do we draw a convincing ethical line between an obscure whitebeam and an elm, say, or between a sperm whale and a salmon? We do not even know enough to draw a practical line.

And, following the same thread, how do you argue for the conservation of a declining species in this place or that unless you attempt to support it at all points on its natural (or potential) distribution? One hears complaints from time to time about the elaborate measures taken in this country to prop up minute populations of plants and animals – lady's slipper orchids and marsh harriers, for instance – which seem to be on the very edge of their range here and incapable of surviving without the wildlife equivalent of intensive care. Ian Prestt, the Director of the Royal Society for the Protection of Birds (RSPB), which has been responsible for the preservation (and re-establishment) of many exceptionally rare British breeding birds, has a firm answer to these criticisms. In an aptly military metaphor, he talks about the importance of 'holding the line'. The 'natural range' of a creature is, precisely, wherever it naturally occurs. If it is having difficulty in surviving somewhere in that range, it is as likely as not because of some kind of human pressure. (Lady's slipper orchid, once comparatively widespread in limestone woods in northern England, has been reduced to a single site almost solely by the activities of collectors.) The wider a species is spread – which usually implies not just physical dispersal, but a certain amount of genetic variety as well – the better equipped it is to escape overall extinction. If you do not bother to 'hold the line' at any point, you diminish that species' overall defences against unpredictable environmental changes. You have also, along the way, set a very bad example to those areas that may be even more important population centres.

Nothing illustrates this better than the changing fortunes of our peregrine falcons. Before the Second World War Britain had something of the order of 700 pairs, a significant proportion of the probable European population at that time, and a great joy to those who were privileged to live near an eyrie – and in the 1950s they were still nesting on the cliffs of Dover.[9] But not everyone agreed about either their numbers or their delightfulness. In 1959 pigeon fanciers began a concerted publicity campaign against the peregrine, labelling it 'the bandit of the skies' and blaming it for the indiscriminate slaughter of exhausted racing birds. Correspondents in *Racing Pigeon* went as far as suggesting that there might be as many as 100,000 peregrines in Britain, and that the government should take immediate action to control them for the vermin they were. In spite of the slight note of hysteria in this propaganda, the Home Office responded and commissioned a census of British peregrine populations. The results are now part of conservation history. Far from multiplying, the birds were found to be in a state of catastrophic decline. In 1962 the population was down to about half of its pre-war level, and in the whole country only sixty-eight pairs were known to have reared young successfully. The next year Derek Ratcliffe published his classic paper linking this massive slump (which was also being observed in other predatory birds) with the accumulation in the birds of toxic agricultural pesticides, passed down the food chain from dressed grain to seed-eater to bird-of-prey.[10] The results of this survey had far-reaching effects upon the control of agricultural chemicals in this country and played an important role in the ecological awakening that happened in the sixties.

Over the next decade the sales of the most insidious and persistent chemicals were gradually reduced. Slowly the peregrine population began to climb back, and more birds began to bring off young. A wardening system was established for the more vulnerable eyries (one of the ironic results of the bird's scarcity being its increased attractiveness to falconers, who raided newly-reoccupied eyries for the young). As I write this (1979) the number of occupied eyries is estimated to be about two-thirds of the pre-war level, so that, although there is still ground to make up, there has been a quite discernible recovery.[11]

But other countries were not so fortunate. Almost all of Europe experienced the same disastrous decline in peregrine numbers as ourselves, and for precisely the same reasons. Some countries did not respond so promptly or firmly, and as a result have driven their peregrines almost to the point of extinction. Others were powerless to act, for all their peregrines migrated south to winter in regions where pesticide use was still heavy, and so became contaminated far from their breeding haunts. In Finland, for instance, the population dropped from a maximum of 2000 pairs in 1950 to sixteen in 1975.[12]

So, from being a minor shareholder in the population of

European peregrines, Britain has, in less than two decades, become the birds' stronghold – an ark for the race.

From whatever point of view it originates – political, scientific, aesthetic, ethical – it is hard to see how conservation can even begin unless there is a kind of Hippocratic commitment to the maintenance of species, and a belief that absolute extinction, like the loss of life in human medicine, is the ultimate sign of failure. Yet this *is* only a beginning (and not even a consistent one; you will not find many voices supporting the presence of dry-rot or head-lice on the planet) and a conservation policy that confined itself to rescuing plants and animals from the verge of extinction would be tantamount to reducing a whole health service to an emergency operating theatre. A species that is rare or endangered is no longer, by definition, contributing much either to the workings of the ecosystem or to our well-being. That is not to suggest that it is 'useless'. It has its own significance as an irreplaceable component of the earth's gene pool, as a potential crop plant perhaps, or the source of unexplored medicinal chemicals. (I hope that ICI, during its current screening programme of Britain's wild plants for possible pharmacological usefulness, will look at the fruits of *Sorbus leyana*, just in case.) Rare species may also be of great scientific interest, particularly if they are located in isolated pockets that may represent the last remnants of more widespread populations. And none of us is immune to the excitement and sense of privilege at meeting what another generation of naturalists called 'curiosities'.

But it is the *common* species that keep the living world ticking over and provide most of our everyday experiences of wildlife, and I would argue that maintaining the abundance of these is as important a conservation priority as maintaining the existence of rarities. It would be invidious to draw up hierarchies of importance for a system whose complexity we have scarcely even begun to understand; yet it is clear, for instance, that the myriads of small animals that maintain the fertility of the soil and prevent the seaward fringes of the land from physically fraying away have a conservation importance of a different order from a scarce bush cricket; and that, in spring, a small and rather plain waterweed on the mud by a Surrey pond does rather less to rejoice the spirit than an abundance of bluebells and buttercups. I am not suggesting that conservation priorities should be based on popularity ratings (though I don't see why these shouldn't be taken into account just as much as the equally subjective 'nuisance' ratings are). But it is worth bearing in mind that, whilst our views about the ecological or economic importance of many endangered species are based on a mixture of faith and speculation, we know for certain about one of the roles of bluebells: people *like* them, and that, even by IUCN's exacting philosophical criteria, makes them a 'useful' species. This is not an argument for downgrading the attention given to rare or little known species, but for paying more heed to the common.

Yet this forces us back to those contradictions and confusions we explored at the beginning of this chapter. The deliberate conservation of common species like the bluebell sounds superfluous, even extravagant. They are 'natural'. They will take care of themselves. Our historically conditioned view of nature (abetted by communications media that have a predilection for the plight of glamorous species in far-off lands, and often, it must be said, by conservation agencies themselves faced with difficult choices about where to allot their limited resources) has pushed conservation – both in its public image and in its practice – into a potentially dangerous preoccupation with the exotic and the rare.

There is a story about one of our most beautiful plants, the snakeshead fritillary, which shows just how insidious the lure of rarity can be. The fritillary is a flower of a rapidly shrinking habitat – damp alluvial meadows – and the Red Data Book states that it is now confined to fifteen ten-kilometre squares in nine counties. In Suffolk, for instance, it grows in a handful of old hay meadows, mostly attached to farms which have scarcely changed since the sixteenth century. One of these meadows is now owned by the Suffolk Naturalists' Trust and, once a year, when the fritillaries are in full bloom, they open it to the public. In 1978, just after 'Open Day', a national newspaper carried a large photograph of a clump of fritillaries at this site, mentioning its recent purchase but quite properly not its location. A television news programme picked up the story and contacted the Nature Conservancy Council (NCC) about the possibility of getting a film of this rare and apparently secret plant. The NCC's spokesman suggested that it was unlikely they would be given permission to make a private and fragile site so explicitly public, but said they would be welcome to come and film the plants on the NCC's own reserve at North Meadow in Wiltshire. This is a National Nature Reserve, but it is also a large area of common land crossed by public footpaths, and with not just a few hundred plants in bloom, as on the Suffolk site, but more than 50,000, it is the finest show of the flower in Britain. No sooner had the figure been mentioned than the story was dead. To the reporter this smacked more of confidence trickery than conservation. How could you describe a plant growing with 50,000 others of its kind as *rare*?

Yet fritillary meadows like this once spread right along the flood-plains of the Thames and other lowland rivers. Before 1930 the snakeshead was known from 116 ten-kilometre squares in twenty-seven different counties. On the Duke of Wellington's estate at Stratfield Saye in Berkshire you could pay a few pence to a lady by a field-gate and pick a bunch for yourself. In Wiltshire it was so abundant that it had a different nickname in almost every village. Now – not so much as a result of picking as of the wholesale drainage and ploughing of old meadows – there are a mere half-dozen fields in Wiltshire in which you can find what was once virtually its county flower. In the whole country there are not more than twenty-five known fritillary sites.

And so, less spectacularly, but by the same process of attrition, a county loses its otters, a village its cowslips, a farm its swallows. These small erosions are not the stuff out of which headlines or Red Data Books are made, yet they are the way that extinction begins, and what, at grass-roots level, the conservation movement should be fighting against. If there is a single starting point, it must surely be in attempting to intervene in the process by which what is common becomes scarce, to *prevent* the stage of rarity and imminent extinction being reached. To begin at the end, as it were, and use 'threat' as the sole basis for one's priorities, could even selectively encourage rarity as a status, by singling out species which have reached that condition for special environmental privileges.

And more often than not it is *erosion* that we mean when we use the word 'extinction', which, unqualified, strictly means complete obliteration. Yet we have already seen the British Red Data Book using it in a restricted, national sense. Read other books, and you will find references to county extinctions, parish extinctons, even extinctions from a single wood. All these small annihilations are 'breaches of the line' and, though the problems of practicality and priority have to be faced, it is difficult to see how we can measure up one loss against another. Is it ecologically more disastrous for a nation to lose its last starfruit than for a village to lose its last primrose bank? They are both tears in the fabric, and neither nation nor village could lay claim to being the more scientifically respectable unit. In some ways, the local extinction may represent the greater overall loss, for here it is not just the species that is lost, but the day-to-day intimacy and associations, the neighbourliness, that builds up around a plant or animal that has lived on close terms with a human community. There is, I think, much to be said for using these human territories as the basic units by which one measures natural erosion, particularly as, in a landscape largely fashioned by man's activities, such territories often correspond to 'natural' habitats, as with an enclosed wood or a local common.

It is this sense of an intimate community of human and natural life that is responsible for so much of the power of Gilbert White's pioneering study in ecology, *The Natural History of Selborne*. I tried, in an introduction written for the Penguin edition of that book, to explore the idea of 'parish' which underlies the book – and which must, I think, underlie a conservation policy which takes any account of human feelings:

'Parish' is a very laden concept. It has to do not just with geography and ecclesiastical administration, but with history and a system of loyalties. For most of us, it is the indefinable territory to which we feel we belong, which we have the measure of. Its boundaries are more the limits of our intimate allegiances than lines on a map. These allegiances have always embraced wild life as well as human, and show themselves no more explicitly than in the universal delight at the annual return of the 'village' birds – the swifts and swallows and martins. I don't think it is a coincidence that these were White's favourites.[13]

Yet so much can make us blind to the losses which occur at this local level, from that persistent myth about the immutability of nature to the practical deficiencies of survey techniques. (What does 'present in fifteen ten-kilometre squares' mean? Represented by fifteen isolated plants, or by 1500 fields full?) Some years there seem to be as many house martins and swallows with us as there must have been in White's day. Yet go back just fifty years, to W. H. Hudson's description of the way they would line the telegraph wires in a Sussex village in the twenties 'for a length of forty or fifty yards',[14] and you know you are mistaken, that you have already started to make the process of adjustment, to trim this year's expectations to last year's realities, and to forget altogether about those sites where there can no longer be any expectations.

PAROCHIAL HISTORIES

The contexts of, on the one hand, global extinction and the protection of the biosphere and, on the other, local erosion are, of course, complementary: unchecked, the one leads inexorably to the other. Yet if we take a second look at the impoverishment of our wild flowers, this time in close-up, inside the boundaries of a specific human community, some new perspectives begin to appear on the nature of 'threat' and what this suggests about conservation priorities.

Hitcham is a small settlement (with a population currently of about 700) lying in the rich boulder-clay country between Bury St Edmunds and Hadleigh. In many ways it is a typical Suffolk village, and its chief claim to distinction is that it was the living of the Reverend John Stevens Henslow between 1837 and his death in 1861. John Henslow was one of the most distinguished natural scientists of his generation, a Professor of Botany at Cambridge University and the man who taught Darwin and encouraged him to make his epic voyage in the *Beagle*. Yet it was in his parish that his most important work was done, and his pioneering experiments in botanical education and village community work made a nationwide impact. He was not just Hitcham's rector but its curator.[15] He opened his library to the parish and gave away most of his glebe land as allotments to the dispossessed villagers. He organized vegetable shows and ploughing matches, formed benefit societies and laid on outings to the coast. And, to the chagrin of many of the new enclosing farmers (who would rather have seen the village children in their proper place, scaring birds in the fields), he began teaching science at the local school and encouraging the children to know and love the wild flowers of their own countryside. His pupils became so skilled in botany that, during the 1850s, Darwin – an ex-pupil himself – frequently made use of their services as paid field-workers, for the gathering of seeds and plants that he needed for experimental work but confessed to some difficulty in identifying! The girls at the school helped Henslow compile his *Flora of Suffolk* (1860), and the additions that they made to the Hitcham list were recorded and accredited by the rector in his parish accounts. You may still read that in 1858 Maria Gosling added 'larkspur and golden saxifrage' and Harriet Sewell 'common thorn apple and branched burr-reed'.

Between them, the village team built up a detailed account of the parish plants (406 species in all) which spans nearly a quarter of a century. Through it we can catch a glimpse of what the old countryside must have looked like – rich, diverse, chequered with woodland and meadow, dotted and crossed with springs and streams. There was even a local herbalist whose mysterious and exotic remedies would occasionally break loose from his garden and spring up in the village lanes. This, perhaps, was the source of Harriet Sewell's 'common thorn apple'.

Between 1944 and 1960 another botanist, Alec Bull, lived in Hitcham and had the rare opportunity of comparing its contemporary flora with that which had been so meticulously logged by Henslow 100 years previously.[16] The changes he found were enormous, yet spread over four generations they had occurred almost unnoticed. Something like sixty native species had gone entirely from the parish. More than twenty woodland species had become extinct, including plants as familiar as woodruff, wood sorrel, mistletoe and wayfaring tree; but then this was hardly surprising, as Hitcham had lost almost all its old woodland. Hitcham Wood (102 acres) and Eastwood (100 acres) had both been cleared by the mid-1860s. Much the same story could be told about the grasslands. Except for a few fragments alongside old lanes, most of this had gone under the plough or been altered beyond recognition by weedkillers and fertilizers. The losses here included wild thyme, marjoram, musk thistle, catmint, betony, and at least six species of orchid. I could go on to list the field-flowers lost to weedkillers, the water-plants destroyed as the streams were either drained away or polluted. But the picture of a radical transformation in the fabric of the village's natural life is already clear. Although there are a handful of rare species in Henslow's tally which have vanished, it is not these that strike you when you compare the two lists, but the casualties amongst the familiar. Corncockle 'not seen for many years'; vervain 'disappeared, 1972'; fairy flax 'roadsides only now'; columbine 'extinct'; whitebeam 'extinct' – reading this epitaph for Hitcham's lost flowers it is impossible not to be reminded of those other memorial rolls in village churches and greens across the country, and their dreadful tolls of lost generations and lineages. It has always been the way for villages. Where men and plants live in close contact, they suffer equally when the land is abused. It was so during the parliamentary enclosures, when commoners of all species lost their livings. It happened again during the First World War, when the young men of the parishes were taken off to fight another society's war, whilst their home woods were gutted of timber to prop up the trenches around them for a few extra hours. The village, the basic unit of natural wealth in our society, has been its perennial victim, and it is a miracle that it has survived at all.

The very ordinariness of what has been lost in Hitcham makes it possible to forget for a moment the special pleadings of rare species (and the special treatment they often demand) and see the pattern of destruction for what it is: the extinction not just of this or that individual or species, but of whole families, whole woods, whole landscapes. This suggests another perspective on conservation priorities. Should we, in addition to the defensive strategy of protecting species at risk, be taking more positive action to identify and modify those environmental processes which pose the most widespread threats to wildlife? This, as we shall see, is an altogether more formidable prospect, as it may mean challenging the conventional wisdom that growth and the increase of wealth are intrinsically desirable social goals. Yet even on its own terms it begs crucial questions about choices and priorities. For, if we are quite honest, what finally makes conservationists of us all is not some generalized reduction in tree cover or percentage increase in herbicide application but, as for John Clare, the loss of quite *specific* living things: 'Langley bush . . . and spreading lea close oak' – the field at the back, the churchyard rookery, the primrose bank along the lane. They are small links in the chain, ecologically, but the largest of all in terms of the human meanings that attach to them, and they cannot easily be replaced or interchanged.

Hitcham still has plantations of trees, for instance, but they are no kin to the old woods that once lay inside the parish boundaries and provided fuel for the villagers as well as woodland flowers. And, just as there are new trees, there are new flowers in the village (indeed, the crude species total in 1960 was only eleven less than in Henslow's day), but many of these are garden escapes and casual weeds and can't really be weighed against the old. I wonder if the villagers were able to find any amongst them to stand in for star-of-Bethlehem (down to a single colony by 1960), whose pure white flowers would have been picked for decorating the church over Whitsuntide?

Alec Bull also remarks that Hitcham had at least one local plant name exclusively to itself – another way of making a plant's local presence irreplaceable. Corn buttercup was always called 'joy' in the area – rather surprisingly, since in much of the rest of Britain it is clear that agricultural workers had a rather low opinion of this bright but unpleasantly spiny cornfield weed. In Yorkshire it was hellweed, in Bedfordshire scratch-burr, in Hampshire the devil's coachwheel (the spines lie on large, round seed-heads). Its most common East Anglian dialect name is gye, which is a generic term in the region for a number of cornfield weeds. It would be pleasant to think that it was the pronunciation of this word with a Suffolk twang and a good deal of Henslowian enthusiasm which changed the devil's claws (Hants) into a joy.

The irony is that Henslow, the champion of mutual aid, was also an ardent proponent of the new 'scientific' farming. He had seen too much poverty amongst the local labourers not to be. Yet where would he have stood if he had realized that within seventy-five years improved farming would have made joy extinct in Hitcham? It is because the conflicts and dilemmas of conservation are all, at their heart, as personal as this that arriving at a workable policy is so difficult. If all that was involved was the preservation of the breeding stock of species and a range of representative natural communities, a few more zoos and high-security nature reserves would solve most of the problems. It would be a grim world for those of us outside the fences, but at least the conflicts with agriculture and development might be settled for a while.

But the fact is that we do not want the natural world preserved as a museum piece. We want the opportunity to experience it face to face, with its qualities of wildness and renewal intact. We want, all of us, to hang on to favourite places and familiar creatures, and to the uniquely private network of meaning and association that attaches to them. And this finally is where the conundrum of conservation rests, for such a complex abundance of wildlife could never in practice be saved in a world where there are so many other legitimate demands upon land and resources; nor could its full range of private significances ever be taken into account – perhaps even understood

– at a public level. And so the necessity of establishing priorities is forced on us, the invidious process of weighing one place against another, one person's interest against his neighbour's. There is no escaping this, just as there is no sense in which conservation can deliberately set out to preserve 'meanings' in addition to the living things they are attached to. What I am suggesting is that the wealth of private (and public) associations which have gathered round the natural world should not be excluded from the consideration of priorities just because they are unquantifiable. They are one of the fundamental reasons why we arrived at the idea of conservation, and they ought at least to be given the best possible opportunities to continue and develop. (Derek Ratcliffe expressed one aspect of this when he talked of 'practising conservationists . . . providing or maintaining the medium wherein people can develop and pursue their interests, be these large or small, trivial or profound . . . '[17] – the conservationist as steward, in fact.)

PLACE AND PROCESS

I have been talking in terms of 'place' rather than 'site' or 'habitat', as this seems to catch the element of human significance better than specialized or abstract words. And it may lead us to at least one set of priorities, those which have to do with the quality of 'uniqueness'. In one sense all natural places (and individual plants and creatures, for that matter) could be said to be unique. But there are clearly some that possess this quality in an especially striking way. We might think, for instance, of the Lizard in Cornwall, where the whole peninsula is based on the beautifully mottled, magnesium-rich rock serpentine, and which supports a remarkable collection of dwarfed plants found together nowhere else in Britain. Or at another extreme, the walls of St John's College, Cambridge, on which grows the only remaining British colony of the naturalized rock-cress *Arabis turrita*. Communities like this are irreplaceable simply by being the only ones of their kind.

But when we look at places that have certain natural features in common we are back once more with intractable value judgements. How, for instance, do we begin to compare the conservation importance of the sites of a comparatively widespread plant like the wild daffodil? Do strong local associations 'count' as much as local scarcity? Wild daffodils are to be found in many parts of western England. Yet people still travel to see the particular colonies which flower on the slopes around Grasmere, and which was seen and immortalized by Wordsworth. The Lakeland daffodils – in poetry and in real life – are part of that difficult notion of 'heritage'. What kind of importance does that give them as against, say, the great number that grow around Dymock in Gloucestershire – probably the most concentrated population in the country – or against a relict clump in a Norfolk churchyard, a county where truly wild specimens are virtually extinct? Association, abundance, rarity, would all seem to give places equal, though different, claims.

And how do we begin to compare places in terms of their importance to *mobile* organisms? Our summer population of nightingales, for instance, has been estimated in recent censuses to be about 10,000 pairs.[11] The bird is on the edge of its range here, rarely nesting north of a line between the Humber and the Severn, and seems to be declining for climatic reasons beyond our control. If we are thinking purely in terms of the conservation of the species, then it could be argued that the British population is of little significance compared to the great numbers that nest in the warmer south of Europe. Yet we would all be the poorer if the bird did not have a *presence* here – even if the majority of us have never had the privilege of hearing a live performance by Europe's most famous songster. We would have lost some of the best poetry of the Romantic movement. We would never have heard that heroic and profoundly poignant record of one singing out against the roar of a flight of bombers crossing southern England during the Second World War. We would not even have been able to entertain the fancy that one might have sung in Berkeley Square.

Whether it is common and predictable, or scarce and unexpected, the nightingale is always a very special and treasured bird. In Kent, for instance, the paramount nightingale county, it is still possible to have the unforgettable experience of hearing a dozen or more singing at one time. (Even the statistics of Kent nightingales have a touch of poetry about them: in the census of 1970, '167 observers heard 977 nightingales between midnight and dawn on the morning of May 24'.[11]) Yet Garth Christian describes what was obviously an equally unforgettable visitation by the bird to a Derbyshire village far north of its usual range. The local miners crowded down the lane to the copse where the nightingale was singing and 'listened earnestly and critically as they did when the parish choir performed *The Messiah*'.[18]

Once most lowland villages in the south had a nightingale thicket, to some or other part of which the birds would return (if one can trust historical records) year after year, even during cycles of cool, damp summers. It was often a wood or scrubby common where the villagers regularly cut, or coppiced, under-wood for burning, and created in the process the kind of bushy growth ideally suited to nightingales (see page 93). When cop-picing became obsolete, nightingales declined. Where it has been reintroduced, they have often returned, sometimes in areas at the extremities of their range (such as the East Mid-lands) where climatic factors would seem to be most strongly ranged against them.

This is, suddenly, a quite new perspective: a species con-served not in a fixed and unalterable spot, but inside the terri-torial framework and everyday life of a specific community; and not by an overweening protectiveness but incidentally, by human activity. This shift of emphasis to the importance of *continuity* rather than immutability is crucial. It is tempting, faced with the crises of loss and extinction, to fall back on the kinds of opposition and contrasts that we use when thinking of the preservation of inanimate objects, to see maintenance as opposed to change, protection as opposed to use. Yet change is an intrinsic quality of living systems. They grow, reproduce, migrate, form communities, evolve, die, yet still keep up a lineage, of a kind. This peculiar combination of development and continuity, in which old forms are not so much replaced by as *contained* inside the new, is characteristic of all living things, including ourselves, regardless of whether we are acting as the agents or the subjects of change. It is like the develop-ment of grain in a tree. A tree's annual rings are not just a measure of its age, but a record of its whole life experience. Drought, defoliation, disease, the lopping of branches, even the clearance of nearby trees, all leave their mark in the pattern and character of the rings. (Oak trees throughout southern England, for instance, almost all possess a cluster of stunted rings that record the effects of the great plagues of defoliating caterpillars that occurred between 1917 and 1924.)[19] Provided such changes are not drastic, the tree lives, the continuity is preserved. The changes have, in a sense, been incorporated in it and actually enhance its 'graininess'.

I think that the metaphor of 'grain', with its suggestions that, where continuity is not broken, change can increase natural intricacy, can be applied to all natural communities and places. It can give us at last a way of regarding and evaluating them that sees them as *dynamic* communities, existing inside a continuously changing world in which we also are a 'natural' agent of change.

But it remains most expressive when applied to trees themselves, which, in the metaphorical sense, have grains 'outside' as well as in. Their shapes, their burrs and branch-stumps and root-stocks, are living records of what has happened to them historically. In their maturity trees are so etched with experience that they become recognizable not just as species but as individuals. (And then yet another kind of grain begins to develop – the accumulating layers of myth and affection that gather round ancient trees.) Yet this, ironically, means that they also display most vividly the effects of the breaking of continuity.

Between 1955 and 1967, R. H. Richens conducted a remarkable and extensive survey of village elms.[20] In the course of those twelve years he visited and took representative leaf samples from the elms growing in the ancient boundaries of more than 500 East Anglian parishes. He found such a degree of variation in leaf characteristics (paralleled by differences in bark texture and the shape of the whole tree) that it was possible to name types of elm distinctive to small groups of settlements, and sometimes even to individual villages (see Figure 1). Partly this was due to the complex genetics and taxonomy of the elm family, and its propensity to bewildering variations and hybridization. (And see Gerald Wilkinson's *Epitaph for the Elm* for the most sympathetic caricature of botanists' attempts to make sense of, so to speak, the elm's family tree.[21]) The East Anglian elms (chiefly the small-leaved group, *Ulmus minor* agg.) reproduce much more successfully by suckers than seed and, where a population was confined to a valley, it tended to reproduce its own kind in a series of vegetative replicas. But ever since neolithic times (when its foliage was used for animal, and quite possibly human, food) the elm had been one of the most widely used trees, and the spread of 'types' was also profoundly influenced by man. In medieval times farmers would take suckers from local elm trees and plant them in the hedges and closes of their parishes. The best specimens often became boundary markers or 'meeting-place' trees, and would be replaced by their

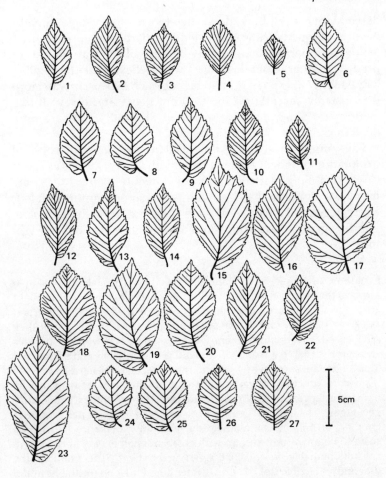

Specimen elm leaves. 1 Frinton; 2 Springfield; 3 Southminster; 4 Epping; 5 Farnham; 6 Colchester; 7 Layer de la Haye; 8 Chrishall; 9 Great Chesterford; 10 Easthorpe; 11 Messing; 12 Little Hallingbury; 13 Tilbury juxta Clare; 14 Marks Tey; 15 Bradwell next Coggeshall; 16 Great Dunmow; 17 Boxted; 18 Kirby le Soken; 19 Great Saling; 20 Copford; 21 Latton; 22 Ardleigh; 23 East Donyland; 24 Chigwell; 25 West Hanningfield; 26 Harlow; 27 North Weald Bassett

Figure 1. Leaves from Essex village elms. From R. H. Richens, Studies on Ulmus.[20]

descendants when they died. The elms of each village came to have a unique architectural identity, partly because of their biological inheritance and partly because of the way they were used. (There are some botanists who believe that the English elm itself, *Ulmus procera*, may be one such type that was more than usually successful.) It is sad but necessary to say all this in the past tense, for nearly half of England's elms are now dead or dying of Dutch elm disease.

The American writer Annie Dillard, in her philosophical exploration of the meaning of biological variety, *Pilgrim at Tinker Creek*, has suggested that this basic quality of life to become *intricate* – a quality that man has exploited and, until comparatively recently, encouraged – is both nature's ultimate safeguard against extinction and the source of our delight in it:

Evolution, of course, is the vehicle of intricacy. The stability of simple forms is the sturdy base from which more complex stable forms might arise, forming in turn more complex forms, and so on. . . . there are, as I have said, six million leaves on a big elm. All right . . . but they are toothed, and the teeth themselves are toothed. How many notches and barbs is that to a world? In and out go the intricate leaf edges, and 'don't nobody know why.' All the theories botanists have devised to explain the functions of various leaf-shapes tumble under an avalanche of inconsistencies. . . . Why so many forms? Why not just one hydrogen atom? The creator goes off on one wild, specific tangent after another, or millions simultaneously, with an exuberance that would seem to be unwarranted, and with an abandoned energy sprung from an unfathomable font. What is going on here? The point of the dragonfly's terrible lip, the giant water bug, birdsong, or the beautiful dazzle and flash of sunlighted minnows, is not that it all fits together like clockwork – for it doesn't, particularly, not even inside the goldfish bowl – but that it flows so freely wild, like the creek, that it all surges in such a free, fringed tangle. . . . Intricacy is that which is given from the beginning, the birthright, and in intricacy is the hardiness of complexity that ensures against the failure of all life.[8]

Perhaps, in the intricate variety of East Anglia's village elms, there is a tree that will prove a match for disease. Dr Richens himself believes the present virulent strain of Dutch elm disease will run its course in another fifteen or so years, and that the best way of conserving the variety of British elms is in the hedgerows where they occur at present – in sucker form if necessary. Even if this proves to be an over-optimistic view, and elms continue to contract the disease as they grow into trees, keeping the suckers going may well add one new touch of variety to the landscape – a kind of bonsai elm.

Variety has been the saving grace of life since its beginning. What must worry us, now, is whether the overall drift of our society towards uniformity is already outstripping the contrary, natural drive toward intricacy. Change, we have been arguing, can enhance intricacy – but only if its pace and scale do not exceed those at which nature can adjust. Most traditional human land-uses stayed within such limits, and in the bird world, for instance, there have been as many additions to the British list over the last few centuries as there have been losses due to climatic change and human pressure. Even since the Second World War, two new breeding species – collared dove and Cetti's warbler – have settled here because a natural expansion in their range coincided with the availability of vacant (and largely man-made) niches.

But can birds as a *group* cope with the abruptness, the repetition, the sheer scale of current environmental change? Every year an estimated half a million Brunnich's guillemots are drowned in salmon nets off Greenland. Every autumn, as many as 150 million migratory birds, which one report estimates to be a quarter of all the migratory birds crossing the Mediterranean, are shot in Italy alone.[22] And just one oil spill (and these are now a weekly occurrence that the Department of Trade seems powerless to control), at Sullom Voe in the Shetlands, turned the coastline into something the NCC's local representative likened to a 'polluted industrial river'. His report on the disaster, with its terse and painful matters-of-fact, was, I think, the most shocking comment I encountered in the whole course of writing this book:

To date (24 January 1979) the figures are as follows:

2841 dead birds including: 104 great northern divers (the breeding population in the western Palearctic approx. 300 pairs, mostly in Iceland), 501 black guillemots, 451 shags, 413 eider ducks, 230 common guillemots.

20 otters picked up dead, but estimated that casualties could be 10–20 times more. Those found died on the spot, others less oiled will return to their holts to groom, then die from oil pollution poisoning.

Countless thousands of oiled sheep. They feed in winter on the seaweeds – heavy snow just after the incident forced them down to the shore to feed.[23]

NATURAL MAN

None of this would be of more than minor importance if wild plants and creatures were simply the 'hobby' of naturalists, and the natural world a kind of specialized pitch, of no concern to non-players. And one can still find naturalists who regard it in this light, and who regret the urgent, populist tone of modern conservation. A speaker at an ecological symposium in 1969 caught the feeling behind this nostalgia very exactly:

Thirty or forty years ago it might have been reasonable to segregate conservation on the grounds of self-defence. There must have been a logic in saying that some values in life were discernible only to a limited number of people at a time when the interests of an exclusive club of, say, wild-life addicts were far removed from the bread and circus approach of a football club.[24]

The dangers and irrelevance of the 'exclusive club' approach had, in fact, been ruthlessly exposed four years before, in the battle over Cow Green Reservoir. This classic case of the conflict between two apparently non-comparable interests in the land is documented in Roy Gregory's sympathetic and perceptive book, *The Price of Amenity: Five Studies in Conservation and Government.*[25] Very briefly, the conflict was over ICI's need for a new reservoir to service its ammonia plant in Billingham on Tees-side. It was not planned to be a particularly big reservoir – it eventually covered 310 hectares (770 acres) – but the most economic site appeared to be in Cow Green, on Upper Teesdale. This remote valley, unhappily, was a unique botanical site which held a special place in the affections of British naturalists. Much of it lay over an unusual rock called sugar limestone which, millions of years ago, had been baked by the intrusion

The lady orchid, one of Britain's most dramatically beautiful flowers, reaches three feet in height on occasions. It is virtually confined to Kent, where it is not uncommon in scrub and light woodland on the chalk (see page 60).

A place in town.

FIND IT IN

The Daily Telegraph

PROPERTY PAGES

FLOWERS O'THE CORN

FLOWERS FRESH IN HUE, AND MANY IN THEIR CLASS
IMPLORE THE PASSING STEP. AND WITH THEIR DYES
DANCE IN THE SOFT BREEZE IN A FAIRY MASS. BYRON
AND...
HOW NEAR THE CORN GROWS

The natural world is a perennial source of images – even highly functional ones.

(Above opposite) *The Chequered Skipper pub (the image of the butterfly on the sign is formed by metal nails) is in the village of Ashton in Northamptonshire, near a group of woods where this butterfly – now almost certainly extinct in England but known in Scotland since the 1940s – previously occurred.*

(Far left) *A poster put out by the* Daily Telegraph *in 1978.*

(Left) *The London Transport poster is from the 1920s, when fields full of cornflowers and poppies were still a common feature of the countryside in high summer, and regarded, obviously, as a sight worth travelling to see.*

of molten rock to the consistency of granulated sugar. The instability and chemical properties of this rock meant that it had never been successfully colonized by woodland. As a result, incongruous communities of plants that had grown in the area shortly after the end of the last Ice Age – rare and localized arctic and alpine plants closely mixed with commoner limestone-grassland species – had managed to survive intact for nearly 10,000 years. The Upper Teesdale communities were living remnants of a flora that had once been widespread in Britain, during the prolonged cool, dry period that preceded the coming of the forest.[26]

The resistance to the idea of even a small portion of this remarkable relic being drowned by an industrial reservoir was so intense that in May 1966 Parliament set up a Select Committee to hear evidence from both sides. To read, only thirteen years later, the arguments that were exchanged during the inquiry is a sad and depressing business. It was not just that the opposing parties were speaking from quite different points of view; they were scarcely talking the same language. I do not think we can blame the scientists for not putting their arguments more persuasively. Inquiries into nature conservation matters were then relatively rare events, and for many witnesses this was the first occasion on which they had been required to defend in public what were to them essentially personal interests. There was no doubting their passion or their sincerity. But in the context of the issues at stake, their arguments sounded remote and narrow-minded. They talked about the scientific importance of plant communities at the limits of their tolerance, about the arcane reaches of genetics and physical geology and, when specific justifications finally failed them, about the value of pure research. Under cross-examination by ICI's barristers, some of them were even made to appear rather less familiar with Cow Green than with their own laboratories. Against the more popular and comprehensible goals of employment and industrial progress the objectors' case looked like a very specialized interest indeed.

The traditional agricultural landscape – buttercup meadows in the Pennines. Already the signs of 'improvement' are evident in the bright, uniform green fields at the top of the picture (see page 111).

It was not until the issue moved into open debate in Parliament that the wider cultural importance of these scientific curiosities began to be championed – especially in a remarkable speech by Lord Strang, who placed the plant communities of Cow Green firmly amongst those unquantifiable values that were being surrendered at every point to the demands of uncritical technological progress. But it was now obvious the way the decision would go, and in March 1967 the private Bill permitting the flooding of Cow Green received the Royal Assent. It is worth quoting the words of Lord Kennet, who summed up for the Government at the end of the Lords' debate:

I think that whatever posterity comes to feel about the presence of the reservoir at Cow Green it may well remember the passage of this Bill through both Houses as the moment when the British Parliament accepted to the full its duty to examine, regardless of tedium and regardless of cost, the fundamental conflict of interests between one ponderable – industrial and economic progress – and two imponderables – pure research and the preservation of natural beauty.[27]

The events of subsequent years might give us good reason to doubt whether Parliament had accepted any such duty. But the conservation movement certainly had, and it would not be made to appear so remote in public again. But what is significant is the way in which the expertise and relevance of its case was built up, now that it was clear there would be many more such confrontations in the future. It would be wrong to over-generalize, but I do not think it is unfair to say that the effort was concentrated less on exploring the richness and associations of the 'imponderables' (which, to be pedantic for a moment, means 'those things which cannot be estimated') than on trying to *reduce* them to 'ponderables'. So the last decade has seen a great gathering of data (including, ironically, a £100,000 research project on Upper Teesdale funded by ICI itself) but rather less imaginative interpretation. If anything, the significance of the natural world as understood by scientists has drifted even further away from the essentially imponderable significance it has for the general public – which is all too often tidied away under that annoyingly vague concept 'amenity'.

We shall see more of this rift in the course of this book. But there was no better example of how entrenched it is – and how potentially damaging – than in a BBC *Horizon* programme on the future of the Somerset Levels, screened in January 1978. The Levels are a large area of low-lying meadows and pasture just inland from Bridgwater Bay and are currently being considered for a large-scale drainage scheme (see page 150). They have a very rich wildlife, and the programme was investigating possible ways of maintaining this in the face of the considerable economic pressures which are building up on the area's natural resources. Amongst these are the deep deposits of peat which underlie much of the Levels, which are being energetically dug for the horticultural trade by Fisons. This is what their spokesman had to say in defence of the excavations:

As a nature reserve, the peatlands in Somerset would be of interest only to a limited number of people. The peatland is scientifically interesting, but it's not an area of great scenic beauty, it's not an area that's of great value to the community in that sense.[28]

If this is a typical attitude – and I believe it is – it is a sad reflection on both the basic philosophy and the public relations of the conservation movement. We must ask ourselves whether it is calculated industrial self-interest or our own narrow-mindedness that has nurtured a widespread belief that nature reserves (and what they stand for) are not 'of great value to the community'; and that between the extremes of scientific interest and scenic beauty there are no other qualities in which natural interest is expressed.

My own belief is that the natural world cannot be evaluated simply in terms of scientific criteria. Nor can it be dismissed as an arena for the amusement of naturalists. Even broader comparisons – for instance with our heritage of art treasures – can be misleading, and return us to that image of a static museum, a collection of living fossils, from which we have had to argue our way clear. The natural world is ubiquitous; it is too pervasive, too much *alive* to be contained within any of these models. It touches us all, physically and emotionally, in every aspect of our lives, even when we are not aware of it.

I will be talking later about the notion of *indicator species* – organisms which inform us about the history and character of the environments in which they live. It is, strictly, a scientific notion. But if we look closely at its resonances, in practice, I think we can see how widely and how intimately we are all involved. One of the best known groups of indicators, because of their remarkable sensitivity to atmospheric pollution, is the lichens. Lichens are the most contingent of all organisms, condemned to the most marginal of existences. They live at the very edge of things, clinging to the face of rocks and the trunks of trees. They do not even have roots and scrimp what nourishment they can from trickles of rainwater across or under their surfaces, and from meagre seepages from bark or rocks. They grow with painstaking slowness, sometimes as little as one millimetre a year, and during droughts can pass into prolonged states of 'suspended animation'. (Some patches on rocks in the Arctic are reckoned to be 4000 years old.) They are as meticulous as chronometers in recording the passing of time and just as delicate. They soak up – with a thoroughness that means it can be measured – considerable amounts of radioactive fallout, which they seem able to tolerate, and much greater quantities of industrial sulphur dioxide, which most of them cannot. In Epping Forest, just downwind from London, ninety species of the lichens which used to grow on the old trees have become extinct in the last 170 years.[29]

Francis Rose has established that there is a group of some thirty scarce lichens so specialized in their demands, so slow to grow and reproduce, that they can only survive where old trees have had a continuous presence.[30] They are indicators of the age and continuity of ancient forests (see pages 98–99). Then again lichens are indicators of antiquity in a much more accessible and generalized sense. They are part of what makes old stonework look old, and ancient woodland *feel* ancient (and damp). And might they even contribute to the longevity of forest trees? Lichens are always described as 'epiphytes' and assumed to have a purely superficial relationship with the trees they cling to. Yet recently they have been found to contain a range of potent antibiotics. Arboreal lichens have distinctly limited prospects on dead, dried-out and fallen trees, and any whose chemical defence systems helped ward off bacterial and fungal infection in a tree would have greatly improved their own chances of survival. . . . It is just a thought, and probably a fanciful one. But it is hard not to speculate when you are caught up in a coil in which biological relationships and symbolic indications are entwined as intricately and sympathetically as a double-helix. Round and round go the spirals; we climb on as observers, as epiphytes, and find we are participants. We see a poisoned lichen, a seabird suffocated in an oil slick – our modern miners' canaries. We begin with a sadness for their fate, then a sharp concern for our own, as a species not so far down the spiral, and end with a larger ethical doubt, embracing the others, about whether these are the terms on which we want to live with the rest of creation.

I have been trying to think of some model which might make sense of our complex and paradoxical relationship with the natural world, which is simultaneously functional and symbolic, continuous and changeable, personal and universal; and the only analogy that will work is that of human language. Stephen Potter and Laurens Sargent have described in their book *Pedigree* (from the Norman *pied de grue*, the crane's foot, whose three splayed toes were used as a conventional sign of origins in early genealogical tables) how much of our language – names, allusions, similes – has been built up from natural imagery, from our attempts to make sense of our own lives by looking at that other society of nature.[31] Perhaps it is not surprising then that our working relationships with the natural world are like nothing so much as the business of using language. Much of the time we get on with both activities without much conscious thought, but it is inconceivable that we could continue without them. Like language, we relish and enjoy the natural world for its own sake. We deliberately preserve some parts and let others change as they will. Dialects develop, new words – and new arrangements of words – arrive, and old ones become obsolete. The whole structure is marvellously enriched by ambiguity, nuance and private reference. Yet through all this intricacy runs a cohesive, organic core of common meaning.

Perhaps it is worth reflecting then that language is at its healthiest when it is being *used*, when we are all busy at it – not, thank heavens, in the same uniform tongue, but at least aware that this particular activity is what holds us all together. The analogy with language may help us realize that our relationship with the natural world is essentially a *creative* one – whether we just stop to glance at a flower or devise a World Conservation Strategy. There is, we can now see, nothing remotely unnatural about our deliberate intervention; as Lewis Thomas said, 'We developed this way, we grew this way, we are this kind of species.'

PART TWO

Nature and Land-Use: Past Harmonies and Present Discord

The idea that the fate of our natural resources depends on the way that we use them seems self-evident. Yet a whole history of artificial contrasts – between man and nature, wildness and cultivation, science and sentiment – has fostered the assumption that the natural world is something intrinsically different and necessarily separate from our own. I think we may be just beginning to accept the idea that human society is more like a rather special kind of natural community than an entirely different category of existence. Yet we still find it hard to acknowledge how *creatively* we are involved, and how much of what we regard as 'natural' survives *because* of its ancient links with us rather than in spite of them.

In Part One I looked at a number of different perspectives on the purpose and priorities of nature conservation. In every case it proved impossible to put an evaluation on the natural world divorced from any human context. The pattern in which it has survived and the meanings it holds for us are consequences of the fact that we have shared some kind of life together. In particular, we saw, they are contingent upon the ways we have organized that shared life into formalized patterns of rural land-use.

In Part Two I will be looking in detail at what I believe to be the three most important of these land-uses – forestry, agriculture and recreation – and how they have influenced our wildlife. In each case I have looked at how traditional practices shaped our natural history and, until comparatively recently, sustained what we have come to regard as our natural heritage; the dramatic ways in which these practices are changing, and the implications of this for the future of our wildlife; and finally whether inside this pattern we can identify any fundamental ecological and social principles which need to be followed if some recognizable fragments of our natural environment are to survive. (I consider ways of putting these principles into practice in Part Three.)

Of these three land-uses, I have concentrated on forestry and on its relations with woodland ecology. I have to confess a degree of personal bias in this, as woodland is the habitat that fascinates me the most. But I think there are also good objective reasons for beginning a study of the relationship between conservation and land-use with a close look at the history and evolution of woodland. Woodland is the most complex and diverse of all our natural habitats. At one time it covered two-thirds of the surface of the British Isles, and it is the condition that most dry land would revert to if abandoned by man. And, in looking at the transition between the primeval forest and our current pattern of tree cover, many concepts which are fundamental to the understanding of conservation in a wider context will emerge.

We will see, for example, that all living communities have a *structure*, and that conserving this may be as important as the maintenance of individual plants and animals; that this structure is profoundly influenced by locality and history and human use; and that, up to a certain level of intensity, use can not only help preserve the continuity of a habitat, but in many cases actually increase its natural diversity.

These principles, which have considerable implications for the way we go about the business of conservation, are relevant to all the other habitats we will be considering in the course of this book.

1
Woodlands and Forestry

Although the Bedford Purlieus is a name very familiar as a household word throughout north Northants yet it is surprising how very little is known about it . . . that only half a century ago it was an enormous forest covering about a thousand acres of land and that today it is only about half that area; that men are still living in the villages of Wansford, Kingscliffe, Nassington and all around who were employed as foresters, woodmen, and oakers; that others are still living who helped grub up nearly half that thousand acres of forest and make it into farmlands; and that all these men can tell stories and incidents of the Purlieus that will come as a surprise to most. . . . If the Duke of Bedford who ordered the clearance could have foreseen how much cheaper wheat would have become, it is probable the old Purlieus would never have been interfered with, for they yielded a good harvest of timber and underwood every year for which there was a ready market, and a large number of woodmen were constantly employed.

Peterborough Advertiser 7 December 1912

THE WOOD AND THE TREES

On 15 March 1978, the Secretary of State for the Environment made a decision which, to those not familiar with woodland conservation, probably seemed perverse and self-contradictory. He confirmed a Tree Preservation Order on a wood in Kent which was at that moment known to be lying flat on the ground. As decisions go it was as much historical as historic, and a medieval woodman would have been amazed that anyone could consider a wood or tree to have been destroyed just because it had been cut down – how else did you harvest them? A great deal has happened to our woods in the last 500 years, and the knowledge of their workings and the forces that have moulded them has, like so much else, slipped away. In a climate of opinion that seems to be polarized between those who see trees as crops that will not grow unless they are planted and those who see them as monuments that should never be cut, the case of Sladden Wood marked the return of a glimmer of common sense about woodland evolution.

Sladden – or the Horizontal Wood, as it is known by those locals who have managed to keep their sense of humour – lies on the north side of the Alkham Valley, just inland from Dover. It covers rather less than seventeen acres (seven hectares), but is the richest of a string of ash and maple woods that wind along the steep slopes of this chalky valley. The character of the country here, and of the plants and creatures that live in it, is absolutely dependent on this mosaic, on the alternation of wood and down and scrub.

All the woods have been cut and cropped in the past, yet the valley has almost certainly been under some kind of tree cover since prehistoric times and carries many of the more sensitive woodland flowers. Sladden has herb paris, green hellebore and half a dozen species of orchid, including Kent's special glory – the statuesque and elegant lady orchid. It also has nightingales, a network of traditional footpaths and walks, and the affection of almost the entire local population.

In 1977, this ancient community of natural and human interest passed into the ownership of a decidedly modern farmer, whose zeal for improvement was well known from elsewhere in the county. He set to work on the valley immediately, with the intention of claiming as much as possible of it for arable crops. He cleared the shelter belts, ploughed up downland and grubbed out the first few patches of woodland. The NCC and many local amenity groups, fearful for the fate of this beautiful and fascinating stretch of country, arranged a number of discussions with the owner, none of which brought anything but gloom about its likely future. And, on 23 November, just seven days before a meeting which had been specifically arranged to discuss its fate, the bulldozers moved into Sladden Wood. Acting with quite commendable speed, Dover Council summoned up a Tree Preservation Order that same day and tried to serve it on the owner. The events of the next few hours had – in more than one sense – all the characteristics of a Whitehall farce. The owner (who had, incidentally, omitted to get a felling licence for the larger trees) refused to accept the Order because, he claimed, he had mislaid his glasses. When they had been retrieved, he attempted to go over to the official serving the Order but, in his counsel's words, 'there were obstructions in between them, and by the time he had got round them the last trees had been felled'.[32]

Sladden Wood that winter looked as if a tank war had been fought in it. In their haste to get the wood down before the Tree Preservation Order was served, the contractors had dispensed with the niceties of tidy felling, and had simply pushed many of the smaller trees over, or snapped them off some feet above ground level. Even some of the larger trees had been treated in this way, sawn half through, then bent over and broken. By any standards that day's work was an act of gross vandalism against what was, by long custom, a public amenity.

Yet the following March, at the time of the inquiry into the owner's objections to the Tree Preservation Order, the splintered stumps had already started to send up new shoots. The inspector at the inquiry accepted the NCC's argument that a tree remains a tree unless it is uprooted or killed, that 'the wood will return to a woodland appearance even without recutting* of the stumps', and that 'the reasonable degree of public benefit which must be established before a tree preservation order can be confirmed can be future benefit'.

Sladden Wood has, for the time being, escaped outright eradication, and a High Court injunction was served against the owner to prevent him carrying out his threat to grub out the stumps. The ground – at present deeply rutted and smothered with rampant weeds and brambles – will take a while to recover from the assaults of the bulldozers. But the seeds accumulated in the soil over the years are still there and will have their chance to sprout again as the trees grow up and start to shade out the weeds. As for the trees themselves, they will bear the marks of the extraordinary woodwreck of 23 November for the rest of their lives. Yet in doing so they may, ironically, become more fascinatingly textured than they were before. If no more is done to them than a touch of tidying and thinning, in 100 years Sladden Wood will carry a distinctive collection of dwarf pollards, sprouting sheafs of contorted branches only a few feet above the ground (perhaps like the famous trees of Burnham

---

* 'Recutting' here refers to the possibility of cutting the broken stumps more tidily at ground level, which would be equivalent to the traditional woodland practice of coppicing (explained more fully on page 73).

Beeches and Epping Forest, which owe their particular shapes to centuries of lopping for firewood). It will have become as much an historical monument as a natural one, a reminder of nature's magnanimous ability not just to heal over the results of our activities, but subtly to incorporate them.

Another wood, another prospect. Wendover Wood is a large plantation (a collection of deliberately planted trees, as distinct from a naturally 'sprung' wood, whether managed or not) in the Chilterns, owned and largely created by the Forestry Commission. Until this century the site was chalk downland interspersed with scattered beechwoods. Some of these have been retained (though extensively replanted) but much of the open grassland has been stocked with conifers. The mix is striking in the grand manner, tumbling over a thousand acres of steep slopes and scarps. As a vista it has a distinct upland flavour, and it would not surprise me if buzzards return to breed here one day. Wendover Wood already has the largest breeding population of firecrests in the country, and great numbers of badgers, for which the Commission has provided little flaps in its fences. The Commission has also considered the needs of perambulating humans, and laid out a network of walks, nature trails and viewpoints. And, to confirm its commitment to public involvement in the wood, in 1969 it arranged for 1700 schoolchildren each to plant a beech sapling.

Yet the striking difference between this wood and Sladden is its comparative absence of natural structure. Since at first sight it may seem absurd to suggest that a wood of standing trees has less structure than what is currently a tangle of stumps and firewood, I think it is worth taking a short while to explore this important term which crops up repeatedly in the description of woods (and is fundamental to understanding the goals of conservation in all semi-natural habitats). 'Structure' is what, at a distance, makes the roof of a wood such a marvellously billowing canopy of greens, contoured and coloured by the intermingling crowns of a dozen different species. It has to do with the arrangement of old trees and young saplings, with the changing patterns of light and denseness and species as you pass from slope to plateau, from the dry to the wet. It is what gives old woods their fascinating and unpredictable variety – yet also their sense of some deeper order, for structure is rooted in the imperatives of geology and climate, and in the slow rhythms of ancient management practices. In a wood where there has been comparatively little disturbance the distribution of the trees will still echo the underlying soil types – alder clumps and aspen groves on the damp patches, spindle and hazel and wild cherry where it is more calcareous. The various generations of free-growing trees will reflect good seed years and the cycles of grazing by stock and wild animals. The shrubs and ground flora will also develop a pattern which parallels that of the trees.

It is of course possible, by block planting, to impose structure of a very different sort, in the sense of a preordained plan or system that may ignore or suppress the pattern that would develop naturally on the site. This is what has happened at Wendover, where the trees grow more according to numbers on a plan than to the interplay of natural forces. In the planted compartments they have little variety of age or shape, and little growing underneath them in the form of shrubs or flowers. It is a wood pared down to its skeletal parts. Only in small patches under the older beeches, where there may have been continuous tree cover, can you find clumps of true woodland species like woodruff and sanicle. Ironically, the best flowers have little to do with the trees. They are relics of the chalk grassland flora that have survived in the rides – candytuft and marjoram and musk thistle. As a consequence you can, in high summer, walk between the dark walls of spruce accompanied incongruously by a troupe of flickering downland butterflies.

From the extremes of Sladden and the conifer compartments of Wendover – the ancient wood with no standing trees and the new plantations with not a great deal else – we can begin to glimpse one of the basic premises of woodland ecology, that woods are more than just collections of trees. They are *places*, landmarks, communities. They have names on the map. They vary enormously with situation, structure and age. Many have minutely documented histories spanning several centuries. In this respect they are more thoroughly four-dimensional than perhaps any other kind of natural habitat. Stretching the point, we could even say they are five-dimensional, if we distinguish between the structure below ground and that above. The parts of a wood that grow above the surface are more obvious and more easily understood. They form an architectural structure of layers and levels, of shelter and communications routes – a complex for moving about and living in. Yet the continuity of the wood as a living whole depends as much on the invisible structure beneath the ground – a scarcely graspable association of bacteria and fungi feeding, and feeding on, root-fibre networks of incredible length; of generations of dormant seeds and rotting leaves; and of worms and dung-beetles and moulds that help recycle the food reserves of the soil.

It hardly needs spelling out that the worst that can happen to a wood is to lose all its dimensions, to have this whole extraordinary complex bulldozed into oblivion, or that any reduction in its diversity – a decrease in area or age range, say – will in some way impoverish its natural interest. Yet in many ways the most conspicuous and heart-rending change in a wood, the temporary loss of its standing timber, may be the least harm that can befall it. It is certainly the feature which is most easily restored, and if the trees are encouraged to regenerate from the existing stock of seeds and stumps – kept in the family, as it were – the wood will soon regain much of its original character. This, with luck, is what will happen to Sladden Wood. Yet it is easy to imagine a more thorough 'restoration' – clearing, grubbing-up, deep trench-ploughing, re-stocking with nursery saplings and spraying out weed trees with herbicide – having a very different result. It would result in a wood with all its dimensions intact except those crucial and inextricably linked ones of age and underground structure. It would lie on a traditionally wooded site in the Alkham Valley. Yet it would hardly be honest to go on calling it Sladden Wood. The continuity would have been broken, the history closed. It would, for certain, take centuries for the community of trees to start forming groves and groupings, with young trees alongside the old, in the way that gives a natural wood its vitality and texture. As for the time it would take for the traditional woodland fungi and insects and flowers to recolonize the floor of the wood, it is quite literally inestimable. For all we know it might never happen at all, and the wood might always resemble a cluster of trees propped up in a field.

Nevertheless the first nature conservation priority as regards woodlands is quite clear: *any* wood, once it has been established, is a better wildlife prospect than a grubbed-out and cultivated memory, even if all it does initially is give a few starlings shelter for the night. But it is not as simple as that. If all woods are different, some are clearly more different than others. Conifer woods, in general, are less interesting than deciduous. Manicured plantations are ecologically more monotonous than free-range woods. The older a wood gets, the richer it becomes. So young conifers planted up (as at Wendover) on botanically rich chalk downland may represent an overall *loss* for nature conservation.

Yet we must not forget, while thinking about conservation priorities in this way, that the growing of timber is also a vital commercial business, and that the chief reason we have any woodland left is because, at some stage in its history, it has been able to pay its way. What does remain can scarcely be compared with the extensive forests in most European countries, but it still covers some 9 per cent of our densely populated land surface. There is consequently fierce competition for its spoils, which are not just its timber but the land this occupies. We should not be surprised that the Forestry Commission wishes to stock its land with the currently most profitable trees, or that the owner of the Alkham Valley wishes to clear his property of woods that do not appear to him to have any economic potential. If it is to be realistic, a woodland conservation policy must take these economic pressures into account and look for ways of reconciling the harvesting of trees with the preservation of the woods themselves.

FORESTRY AND FORESTS

The complex structure of woods – and indeed of the ways we regard them – has meant that they have always been used for a multiplicity of purposes. We tend to think of 'forestry' purely in terms of the production of timber, yet it has always meant more than this. Even the origins of the word some time during the Dark Ages have an intriguing ambiguity. On the one hand 'forest' meant simply the unclaimed waste beyond the islands of civilization – the Wildwood, as Oliver Rackham (borrowing from A. A. Milne) has called it.[33] Wild it may have been, but for most of the population it was the source of everything that was not provided by their little patches of cultivated ground, from herbs for fertility to wooden grave markers. On the other hand the word was used in the sense we see in the phrase 'Royal Forest', to describe a tract of land (which might or might not be predominantly wooded) subject to special laws, usually concerned with the conservation of game. As the area of woodland began to dwindle before the spread of towns and organized agriculture, the two meanings converged and forestry began to mean the craft of managing and harvesting the various products of uncultivated, and therefore usually wooded, land.

By the early medieval period, when probably less than one-fifth of the original forested area remained under woodland cover, forestry was an exceptionally complicated business, with its own laws and codes of practice. The few thousand remaining square miles of tree-land provided (though not all at once from the same sites) the nation's firewood and building timber, acorns for its pigs and cob-nuts for their keepers, dyes, herbs, fruits, Christmas mistletoe and Easter palm, birch besoms and wattle hurdles, the odd rabbit or hare for the pot, shelter for cattle, footpaths for workers and sport for the gentry.

With a few amendments (most of the 'small business' of woods, for example blackberrying and bird-watching, is now carried out for enjoyment rather than necessity) this list would be a fair description of the range of provisions of modern forests, though there have been massive shifts in the scale and balance of the various uses. Medieval woodmen talked of *housebote, firebote, haybote, pannage, agistment* and *fugerium*; twentieth-century planners speak less elegantly of multiple-use environments. Yet the idea of the bountifulness of woodlands is common to both. No other kind of natural habitat can match the complexity of a wood's living space or the variety of lives which can be pursued in it.

In its most recent statement of objectives, the Forestry Commission placed the 'protection and enhancement of the environment' second only to the commercial production of timber. I think it is worth quoting this section of the document in full, for it captures succinctly both the great contribution which forestry can make to wildlife conservation and the limitations of its current philosophy:

As trustees for all sectors of the community and for future generations, the forester's duty is to respect our woodland inheritance and shape its lifecycle by the best of traditional and currently evolving standards, leaving options for further evolution. The Commission applies and continually develops this policy with distinguished professional advice, and accepting some reduction in financial returns. It seeks to perpetuate the predominantly broadleaved character of the typical southern lowland landscape, while giving conifers an appropriate place there, which is widely accepted. In the uplands, where often only conifers can be grown, it seeks effective landscaping at every opportunity.

The importance of forests as natural wildlife reservoirs places upon the Commission a special responsibility for following enlightened con-servation management policies, one it gladly accepts. The type and intensity of such management varies from forest to forest though there are virtually none of the Commission's forests which are unfit to serve as refuges for wildlife. It is the Commission's aim to improve forests as wildlife habitats and to integrate balanced conservation and wood production in a pattern of good land use and sound management.[34]

This is a heartwarming statement coming as it does from the largest woodland owner in Britain, yet it is almost exclusively concerned with the conservation of wildlife *in* woods. Its des-cription of woods as 'refuges' and 'reservoirs' suggests that the Commission regards a wood as a kind of building inside which creatures live, rather than a community with a life of its own, greater than the sum of its living parts. The conservation *of* woods – the preservation of their continuity and the features which depend on it – is, as we have glimpsed with Sladden Wood, just as important and it cannot be guaranteed by blanket policies such as perpetuating 'the predominantly broadleaved character' of southern England. A new beech plantation may be attractive from a distance, but inside it can be as thin in wildlife – and for that matter wild liveliness – as a young conifer plot.

We have to face the fact that conservation in relation to wood-lands means different things to different people. To a commer-cial forester it means guaranteeing a continuing supply of timber. To a forest ranger it may chiefly mean tolerating deer and protecting birds and badgers. To an ornithologist it will include the conserving of thickets of undergrowth and the pro-vision of nest-boxes on trees. To most parish amenity societies it means the preservation of fine old standing trees and the planting of new ones. Yet it was the lady who wrote to *Woman's Hour* in December 1977 who demonstrated just how diverse views of woodland conservation can be. Her plea to the public was to buy plastic Christmas trees, to save our plantations of young spruces from premature decapitation. It is easy to ridicule a view of ecology and conservation which supports the manu-facture of highly energy-consumptive synthetic trees in order to conserve stands of alien conifers that were planted for the pre-cise purpose of being cut for Christmas; but this lady, like the rest of us, is living in a century in which the predominant forestry activity has been the growing of tree species which, unlike hardwoods, do not sprout again when cut down. They die. It is no wonder that she considered that their protection would be a blow struck for conservation, a gesture on the side of the living.

The unspoken assumption running through all these various images is that where there are trees there's a wood, and there-fore – perhaps in some kind of biological tautology – woodland plants and creatures: nut bushes, crabtrees, sheets of bluebells, glades, a nightingale in a thicket, and a few venerable trees distinctive enough to be places in their own right, with their own mosses and hollows and woodpeckers. But the hard truth is that modern forestry practice cannot guarantee the survival of these features in woodland. They are the products not simply of tree cover, but of long periods of woodland stability. It is especially ironic that, just as the area of land under trees is on the increase again for the first time maybe since the Black Death, so the features that we take for granted as the quintessential ingredients of woodland should be most seriously threatened. The origins of this 'credibility gap' in woodland history (it strains public understanding as much as wildlife's tolerance) seem to lie in the breakdown of traditional woodland manage-ment that occurred during the eighteenth and nineteenth cen-turies. Up to that time most woods that had survived were 'taken as they grew'. They were relics of the primeval Wildwood – thinned, sifted through, cut back here, restocked there, but still retaining vestiges of their original community structure. They were rarely disturbed beneath the ground and, above ground, management often positively enhanced their richness.

But for the last 150 years trees have been increasingly treated as a long-rotation arable crop – planted, harvested, their 'stub-ble' ploughed out ready for the next planting. Plantations rarely have the dimensional richness of natural woods. They have no chance to develop a history, a structure dependent on time. Only the most opportunist and adaptable organisms – the squat-ters of the natural world – can cope with this kind of insecurity of tenure.

The problem is that our expectations of woodland wildlife derive largely from the immensely rich and varied communities of plants and creatures, the native inhabitants of our woods, that survived alongside the old management systems. Yet our belief about how woods 'work' is based on the modern plan-tation system. The confusions produced by these contrary images are formidable. At the risk of a gross, but I hope not too unfair, piece of simplification, the popular image of woodland development might be summed up like this. Most woods had the same origins as the plantations we see in increasing profusion. They were planted by man, and therefore the chief aim of woodland conservation must be to plant new trees in the unfortunate but likely event of old ones being cut down. Yet woods are also archetypally wild places, and we find it hard to believe that any of their interesting inhabitants or features – beyond their existence in the first place – could be due to anything as contrived and restraining as *management*.

Between this view and those of commercial foresters and woodland ecologists, there is not much common ground. Yet it is vital that we find some, for, although the area of land covered by trees is increasing, *old* woodland is fast disappearing, and the pressures upon all kinds of existing tree-land from agriculture and intensive forestry are accelerating. If we are to be clear about how these current pressures may affect woodland – both as a community and as a collection of particular, wild components – we need to look in more detail at the history of our woods and how their past uses shaped them.

THE PRIMEVAL FOREST

About 7000 years ago, when the climate was agreeably warm and man had made virtually no impact on the landscape, about two-thirds of the British Isles was covered by woodland. The only areas clear of trees were mountain slopes above about 2500 feet, the unstable rocks of cliffs and screes and beaches, and the considerable expanses of wetland. The remainder was the Wildwood, the primeval wilderness. This 'deciduous summer forest', as ecologists have rather evocatively named it, was (and still would be) the natural climax vegetation on these temperate islands, the culminating, stable plant community which would always tend to cover most dry land if only man (and drastic climatic change) were to stay in the background.

Yet this picture suggests something altogether too static and monotonous. Was the Wildwood really that uniform, that *finished*? Both everyday experience and archaeological evidence suggest that the traditional vision of a huge forest of mighty oaks, interspersed here and there with various inferior species, has more to do with a mixture of sentimentality and the plantation mentality than with fact. The best evidence of all – and the most relevant for conservation – is the immense variety of woodland types that have come down to us today. If for a moment we can accept the argument (there will be more to support it later) that the best of these semi-natural woods are modified relics of the original forest, we can see how vital and varied the fabric of the prehistoric Wildwood was. These remaining fragments are living woods, not fossils, and therefore not literal representations of the old forest; yet they are time capsules, in a way, and scanning them today we can catch a glimpse, an echo, of the richness and variation of the Wildwood.

There are beechwoods in the Chilterns, ashwoods on the Pennine limestones, pinewoods in the central Highlands of Scotland – and unplanted oakwoods and ashwoods for that matter, north of Loch Maree in Ross-shire, despite the Forestry Commission's scepticism about the viability of hardwoods in northern latitudes. There are smaller, more remarkable, types too, some represented by only a few remaining relics. Yew woods grow here and there on the southern chalk, most spectacularly at Kingley Vale National Nature Reserve in Sussex, where in spring their dark tiers – more black than green – are gashed with the felted white leaf-buds of whitebeams. A scrubby expanse of almost prostrate holly and blackthorn grows close to the sea on the Dungeness shingles. Tycanol Wood in Dyfed, which straddles an exposed west-facing crag five miles from the Atlantic coast, also has dwarf trees. At no more than 590 feet (180 metres) above sea level some of its windshorn oaks are reduced to a metre or so in height, yet more than 100 species of tree-borne lichen have been recorded for the whole wood.

To describe any wood in terms of its most persistently occurring or dominant tree is a convenience but rarely catches the associations of trees that give most woods their character. Oakwoods in north-west Scotland would be more properly called oak-birch-rowan-hazel woods. At another extreme, in Bardney Forest, Lincolnshire, they appear as an extraordinary series where oak shares dominance with small-leaved lime – a very fitting association, for this little-known tree may once have been the commonest in the lowland climax forest. It also occurs in the woods along the River Wye, especially those that hang on both sides of the spectacular meandering gorge cut out by the river in its lower reaches. The Wye here has worn down through geological layers that range from stony limestone to heavy clays, and the steep valley slopes carry almost our entire range of native trees and shrubs (more than sixty species) in apparently natural groupings. There are stands of an even rarer native lime – the large-leaved *Tilia platyphyllos* – with wych elm, field maple, wild service tree and many of its rare cousins. And, except in plantations, there are invariably woods within woods. In Hayley Wood, in Cambridgeshire, a mere forty-nine hectares (121 acres) in extent but with a written history extending back as far as 1251, Oliver Rackham* has identified six different woodland communities: ash-maple-hazel coppice with oak timber trees, which covers the bulk of the oldest parts of the wood; a variant of this on waterlogged soils in which aspen groves occur; an ash swamp; a strip of slightly younger woodland which has developed along an abandoned lane; the Triangle, a new wood sprung up this century in an abandoned field adjacent to the main wood; and patches of elm scattered throughout the wood, which form altogether seven distinct family groups (clones).[35]

George Peterken has likened these highly localized variations in the community structure of woods to 'dialects' in the trees and shrubs. They are paralleled by the variations in physical structure. Woods can include slopes so sheer that they are quite free of trees, and extensive natural clearings created by fire or the falling of large trees. (Dead wood in some form or another must have been a major element in the Wildwood and a great influence on its animal life. In some of the forests of Poland, which are believed to be amongst the closest remaining approximation to genuinely natural woodland in Europe, as much as 50 per cent of the timber is dead or dying.) Water too can radically change the pattern of tree cover. If a river flows through a wood it creates a strip entirely free of cover and fringed by unusual habitats like gravel beaches and rocky ghylls. If the water is moving (or held in the ground) the patchwork of cover and open habitats will be different again – fen, alder swamp, perhaps ponds and springlines.

Weather, fire, water, even large animals (of which we are just

---

* Oliver Rackham, whose name has occurred already and will do so again in this chapter, deserves a note to himself. His detailed studies of the ecology and human history of woodlands have revolutionized our view of their development, and his introductory book on the subject, *Trees and Woodland in the British Landscape*, is already a classic, a work of literature as well as of imaginative history and science.

the latest example), all play a part in shaping the architecture of a wood. Deer, for instance, not only beat out regular tracks through the undergrowth, but can convert a temporary clearing to permanent pasture by regular grazing. Left to its own devices and given enough time and space, a wood will quite naturally generate a variety of habitats that range from open, sun-lit glades to dense thickets, and from creeping mosses to huge, ancient trees and the extraordinary collections of birds, lichens and insects that live in association with both their live and their dead branches.

Given this wide choice of habitat and the extent of the original forest cover, it is no wonder that large numbers of our plants and animals are adapted to living in woodland conditions. Two-thirds of our breeding land-birds, more than half our butterflies and moths and one-sixth of our flowering plants are exclusively or chiefly dependent on woodlands. If we were to add those more adaptable species that occur in other habitats as well, and those that use woods casually from time to time, it would be possible to find, somewhere in the complex of woodland habitats, virtually the entire range of our flora and fauna. Only those species confined to extreme and highly specialized habitats like mountain tops and saltmarshes will not, at one time or another, have been able to find a living in the forest.

THE BEGINNINGS OF MANAGEMENT

This was the woodland estate that our prehistoric ancestors inherited, a vast and infinitely varied resource that must have seemed beyond ordering and simplification. Yet, from the moment that early men began to establish settled communities and clear the trees for their villages and crops, they began to use the forest. It was the source of their firewood and building timber and a good deal of their food. It provided browse and shelter for their cattle. Whilst there was still a small human population and an almost boundless expanse of woodland, these uses were entirely compatible. If cattle grazed out young saplings and held back woodland regeneration, or appropriated the most accessible lower branches of existing trees for browsing, there would always be, just a little deeper into the forest, an abundance of trees of all shapes and sizes. But, as the area of uncleared woodland declined and the demands for usable timber became more complex and specialized, it was inevitable that some deliberate management principles would be developed. There must have been two overriding needs. The first was to prevent cattle eating away the new tree growth as soon as it appeared. The second was to try and make this growth more regular and predictable. Underwood for burning can be rough and ready stuff, but for making baskets or the shafts of forks and ploughs you need poles of a straightness and evenness that cannot always be guaranteed by free-growing branches.

It would be hard to say when the answer to this need – the coppice – was invented. But it cannot have escaped the attention of early woodmen that most of our deciduous trees, when they were cut down, regenerated naturally by sending up sheaves of vigorous, straight new shoots from their stumps (more usually referred to as 'stools', to distinguish them from dead stumps). It was then only a short step to the deliberate felling of trees, not just for their immediate timber yield but for the multitude of even poles that would sprout from their bases and continue to sprout almost indefinitely after each new growth was harvested – and from there to physically separating the woodland areas where cattle were pastured from the areas where coppice poles were grown. (These, incidentally, are what are traditionally referred to as 'wood'. 'Timber' refers to mature, uncropped trees, cut for more substantial works.)

The formal coppice, where the stools were cut on a strict rotation and the young shoots protected from browsing cattle by banks or fences, is sometimes accredited to the Normans. Yet the informal practice is much older. Amongst the oldest surviving wooden artefacts in the world are the 'corduroy' roads that were built to provide ways across treacherous peat bogs. The most sophisticated of the trackways so far discovered is also the oldest. It was excavated in the Somerset Levels and contains oak logs, poles of ash and alder and holly, and smaller wands of hazel and small-leaved lime – all selected to fulfil different functions in the structure. Most of the poles are too straight and uniform to be branches of trees or casual cuttings from scrub. Oliver Rackham believes that it is 'very unlikely that such poles could have been *found* in the Wildwood; they must have been *grown* in managed woodland . . . . The sizes and shapes of the poles are remarkably like those produced by a medieval mixed coppice on a rather long rotation. An exact replica could easily be built out of the Bradfield Woods.' This trackway has been placed by radiocarbon dating to somewhere between 3000 B.C. and 4000 B.C.

The Bradfield Woods in west Suffolk are perhaps the finest surviving example of a worked coppice. One of the group, Felsham Hall Wood, has an almost unbroken record of coppicing going back to at least 1252, when it was owned by Bury St Edmunds Abbey. There are woods still in existence with even older pedigrees (though, unlike Felsham, most of these are no longer actively coppiced), and it is clear that, by the early medieval period, what remained of our forest cover was being run efficiently and intelligently as a self-renewing resource, and that a formal distinction between coppice woodland and pasture woodland had already been established.

The clearest evidence for this is in Domesday Book (1086) which, in literally thousands of references, records six out of ten English parishes and villages as having woodland of some kind.[36] The statistics and nomenclature of Domesday are notoriously inconsistent, and are difficult to translate into modern equivalents. But the frequent references to *silva pastilis*, particularly in the north and west, almost certainly refer to woods used for pasture, and those to *silva minuta* (with variants like *silva parva* and *silva modica*) to underwood or coppice. In some areas *silva* is replaced by the word *nemus*, and there are references to *nemus ad sepes* (wood for fencing) and *nemus ad domus* (wood for house-building, or perhaps just domestic use in general). Remarkably, the entries for twenty-nine close-lying villages on the boulder-clay of west Cambridgeshire are all in these last two forms, which may indicate a local scarcity of woodland, necessitating the intensive management of what remained as coppice. 900 years later this corner of Cambridgeshire still has a fine concentration of medieval coppices, and they are still oases in an ocean of open farmland.

The entries for much of the rest of eastern England are given in terms of numbers of swine and are more difficult to interpret. It is now generally realized that the 'swine number' was a notional unit of measurement and bore no relationship to the actual numbers of pigs owned by a village and allowed to forage in its woodland. Underwood or coppice in these regions may simply have been ignored, or measured in terms of a swine number even if pigs never entered them. Yet pigs were probably allowed into the coppices when acorns or beechmast were in short supply – and provided the coppice shoots were well enough developed to be able to sustain a certain amount of damage.

For all its uncertainties Domesday gives a good idea of the distribution of woodland in eleventh-century England. The similarities with the current pattern of deciduous woodland cover are striking. The clay lands of the Weald, for instance, and the Wye and Severn valleys stand out as conspicuously wooded areas, just as they do now. The extent of local woodlands no doubt influenced the style of management. In well-wooded areas – and in the thinly populated upland areas of the north and west – coppicing was probably done on a fairly haphazard basis. In areas of the lowlands where the forest was cleared early and an arable bias (and often early enclosures) had been established even by the middle ages, the remaining woods were smaller and were of necessity managed very intensively. Felsham Hall Wood was typical of these lowland coppices and probably looked much the same 700 years ago as it does today.

The whole wood is surrounded by a huge boundary bank and ditch – a characteristic feature of ancient coppices which was vital to keep out wandering deer and cattle. The underwood is cut on a short rotation (about ten years) so that at any moment there are compartments in the wood which are completely open, having recently been cut, and others at all stages of regrowth up to the dark and densely packed thickets, thirty feet tall or more, that are ready for their next cut. From casual notes in court rolls and accounts it looks as if the composition of the underwood was much as we find it today – a mixture of ash, hazel, maple, lime, birch, crab apple and willow. Very little went to waste. The finer cuttings were bound up as faggots for firewood. Hazel was especially valuable as it could be woven into wattle hurdles, for use in fencing and house-building. Selected stools of species such as ash and maple, which supplied finer quality timber (useful for making farm implements or in small-scale turning), might be cut on a longer rotation of up to twenty years. And, scattered amongst the stools, which would continue to provide these poles indefinitely, a few standard or 'maiden' trees (particularly oak) would be allowed to grow to maturity. Sometimes these trees were promoted coppice poles. Sometimes they grew from seedlings which became established in the open conditions just after a compartment had been cut. In later centuries they were also deliberately planted. These timber trees were often cut highly selectively, being taken out because a certain pattern of branching or a curve in the trunk fitted the needs of a particular piece of building work. The skills and conventions of medieval carpentry relied upon exploiting the natural characteristics of trees and thus avoided the waste and loss of strength involved in attempting to turn naturally eccentric logs into uniform timbers. In every way the management of the medieval coppice was integrated with the social life of the village, from supplying its firewood and the raw material of its craftsmen to influencing the design of its buildings. (In many woods – Hayley, for instance – these links were direct and parishioners had explicit rights to cut their own wood and to gather bark and nuts and other by-products.)

So too was the system of wood-pasture – though in this case it was the social organization that was complex and the management that was simple. 'Wood-pasture' is a term used for any type of land on which the growing of trees was combined with the grazing of stock. The animals fed on the grass and herb layers beneath the trees, browsed the lower branches, and foraged acorns and beechmast when these were available. There was, as a result, very little tree regeneration from seeds or suckers, and no usable new growth from existing trunks at any level which was within the reach of the cattle. So the usual technique of harvesting wood in pasture land was *pollarding*, the lopping of often quite sizable branches at a height of between six and ten feet above the ground. Like a coppice stool, the pollarded boll grew new branches to replace those that had been cut. But the cutting cycle was usually less regular than in a coppice, as lopped branches were really only useful for firewood or rough timber. Perhaps the most important factor regulating the length of the rotation was the need to keep the underlying grass well-lit and productive.

As well as providing a continuous supply of wood and promoting grass growth, pollarding greatly increased the life-span of the trees themselves by reducing their liability to wind damage and toppling and the demands on their above-ground resources. (Stag-headedness is now generally regarded as a kind of auto-pollarding by trees whose budgets have become over-taxed.) Prolonging the life of existing trees helped compensate for the fact that very few new trees could be expected to grow under conditions of heavy grazing.

Traditional wood-pasture was a close approximation to our popular image of an ancient forest and is the kind of woodland we can still find in places like Sherwood and the New Forest. It had a scatter of large, old trees – often sculptured in extraordinary shapes because of centuries of pollarding – dappled clearings, a rather sparse ground flora, no undergrowth, and a good deal of dead and fallen wood. This comparatively simple picture belies the immense variety of administrative systems which regulated wood-pastures. Many were wooded commons, the open wasteland of the manor on which the rights to graze stock and cut wood (though not to fell trees) were vested in the local villagers. There were also enclosed parks, which usually contained cattle or native red deer, though there were a few curiosities like hare parks. But, after the introduction of the fallow deer by the Normans, these parks were increasingly devoted to private hunting interests. The fashion for 'the chase' raised the number of private parks from thirty-five in Domesday to something like one in every fifteen square miles by 1330.

Both wooded commons and enclosed parks could be found in the Royal Forests. 'Forest' here is a strictly legal term, indicating that certain laws operated over an area of land rather than describing its woodland characteristics. These laws were biased towards the conservation of deer (though this was as much for commercial reasons as to provide an object for sport) and they often included provisions designed to preserve tree cover. Yet the king's rights rarely extended beyond deer and timber and, even in the much reduced Royal Forests of the late medieval period (when the word had come to mean just those parts of the original Forest which were not farmland or private wood), there were common pastures and worked coppice. The Royal Forests were classic early examples of what we would now call multiple-use habitats. Hatfield Forest in Essex (now managed by the National Trust) is unique in that all the elements of the medieval Forest system survive: deer, cattle, grassland, pollards, coppices, ponds and moats, and even a seventeenth-century rabbit warren.

USE AND CONTINUITY

The detailed records of medieval woodland management, fascinating though they are, can only give us circumstantial evidence about the origins of woodland wildlife. Yet they all point to the likelihood that both coppice and wood-pasture were modified relics of the Wildwood, carved out of the forest rather than specially planted. There is some support for this view in the similarity between the composition of the tree cover in medieval woods and that suggested by archaeological remnants of the prehistoric forest (chiefly pollen grains and wood fragments preserved in peat). Considered by themselves, of course, neither coppice nor wood-pasture bears much resemblance to 'natural' woodland. But, added together, they represent most of the elements we imagine made up the primeval forest. What medieval woodmanship did, in effect, was to split the two chief layers of a natural forest and conserve them under separate management systems. The coppice preserved the continuity of the ground flora, the shrubs and young trees, and the animals and birds that depended on them. Wood-pasture preserved ancient trees and dead wood and their associated communities.

Often management actually heightened a wood's diversity, by changing the balance between different species and communities, and occasionally by introducing quite new habitats. Commercially valuable species like hazel, for instance, were encouraged and so tended to increase; but then so, incidentally, did many other shrubs, as a result of the regular increase in the light reaching them which followed coppicing or the felling of trees. Coppicing also gave an enormous boost to the blossoming and seeding of woodland flowers.

Artificial habitats, such as the rides which were cut to provide access to the wood and exit routes for the cut timber, extended the permanently open habitat that in natural forest only occurs in clearings and along the edges of wide streams. Boundary banks and ditches increased the opportunities for plants of both damp and well-drained situations. Ponds were dug to water horses, and very occasionally hedges constructed *inside* a wood to protect young shoots.

All this work meant not just alterations in the natural structure of the wood, but considerable physical stress. Anyone who has worked in a coppice will know the ravages that the ground suffers as the wood is being cut and sawn and carted out. When coppicing was still an important part of rural economy the activity inside the woods during the winter cutting season must have been intense. The woodmen would often live in the woods during the cutting season, building cabins out of spare timber. Not having the benefit of circular saws, they used long two-handers to slice up the standard trunks and had to dig deep pits for one of the sawyers to stand in. The heavy, horse-drawn

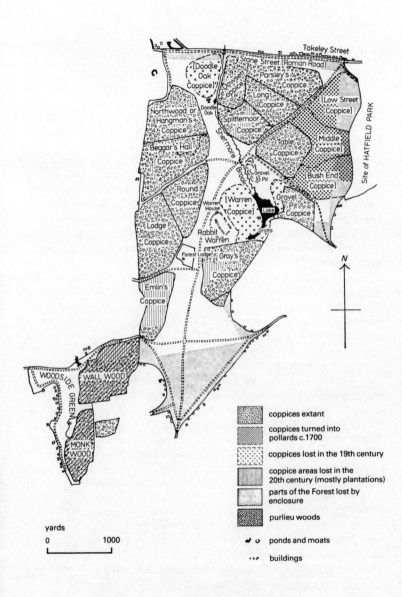

Takeley Street
Stane Street (Roman Road)
[Doodle Oak Coppice]
Parsley's Coppice
Dove Coppice
Long Coppice
[Low Street [Coppice]
Northwood or Hangman's Coppice
Doodle Oak
Spittlemoor [Coppice]
[Middle [Coppice]
Site of HATFIELD PARK
Beggar's Hall Coppice
Table Coppice
[Bush End [Coppice]
Shermore Brook
Round Coppice
Gravel Pit
Warren House
[Warren [Coppice]
Lake
Gravel Pit Coppice
Lodge Coppice
Grotto
Rabbit Warren
Forest Lodge
Gray's Coppice
Emlin's Coppice
N
WOODSIDE GREEN
WALL WOOD
MONK WOOD

coppices extant
coppices turned into pollards c.1700
coppices lost in the 19th century
coppice areas lost in the 20th century (mostly plantations)
parts of the Forest lost by enclosure
purlieu woods

yards
0   1000

⌁ ○   ponds and moats
···   buildings

Figure 2. Hatfield Forest, an ancient multiple-use habitat, now owned and managed by the National Trust. From Oliver Rackham, Trees and Woodland in the British Landscape.[33]

Pollards appear many times in this book, and there is a good case for saying that they are the most vivid demonstrations of what can result from a co-operative working relationship between man and nature.

The idea of lopping the branches of trees (for firewood, cattle fodder, etc.) above the level at which animals browsed was one of the first inventions of formal woodland management, and the practice was almost certainly well-established by 3000 B.C. Its original intention was to ensure that replacement shoots could grow – and be cropped in their turn – without being eaten away. But the many other benefits that resulted must have been obvious very soon. It encouraged the growth of grass beneath the trees. By reducing the demands on trees' food resources, (and also their top-heaviness) it reduced their susceptibility to disease and windthrow, and often doubled their life-span. This longevity, combined with the unique shapes and textures produced by centuries of lopping, meant that pollards often became important as meeting-place trees and boundary markers. It also meant that they could become extraordinarily rich and diverse wildlife habitats. Lichens grow on their trunks, and ferns in the damp cracks in their bark. Owls live in the hollow centres and insects in the patches of dead and rotting wood. Pockets of humus often accumulate in the crown of the tree, and an immense variety of bird-sown plants can grow here. The seventeenth century botanist John Morton even discovered wild columbines in pollard willows. I have found four different species of tree growing from a crown of a single willow not more than fifty years old, and a farmer nearby, who has a willow similarly blessed, boasts that he is the only local fruit-grower who has to climb a ladder to pick his gooseberries.

Pollarding is responsible for the gnarled shapes we traditionally associate with ancient trees. Yet (willows excepted) virtually no new pollarding has been done this century, so we are living on the rapidly decaying legacy of another generation's good sense. If we wish to have pollards in the future we have to begin to create them now, with young trees, and be prepared to put up with the rather unattractive and bristly appearance they present for the first few years after cutting.

A Dutch poster, showing the range of natural life that can find a home in a pollard willow.

(Left) *Tree lungwort* (Lobaria pulmonaria) *in Rassal Ashwood NNR, in the old county of Ross-shire. Lichens like this are not just indicators of damp forest conditions free of atmospheric pollution, but of the continuity of woodland cover (see page 99).*

(Below) *Bluebells under old hornbeam coppice, Hertfordshire. Although the trees were last coppiced forty or fifty years ago and cast a heavy shade, the wood has never been seriously disturbed. Bluebells, and many other flowers, are, like the lichen above, associated with continuous, settled woodland conditions (see page 86).*

(Above) *House martins, one of the favourite 'parish birds'. Marvellously adaptable, they have taken recently to nesting in plastic nestboxes, on concrete water-towers and even under motorway bridges. One of the very few threats they face is from the occasional householder who illegally destroys their nests in the interests of 'hygiene'. In most continental countries they are believed to bring luck to the houses they lodge at for the summer months (see page 36).*

(Left) *A young grey seal: another much-loved creature but, unlike the house martin, only partially protected by law, and with a life-expectancy very much dependent on the level of current culling programmes. Should public affection, in cases like this, override scientific and economic pressures to control populations? (See pages 24–25)*
  (Alan McGregor)

wagons in which the underwood and timber were carried out must have churned up the ground just as thoroughly as a modern tractor.

Yet ancient woods seem impervious to this kind of treatment. Felsham Hall Wood has been subject to the pressures associated with coppicing almost every winter for the last 700 years. Yet it is still one of the richest woods in England, containing over one-fifth of all our flowering plant species and forty-two species of native trees and shrubs. Every spring the compartments which were cut the previous year are dashed with brilliant patches of oxlips and wood anemones and early purple orchids.

Phyllida Rixon's history of another East Anglian wood, Bedford Purlieus, gives an even more persuasive picture of the capacity of working woods to survive wear and tear.[37] The Purlieus (originally known as Thornhaw Wood) is a surviving remnant of the Royal Forest of Rockingham, which once covered much of Northamptonshire. Its early history was mixed, and it appears to have gone through periods both as a grazed wood and as a coppice. One of the striking features of the records is the degree of pressure the wood had to bear. The manorial rolls of 1597 list the offences of a steward called Nicholas Thorogood, who dug up thorn trees for fencing his own lands, felled and purloined timber including 'two great crab trees, one servis tree, 2 ashes and divers old sallows', and repeatedly allowed his sheep and horses to stray into private coppices in the wood, where 'they do great spoil in the springtime by eating the spring of the same woods. . . '. Later the estate hired men for the express purpose of 'catching nutters' and guarding the timber on the eve of May day, when the local commoners apparently always tried to poach a little extra underwood and a few straight trees for use as maypoles. But between 1862 and 1868 there was a much more calamitous attack upon the wood: 600 acres – half its total extent – were grubbed up by the Duke of Bedford, at a cost of nearly £19,000.

The common buzzard, known in parts of Scotland as the 'tourists' eagle'. It would perhaps be less easily misidentified if illegal killing by keepers was not preventing its becoming a familiar bird in the lowlands again (see page 192).
(Alan McGregor)

(With the fall of wheat prices to sixty shillings a quarter this proved to be a financial disaster, and the cleared ground was soon allowed to revert to rough pasture.)

During this century the pressures on the Purlieus have accelerated. Most of the standing timber has been clear-felled, and in places the derelict coppice stools have been interplanted with oak, beech and a few exotic species. During the Second World War 150 acres (sixty hectares) were occupied by the army. In the 1950s the British Steel Corporation leased the mineral rights (there is ironstone under the ground) and began quarrying. . . . The story goes on, and the future of the Purlieus is by no means assured. Yet, through all these upheavals and the incursions of earlier centuries, the surviving 500 acres (200 hectares) have remained as *woodland*. Phyllida Rixon's detective work has established an historical continuity back to 972 A.D. and that is about as far back as one can go with historical records. It is a reasonable assumption that any wood which was in existence at this time was a genuine prehistoric relic and that Bedford Purlieus has, in consequence, been a continuously wooded site for 7000 years. The richness of the flowering plants certainly points to ancient origins: there were 462 species at the last count (including forty-five species of trees and shrubs) – the most recorded for any single wood in Britain.

Like Sladden, Bedford Purlieus is at present a ragged and incongruous wood, and the evidence of the intense pressures of the last fifty years is inescapable. Yet I find it a curiously heartening place. When you see that prehistoric survivor, the small-leaved lime, continuing to sprout amongst the newly planted chestnuts, and lilies-of-the-valley crowding amongst the bracken up to the very edge of the quarry tracks, it is hard not to feel a sense of hope about the resilience of our ancient woods.

Yet it would be dangerous to become complacent about the immutability of woodland, or to assume that employment necessarily increases their natural interest. One of the less happy consequences of the organized management of woods was that they became defined and discrete. In acquiring boundaries and names they became separated from one another. This made little difference to the lives of their more mobile inhabitants. Mammals, birds, flying insects, even plants with light, wind-borne seeds, could easily migrate between woods over quite large areas of farmland. Yet a less aggressive woodland plant (like the wood anemone, say), cut off in an isolated fragment of wood, was in a much more precarious position. If, by any accident, this species was wiped out in the wood, there was no easy way in which it could reappear by natural colonization. The source of new plants was too remote. And the shrinking in size which inevitably accompanied isolation made such localized exterminations that much more likely. The smaller a wood (or for that matter any kind of habitat) becomes, the more vulnerable to extinction are the species that live in it. It is not simply that there will be fewer numbers of each kind of plant and animal; the genetic variability will be less too, which will reduce the chance of there being any individuals adapted to survive a drastic change in local conditions. The fortunes of species hanging on in these isolated pockets of woodland so closely resemble those of species on real islands that the process of woodland clearance is often compared to 'islanding' – a movement from a continental land-mass of forest, broken here and there by lake-like clearings, to a cluster of wooded islands in a sea of farmland.

Yet it was precisely this highly organized pattern and the intensive use of the remaining islands that helped ensure their survival. By the middle ages woodland was too scarce and valuable a resource to squander. One of the most intractable historical myths that has grown up this century – and which must bear a good deal of responsibility for our modern horror of cutting trees – is that our woodland was destroyed by being *used*: burnt up in the furnaces of the iron-smelters and sunk with the great ships of successive battle fleets. It is now clear that this theory is not supported by historical evidence (see Rackham again).[33] Iron-smelters or builders who destroyed one of their basic resources in the ordinary pursuit of their trade would rapidly have gone out of business. They relied absolutely on a continuous, reliable local supply of wood. And the joy of the coppice, as we have seen, is that it can meet this need, and continue to grow bushels of firewood indefinitely. I doubt if it is a coincidence that many of the surviving concentrations of one-time coppice (in the Forests of Wyre and Dean, for example, and the Loch Lomond oakwoods) coincide with areas of heavy ironstone quarrying in the seventeenth and early eighteenth centuries.

The felling of *timber*, for house- or ship-building, say, had a more conspicuous effect (especially if it was taken from heavily grazed wood-pasture, or from areas where natural regeneration was slow, such as the Highland pinewoods). But felling alone would only result in temporary treelessness. All of our native species will regenerate from seed or suckers if they have sufficient light and are protected from over-browsing, and even a wood which was clear-felled should have had useful extractable timber again within forty or fifty years. What destroyed our woodlands was not employment but redundancy. If a wood was felled at a time when wheat or sheep or speculative building were more profitable than timber, then the cutting of the trees was often followed by the clearing of the ground. The use of the land itself changed.

The increasing availability of cheap coal and imported Scandinavian timber (and in our own time of synthetic substitutes for wood) increased the economic irrelevance of our native woods. By the late eighteenth century the area of woodland in Britain was probably lower than at any time since the immediate post-glacial period (and certainly lower than now). It was this drastic reduction in tree cover that led John Evelyn and others to campaign for a nationwide programme of planting. The early plantations of the eighteenth century were superficially not unlike many of the woodlands they were meant to replace. They were mixes of native hardwoods, often established on areas that had not long lost their tree cover. Parkland on private estates and downland in areas where sheep had become uneconomical were favourite sites. The chief physical difference between them and the old 'natural' coppices was that they were managed almost exclusively for their timber crop, not their underwood. They were what we now call 'high forest'.

But by the early part of the nineteenth century the idea of tree monocultures began to take a grip. In the Chilterns, the coppices were promoted to beech high forest (and augmented by extensive plantations) to feed the furniture industry in High Wycombe. Exotic trees began to appear. In 1829 the Duke of Atholl began planting up hundreds of thousands of acres in Scotland with larch. The process led inevitably to our present forestry pattern, with its massive plantations of alien conifers, planted up on sites with a low agricultural potential, including, all too often, existing ancient woods.

The effect of the introduction of the plantation system has been that, over the last century, the net area of land under trees has actually increased and is likely to go on doing so. In 1895 there were 2,725,000 acres. In 1965/7 there were 4,305,100 acres – an increase of 1.58 million acres or 58 per cent.[38] Yet these figures disguise dramatic changes in the character and location of woodland. Although the area of woodland shrank between the middle ages and the beginning of this century, its pattern of distribution across Britain remained substantially the same. Today traditionally well-wooded areas like Hampshire and the Chilterns have been overtaken in woodland density by the Norfolk Brecklands and the hills of eastern Scotland, which have had scarcely any woodland for hundreds of years. In individual areas, too, the nature of the woodland cover has altered. George Peterken, the NCC's woodland authority, has examined in detail the changes in the composition of Rockingham Forest over the last three centuries.[39] The total area dropped from a figure of 8442 hectares in 1650 to a low of 4900 hectares in 1885, creeping back to 5525 hectares in 1972. Yet the area of *ancient* woodland declined consistently throughout this period. As far as can be told, all the woodland in 1650 had been there in medieval times and therefore was probably descended from the original, natural Wildwood. By 1817, 1260 hectares of this ancient woodland had been cleared and 460 hectares of plantation established on previously unwooded ground. By 1972, only 3558 hectares of the old woods remained; 4251 hectares had been cleared and not replanted, and 1967 hectares of new plantation had been created. Throughout Britain there has been the same drastic decline in old woodland. In eastern England not far short of half the ancient woodland that remained in 1946 had been destroyed by grubbing out or coniferization by the mid-seventies.[33]

WOODS, ANCIENT AND MODERN

The differences in the ecology and character of ancient and modern woods are so extensive that a distinction based on their origins is now used as a way of classifying woods. So, in addition to grouping them according to underlying soils, dominant tree communities, management styles and so on, we can also describe them as *primary* or *secondary*.[40] Primary woodland is on sites which have been continuously wooded (that is, not converted to arable or meadowland, for example) during the historical period, which is normally assumed to indicate continuity back to the days of the Wildwood. Secondary woodland is that which now occupies sites which have *not* been continuously wooded. The management of the woods does not affect this classification. Primary woods can have been clear-felled repeatedly without their continuity being broken. And secondaries can be entirely spontaneous, 'natural' woods which have sprung up in abandoned arable fields.

It is sometimes hard to believe that a small and unexceptional copse, in which none of the individual trees looks particularly old, may be on a site which has been continuously wooded since the Stone Age, and that its present structure and wildlife may be the result of 1000 years of interaction between human and natural forces. Yet so deeply does history etch itself on a wood that even the least prepossessing primary woodland can possess a range of features that simply cannot occur in secondary woods. The genetic variety of the trees, which represents some of the variations which have occurred over several thousand years (and which is evident in the characteristically 'quirky' shapes of woodland oaks, for instance), is one example. Another is the soil structure, which by definition has never been seriously disrupted in a primary wood. (Hayley Wood, in Cambridgeshire, now a county Trust nature reserve, is used as a site for the monitoring of radioactive fall-out because of the reasonable certainty that the soil strata of all but a small area have never been disturbed and are unlikely to be so.) But perhaps the most striking difference is that a whole range of woodland plants and animals appear to be confined to primary woods and find it hard to colonize, and in some cases even survive in, secondary woods. In a group of about 300 woods in central Lincolnshire, George Peterken was able to distinguish eighty-five probable primaries by an examination of maps, written records and archaeological evidence. Comparing their flora with that of the newer woods, he found that at least fifty species of flowering plant were more or less restricted to the continuously wooded sites.[41] These were not for the most part great rarities, or where they were it was usually because primary woods themselves were becoming scarce and fragmented. They included many of the plants that we usually look on as the traditional flowers of our woodlands. Wood sorrel, yellow archangel, sweet woodruff, wood anemone, lily-of-the-valley, yellow pimpernel, greater butterfly-orchid, goldilocks, early dog-violet and herb paris were almost completely confined to primary woods. Moschatel, ramsons, sanicle, early purple orchid and primrose had most of their localities in primary woods, and their other sites were in long-established habitats – ancient hedge banks, old meadows – that had clear historical or geographical links with primary woodland.

This is a list compiled from a specific group of woods in central Lincolnshire and cannot be transferred as it stands to other parts of the country. But comparable lists are being drawn up for other areas using methods similar to George Peterken's. In the Cotswolds, for instance, meadow saffron, red helleborine and angular solomon's seal are quite reliable indicators. In the drier parts of East Anglia even bluebell is confined to ancient woods (though it becomes much more adaptable as you move west). And it is becoming clear that there is a basic list of plants that are far commoner in primary woods than in secondaries right across lowland Britain – a list that would include, for instance, wild service tree, small-leaved lime, herb paris, wild columbine and lily-of-the-valley.

In the boulder-clay regions of East Anglia, the true oxlip, *Primula elatior*, is not a bad indicator, but it does crop up in some secondary woods in circumstances that give a clue as to why there are such differences between the flora of the two types of wood. It is, for instance, slowly invading (at a rate of about four feet a year) the Hayley Wood Triangle (page 71) which has only been under trees since the 1920s, but which abuts directly on to the ancient core of the wood. Bluebell, dog's mercury and bird's nest orchid are also colonizing the Triangle, and Oliver Rackham reckons that it will take something like 150 years for the pattern of vegetation to resemble that in the old wood.

The chief factor which keeps so many plants 'loyal' to ancient woodland seems to be their poor colonizing ability. Some scarcely seem able to extend their range where they are already established, let alone find their way cross-country to newly-formed woods. As a group they are, typically, slow-growing perennials with rather low reproductive capacities. Even if they are successful in reaching secondary woodland (or are deliberately introduced), they stand little chance in the short run amongst aggressive and adaptable colonizers like cow parsley and hedge garlic. But the less demanding primary woodland species can, as we have seen, persist in other long-established habitats. In southern England, for example, archangel and woodruff are quite common in old hedge banks, and pignut and goldilocks in unimproved grasslands. From these reservoirs they can recolonize adjacent secondary woods. In areas of countryside where there is an abundance of woodland of all kinds, probably linked up by relatively undisturbed hedgerows and stream banks, there are consequently less marked differences between the flora of primary and secondary woodland.

Yet there are fewer and fewer areas of compact countryside where such opportunities for colonization occur, and in general it is true to say that, the more primary woodland we lose, the more many of our favourite woodland flowers will be reduced. No amount of new tree planting will conjure them back if there is nowhere for them to come back from. Trees are not magic wands that, when waved over the earth, spontaneously generate woodland flowers.

Nor are flowering plants the only group to contain sensitive species which are restricted to long-established woodland. There are lichens and invertebrates dependent on the old trees and dead wood of ancient high forest, and mosses confined to the rocky floors of damp westerly woods.

What all this amounts to, in short, is that primary woodland is irreplaceable. In neither a philosophical nor a physical sense can it be re-created. Its gene pool and community structure, even many of its actual inhabitants, are dependent on an uninterrupted (though by no means uneventful) history that may go back to prehistoric times – and promises by developers to 'restore' woodland which has been destroyed by quarrying or road-building should be viewed with considerable scepticism. They may re-establish the trees but they will not re-create the wood.

The idea of 'non-re-creatability' could be regarded as the equivalent for communities to irreplaceability for species. Not just individual habitats, but whole habitat types, could become extinct in the same way as individual plants and animals – and would likely take a good deal of these with them. If this is so, then the conservation of living communities which are non-re-creatable (it is a clumsy phrase, but there is no other which quite catches the meaning) could be our second Hippocratic rule (see page 33). This is especially true as, on George Peterken's estimation, primary woods account for not more than 20 per cent of our current woodland area (50 per cent if we include mature secondary woods which have begun to assume some primary characteristics). They clearly have a good case for priority treatment if we are not to lose their 'loyal' species and most of the other features we traditionally associate with woods. (But, again, it is only a baseline rule, not the guiding principle of a whole policy for habitat conservation. A twenty-year-old mixed plantation is not something to be given up lightly just because a wood resembling it could conceivably be grown inside a generation.)

The conservation of these remaining primary sites presents rather more problems than their identification. Some, it is true, are fairly well protected by their topography, for instance the little dingles that lie in steep-sided valleys all along the Welsh marches, and the wooded ravines of the western Highlands. Woods in deep gorges and on precipitous slopes have probably been less modified by human influence and grazing pressure than any other type. They often possess a much wider range of primeval forest components than have been able to survive in accessible lowland woods. At Inverneil Burn, for example, a ten-hectare (twenty-five acre) wooded gorge in Argyllshire, there are not just moss-covered boulders, a rich herb layer of woodruff, meadowsweet and beech fern, but lichen-draped hazels, mature ashes and wych elms, and a good deal of dead and rotting wood – elements that have normally been fastidiously separated by traditional woodland management. (Yet the presence, even here, of naturalized rhododendron shows just how hard it is to find examples of truly natural woodland in Britain.)

Sites such as these can also provide opportunities for the development of some of the most interesting examples of secondary woodland. When a massive landslip in the mid-nineteenth century created the famous undercliffs between Axmouth and Lyme Regis (now protected as a National Nature Reserve), it opened up a chasm which has become covered by a mosaic of ash and field maple and a thick scrub layer of hazel, dogwood, spindle and blackthorn.

The problems arise with the two major kinds of surviving primary woodland – coppice and wood-pasture – both of which have lost the economic importance they once had and the management techniques that reflected this. In many landowners' eyes they are already derelict and redundant – and that, as we have seen, is the surest prelude to clearance. They badly need new social roles, and styles of management designed to fulfil these which are practicable, economically viable and capable of sustaining the potentially rich communities which hang on in these woods. It would be no real answer – even if it were possible – to establish them as 'woodland reserves' and simply leave it at that. Although they only make up one-fifth of our current woodland estate, that is not far short of 1 million acres (400,000 hectares) of trees. It is scarcely feasible that such an area of potentially productive woodland should be exempt from contributing – as it previously did – towards its keep. Not that we should want it to be exempt. The idea that conservation and economic use are in some way fundamentally opposed is, as we saw in Part One of this book, a fallacy. In the case of our surviving woodlands, major elements in their ecological make-up are a *consequence* of use and, if it is these elements that we wish to conserve, the traditional pattern of use – or something which fulfils the same function – will need to be continued.

I will be looking in the final section of the book at ways in which new social and economic roles might be found for supposed 'archaic' habitats and land-uses. For the moment I want to look at the current state of our coppices and wood-pastures, and at what is needed if their special natural features and inhabitants are to survive. What follows, in effect, is a set of scenarios of the likely ecological impact and practicality of a number of possible futures.

FROM COPPICE TO COPSE

Now coppicing has largely ceased it is often hard to tell ancient coppices from other woodland types, but they probably account for 90 per cent of our remaining primary woodlands. They are concentrated in the lowlands, but remnants can still be found even in mountainous areas of Wales and Scotland. They range in size from vast tracts like Cranborne Chase to half-acre village spinneys and, as discrete, individual woods, they must be numbered in tens of thousands. The one thing the vast majority have in common is that they are no longer cut. The value of coppice woodland as a source of fuel and domestic timber began to decline in the nineteenth century. By the 1920s a complex range of social changes – cheaper coal, better transport, the running down of local craft shops, the gutting of whole woods during the First World War – had made the vast majority redundant as a component of the village economy.

The fifty years of relatively unchecked growth since then are responsible for the current appearance (*not* the structure – except in terms of age) of most of our coppices, and of what we probably regard as the typical English wood – the late-twentieth-century parish copse. It is a smallish wood, usually between five and fifty acres. It has one or two old trees which escaped the axe at the beginning of the century, but very few dead ones. Some of the others look old, but even inside a wood a tree with a girth of four feet probably represents no more than sixty or seventy years' growth. Many of these trees appear to have more than one trunk and, if you examine their bases, you will see that they have developed from neglected coppice stools. The wood is quite dark inside, and the shrub layer – probably a mixture of hazel, holly and hawthorn – is tall and leggy. There will be patches of bluebell and dog's mercury under the trees, and a few clumps of primroses along the paths (though, as older citizens will tell you, 'not like there used to be'). There may be a large number of birds, but these will chiefly be familiar and adaptable garden species like thrushes and tits, and warblers will be the exception. Add a few larches and pines, planted by a previous owner in a fit of fashionable enthusiasm, some invading sycamores and an old marl pit now filled with very contemporary rubbish, and that is as far as you can get with generalities. It is, in short, a wood which will appear virtually worthless to a commercial forester and a positive waste of land to an ambitious farmer. Left to itself for 100 years or so, it would begin to develop a more natural structure, and maybe even produce some acceptable timber trees into the bargain; but its fate will have been decided long before that. In many cases it has been decided already. A minority of these woods are still being coppiced. Cranborne Chase, for instance, is still extensively cut for hazel wands, which are used in the making of hurdles, and many thousands of acres of worked coppice survive in Kent. A rather larger number have been selectively promoted to high forest. The Chiltern beechwoods are the classic example of this process, to the extent of having gone through a stage intermediate between coppice and high forest in which compartments of young, straight beech standards were clearfelled for turning into chair legs. (The bodgers, who did every stage of the work from felling to shaping, purchased areas of 'wood' just like freelance coppice workers.[42])

The majority, though, hang in various kinds of limbo. In East Anglia and the Midlands many are used as game coverts. They have been gutted of most of their timber, and the nearest they get to management is an occasional, sporadic cut to increase the density of the undergrowth for the pheasants. At another extreme, the coppices in the uplands are used for little more than shelter for cattle. Most of the shrub layer and ground flora has been grazed out (though it may conceivably have survived in the form of depauperate plants and dormant seed) and the remaining trees, mostly emaciated oaks, form a kind of immature wood-pasture.

What options are open for these derelict coppices? One suggestion often heard is that naturalists ought to welcome the end of 'unnatural' management and leave the woods alone to develop in their own way. I do not need to repeat the economic obstacles to such a policy. What may be less widely appreciated are the ecological dangers it presents. To begin with, most of our coppices are simply not big enough. A wood needs room to shift, to 'flex' at the edges, if it is to mature and still retain its identity. It also needs time, and there will be long periods during a coppice's transition to high forest when it will present a rather unattractive prospect – ragged and impenetrable, too clogged to produce timber of any value and too dark to support many flowers. Because there is nowhere for them to spread to, many plant and insect species which are dependent on light may become extinct during this stage. The process of transition is, of course, ecologically fascinating in its own right, but such intangible assets are not looked on too kindly, particularly when they are happening over a time-scale that is measured in centuries. The deliberate abandonment of a coppice is, in short, a risky business and certainly not a way of creating that perfect forest of the imagination where great trees preside immemorially over carpets of spring flowers.

A rather safer future for these woods, both ecologically and economically, would be to return them to the traditional management under which they evolved. This would restore their structure above ground and greatly enrich the herb layer. It is quite likely that the traditional spring brilliance of our woodland flowers is a result of the regular coppice cycle – the sudden opening to the light of a compartment, followed by a period of increasing shade during which the plants store up reproductive resources. When Buff Wood (one of the west Cambridgeshire boulder-clay woods, now owned by the University of Cambridge) was restored to coppice rotation in 1955 after a long period of neglect, the primrose population responded with a prolonged burst of flowering which lasted for eighteen months, and produced blooms that were estimated as a hundred times more profuse than they had been before coppicing began. (Nightingale nesting is also influenced by the cycle. A survey by K. Williamson and P. Stuttard in southern England showed that nightingales prefer coppices of between five and eight years' growth. The highest concentration of nesting pairs – in a six-year-old coppice – was *ten times* higher than that in old or recently cut underwood.[43])

A widespread restoration of coppicing would depend on the availability of a relatively skilled labour force and a market for the crop, and in these respects Buff Wood is an exception. It is managed by the University Botanic Garden, and its coppice products are used in a variety of ways in the garden – a neatly self-sufficient cycle which could be copied elsewhere. Most coppices run as nature reserves are forced to burn their cut wood for want of an outlet. But there are signs that the coppice market may be expanding again. The resurgence of thatching in weekend-cottage belts has greatly increased the local demand for hazel spars. A small lorry-load of hazel wands (the amount picked out from an acre of mixed Suffolk coppice) was fetching about £100 in 1978. Some of the new outlets are, paradoxically, the products of modern technology. Wattle hurdles are proving very successful as motorway sound screens. Manufacturers are buying mixed coppice to pulp into packaging material. The greatest hope for the reinvigoration of coppice woodland may lie in the wood-burning stove – a marriage of the most ancient use of underwood with the most modern ideas of energy conservation.

But I do not think we can regard a return to coppicing as a universal answer to the identity crisis of ancient woods. As well as the practical and economic difficulties I have touched on above, there are circumstances in which the reintroduction of coppicing after a long gap might seriously damage a wood. (This is particularly true of the northern oak coppices, where the trees are mostly growing on thin, depleted soils and are only able to live at subsistence level.) We should also remember that coppices are, by definition, abbreviated woods. They are especially short of mature trees, which are amongst the most attractive and biologically rich features of woodland – and the most commercially valuable.

The ideal future for old coppices, then, may be to convert them gradually to a more mixed type of woodland, retaining a small area of worked coppice for diversity's sake, or a larger area where there is a market for the wood, and 'promoting' the remainder to well-spaced high forest. High forest, as we have seen, is what a neglected coppice will eventually turn into anyway. But, if the conversion is carried out as a deliberate act of woodland management, it can result in a wood which is different from a 'spontaneous' forest in two important respects. Firstly, the density of the trees can be controlled so that the ground flora is not shaded out. Secondly, trees can be selectively encouraged with at least one eye on their potential timber value. The gross timber output of such a wood is obviously not as high as in a plantation, but it is much more diverse and is achieved with a very low input.

This is the policy that is being followed in parts of Ham Street Woods National Nature Reserve in Kent. Under the inspired hand of the warden, John Maylam, this 233-acre (ninety-four-hectare) wood has become one of the most attractive and exciting in southern England, and a case study of the way that commercial forestry and nature conservation can co-exist. There is still a good deal of coppice. The hornbeam is cut for pulpwood on a twenty-year cycle, small quantities of hazel for hurdles, and the planted sweet chestnut – probably the most economically valuable crop in the wood – for fence paling. In other compartments oak and ash stools are being promoted to timber trees by careful selection of the most promising leading shoots, by interplanting with saplings grown from Ham Street seed, and by a progressive thinning-out of side shoots and underwood until the canopy closes. When they are mature, these trees will be selectively felled in small groups, leaving areas very like those in a recently cut coppice. In these temporarily open compartments the ground flora will be able to flourish and a new generation of timber trees form by natural regeneration – fed by the few standard 'seed' trees left standing for this purpose.

After only twenty years' growth the quality of the timber, and of the oak in particular, is remarkable – as straight and clean in the bole as in most plantations, yet showing that marvellous diversity of shape and branching in the canopy that is characteristic of the richly varied genetic stock of primary woods. Even commercial foresters have been impressed. Peter Garthwaite, lately a conservator with the Forestry Commission and now an independent consultant, was asked by the NCC in 1976 to prepare a report on the commercial potential of deciduous woodlands in south-east England. This is what he had to say of Ham Street:

> . . . one cannot help comparing the results of this careful sylviculture with the neighbouring Forestry Commission area, in which, from a similar starting point, the general policy has been to clear the hardwoods and replant with conifers. Many of these crops have suffered severely in this cold wet ill-drained soil. I have no doubt that with only a slight change of emphasis and acceleration of the tempo the long term results of the hardwood sylviculture as practised at Ham Street Reserve will prove better in purely financial terms than the conversion to conifers.[44]

The remarkable thing is that this financial potential has been achieved at no cost to the wood's natural interest. Ham Street is as exciting and varied a wood as you could wish to find, a mosaic of maturing trees and bushy young coppice, with a density of song-birds so great that there are moonlit nights in May, John Maylam will tell you, when you have to raise your voice to be heard above the nightingales. There are rides and glades and ponds, and a list of insects that would do credit to the tropics. There are bewitchingly secluded gullies of alder and downy birch, dark and tangled and deliberately allowed to go wild (the official term is 'non-intervention zones'), and here and there scarcer trees like wild service and aspen, which are allowed to grow to maturity among the oaks. They may be harvested in their time or they may be left. There is no urgency about the decision. The point about this wood is that, being first and foremost a nature reserve, it does not have to have the last drop of marginal profit wrung from it. There are even examples of that anathema to the commercial forester – dead trees which are allowed to remain standing. One of John Maylam's proudest exhibits is a dead oak (and not a very old one) in which all three species of British woodpecker have nested, one above the other.

It would be foolhardy for any conservation body to depend too exclusively on the expertise of particular personalities (they

are scarce and non-re-creatable too). Yet there are good reasons
for stressing that skill and sensitivity are required in looking
after a reserve like Ham Street. In the hardbitten worlds of
commercial forestry and agriculture, nature conservation is
often undervalued because it is thought of as an *abandonment* of
skill, an opting out of responsibilities. Conservationists stand to
gain a good deal more regard from other landworkers if they
can show that they, too, know about husbandry.

Examples like Ham Street have demonstrated that conservative woodland management, based on coppice promotion and
natural regeneration, can be both economic and efficient. (The
Forestry Commission itself, on advice from the NCC, is following a similar policy in the Lincolnshire limewoods.) With the
market for native hardwoods already showing an upswing, I
have a feeling that the prospect for our derelict coppices is
looking rather brighter than it has for a long time. And any
number of factors could easily swing the balance in favour of
bringing them back into working order on an increasing scale
– escalating fuel prices, shortage of imported timber, the impoverishment of the soil which looks as if it may be one of the long-
term results of intensive conifer harvesting. But the decisions
really need to be made now, if many of the irreplaceable natural
features of ancient woodland are not to be lost, and the range
of wood and timber we will need by the end of the century is
to be guaranteed.

It would be foolish to pretend there are no disadvantages to
conservative management policies. Promoted coppice does
sometimes produce crooked or soft-hearted timber. Natural
regeneration is not always as quick or reliable here as it is in
warmer climates on the continent. (Oak is particularly tempera-
mental in this respect, and much of the Botanical Society of the
British Isles' symposium on *The British Oak* was taken up with
a debate about the conditions which control natural oak
growth.[45]) The real scandal is that too often foresters fail to take
advantage of natural regeneration and promotion when they *do*
occur well.

But even where this is impracticable, and a forester feels he
must rely on planted trees, he can still conserve some of the
elements of the original wood with little extra trouble or cost.
He could, for instance, clear-fell the entire wood, plant up with
nursery-grown hardwoods and preserve the coppice structure
in an attenuated form as the shrub layer. It is even possible to

follow this policy using exotic conifers as nurse trees provided they are planted far enough apart. Parts of Bernwood Forest in Buckinghamshire have been managed in this way, and one of the results has been a great increase in the proportion of wild service trees amongst the remnant hardwoods, which the Forestry Commission seems prepared to tolerate. The wood is an extraordinary sight in autumn, with the dark conifers lit up by the flaming crimson leaves of the service trees. But close planting of conifers on an ancient woodland site soon has a disastrous effect on the ground flora and woodland insects. Research by the Institute of Terrestrial Ecology, for instance, suggests that seeds of herbaceous flowers and shrubs can remain viable for up to fourteen years under the accumulating layers of toxic pine litter, but that after that period their chance of germinating falls rapidly.

BILLY WILKINS (FLORUIT 1200– ?)

In one of our few surviving and still functional medieval deer parks, Melbury Park in Dorset, the most venerable trees have had their age and individuality honoured by being given their own names. They are not functional or official titles, as in the considerable number of Gospel and Queen's Oaks scattered round the country, but more intimate tributes. Billy Wilkins, reckoned to be at least 800 years old, is named after one of the local families. Billy is a partially pollarded oak, so vast and architecturally complex that a walk round him is like a journey between two quite different landscapes. The south-facing side, dry and airy, is festooned with lichens in the dappled sunlight. As you move round to the north the climate changes. The trunk moistens and the light fades. There are patches of moss and ferns, and dwarf pools of water caught in the crotches between the roots. To the south you can believe you are in woodland, but round here in the dark it has the feel of a forest in the romantic sense, the haunt of owls and beetles and toadstools.

These old trees are the very heart of wood-pasture and make this the one kind of primary woodland that actually *looks* ancient. And the fact that individual trees are capable of outliving whole eras of agricultural policy is the one reason that this habitat has not become extinct. For despite their aura of stolidity, wood-pastures are the most redundant and threatened of all our primary woodlands. There is no conceivable use in foresty for over-mature and dying trees, or in modern agriculture for grasslands whose growth is suppressed by overhanging foliage. (Pollarding, of course, previously avoided this.)

The decline of pasture woodland set in well before that of the coppice. The Crown's interest in deer waned during the late middle ages, and gradually nearly all the Royal Forests, like Dean and Alice Holt, were enclosed and devoted to timber production. Only the New Forest retained most of its ancient structure and land-use. The wooded commons suffered continual attrition at the hands of the enclosers, and those that remained consequently became increasingly over-stocked. Since it was illegal to erect fencing on common land, young trees could not be protected from grazing, and the tree cover eventually vanished altogether from most of them.

It would be wrong to regard these changes as being wholly destructive. Many of the hardwood plantations that were set up in parks and chases during the seventeenth and eighteenth centuries (particularly in areas that were well-wooded anyway) have developed into rich high-forest woods in their own right. Many commons, too, have evolved into interesting new habitats. The Gloucestershire Commons, for instance, (now typically fragmented into woods *and* pastures rather than wood-pasture) contain, because of their long tradition of grazing, some of our finest stretches of limestone grassland and are particularly rich in orchids. And many of the common 'greens' of southern England, where grazing ceased altogether early this century, have reverted to diverse, albeit rather immature, secondary woodland. Regenerating on soil which has rarely been seriously disturbed, and often from genetic relics of earlier woodland surviving as nearby hedgerows, isolated pollards and clumps round ponds, they develop into much richer woods than those that form, say, on abandoned arable fields. They have a peculiar, hybrid ancestry, closer to interrupted primaries than to secondaries, and maybe deserve a title of their own. (Naphill Common in Buckinghamshire is one of the finest examples.)

But all these conversions have entailed the loss of the principal, irreplaceable features of primary wood-pasture – the continuity of ancient timber in a well-lit woodland context, and the lichens and invertebrates that are dependent on this particular combination of conditions. It was only in wood-pasture that these features of natural forest survived in any quantity. It is reckoned that there are now no more than 400 wood-pastures remaining in Britain south of the Clyde and Forth which have some ancient features, and of these Francis Rose and Paul Harding have singled out just sixty-eight which have populations of lichens or invertebrates 'faithful' to old woodland.[46] Even in this shortlist there are areas like Epping and Sherwood Forests which, despite their fine old trees, have been stripped of most of their lichens by atmospheric pollution. Conversely, the Mens in Sussex, a wooded common which was abandoned about 100 years ago and has regenerated into mixed high forest, has few ancient trees but one of the richer assemblages of woodland lichens in south-east England (seventy-seven species to date – though lacking, not surprisingly, the most sensitive indicators of ancient woodland, such as lungwort lichens).

The outstanding feature of the fifty-six special sites that are in England is that two-thirds of them are parkland of some kind, and these in turn are often direct descendants of medieval deer parks. This was the one kind of wood-pasture which found a new role – in the form of 'landscape' parks – during the decline of traditional woodland management. After Tudor times, deer parks were treated more and more as private pleasure grounds rather than as the economic venison ranches which had been their chief original function. When the fashion for 'pastoral' flowered in eighteenth-century painting and poetry, it was no great surprise that privileged landowners took the mellow prospect of the deer park, with its clumps of ancient trees, glades and groups of cattle – a scene which was rustic without being too threateningly wild – as the model for their 'landskips'. (It is still regarded as one of the archetypal English landscapes: see page 164.) Many ancient parks, such as Melbury, were virtually taken as they stood and simply had a few groups of exotic trees added for a classical effect. (Sycamore was especially popular – and this is one situation where conservationists ought to be more hospitable than they usually are to this alien species: it is the fourth most important tree for lichens of any kind in Britain, being host to at least 183 species.) Lowther Park, in Cumbria, which is reputedly over 1000 years old, kept its old oaks and ashes, and had spectacular avenues of lime, yew and sweet chestnut added to them. Even the formal arrangements of Capability Brown – as in Heveningham Park in Suffolk – retained many of the existing pollards of the original estates. At Sotterley, nearby, part of the park was created by enclosing an area of farmland and small copses. The hedgerow trees supplied the obligatory ancient timber component, and you can still see the pattern of the old field boundaries in the lines of great oaks and elms.

Yet here and there parks survived with almost all their traditional elements intact and in working order. Melbury Park is one of the best examples remaining, with 202 epiphytic lichens in its two square kilometres (0.8 of a square mile). (Only one other wood of a similar size in Europe is known to have more.) Moccas Park, in Herefordshire, is another fine example and was a favourite of Francis Kilvert. His description of it in his diary entry for 22 April 1876 is the most graphic account we have of the feel of an ancient wood-pasture – and a forceful demonstration that the features responsible for their ecological importance and aesthetic appeal are not so very far removed from each other:

We came tumbling and plunging down the steep hillside of Moccas Park, slipping, tearing and sliding through oak and birch and fallow wood of which there seemed to be underfoot an accumulation of several feet, the gathering ruin and decay probably of centuries. As we came down the lower slopes of the wooded hillside into the glades of the park the herds of deer were moving under the brown oaks and the brilliant green hawthorns, and we came upon the tallest largest stateliest ash I ever saw and what seemed at first in the dusk to be a great ruined grey tower, but which proved to be the vast ruin of the king oak of Moccas Park, hollow and broken but still alive and vigorous in parts and actually pushing out new shoots and branches. . . . I fear those grey old men of Moccas, those grey, gnarled, low-browed, knock-kneed, bowed, bent, huge, strange, long-armed, deformed, hunchbacked, misshapen oak men that stand waiting and watching century after century. . . . No human hand set those oaks. They are 'the trees which the Lord hath planted'. They look as if they had been at the beginning and making of the world, and they will probably see its end.[47]

Kilvert did not foresee the pressures that would challenge the immortality of old oaks in the twentieth century. Yet, although the 'several feet' of dead wood and some of the great trees have disappeared, his account is still a recognizable description of Moccas today. It is a measure of the isolation of these parks, and of the continuity and individuality of their trees (their 'grain' again), that Moccas is host to three species of beetle that have not been found anywhere else in Britain. One was recorded from a solitary lime and has not been seen again since this tree blew down and was removed in 1976. Another has been found in half a dozen of the oldest oak pollards but not in any of the over-mature maiden trees.

The Moccas beetles are one reason why this park is of national importance to conservation, as are its ninety-seven species of lichen. Yet it would be a narrow view of the park which reduced its natural interest to these fragmentary details. They are tokens of its character rather than a complete picture. Every one of Moccas's ancient trees is a unique and irreplaceable monument. Those 'gnarled, low-browed, knock-kneed' oaks are living records of centuries of interaction between natural growth and human work, and their like may not be seen again. The whole park has an identity which could never be imitated, let alone re-created. Even Kilvert's presence and the record he left – see him as another rare creature with an affection for old timber if you like – have added their own indefinable trace.

Moccas Park, fortunately, is being managed sympathetically under guidance from the NCC. New trees are being grown from acorns of the stock that produced those fantastic shapes and are being protected from grazing deer and cattle. A similar policy is being followed at Sotterley and at a few other wood-pastures of great natural interest. The problem lies with that rather larger number of ancient parks that are not being managed with help from conservation bodies. Old oaks linger on for centuries, but gradual replacement is required to ensure that the special features of these parks survive. But whether this happens may depend on whether some new social role can be found for substantial areas of fine, over-mature trees. Yet another amenity transformation – the change from private landscape park to public country park that we are already seeing on many estates – may be one of the answers.

FORESTRY AND TREE-PLANTING

I imagine it will be clear by now that woodland conservation has very little to do with the planting of new woods. Forestry plantations can provide useful refuges for the more adaptable forms of wildlife, but most traditional woodland species can neither reach them nor survive in them. And, as *structures*, plantations are by definition no more 'natural' than a garden shrubbery. With the Forestry Commission currently thinking in terms of doubling its acreage of conifers by the year 2025, by invading areas of ancient natural interest such as Dartmoor and the Yorkshire Dales, afforestation could well become one of the gravest threats to our natural heritage. Nevertheless, plantations can make some contribution to conservation. In time they develop what we might call natural 'aspects'. Their trees begin to weather, to break ranks and drop branches. They are invaded by insects and birds, and rotted by fungi. Slowly (if the management is not too intense) the more enterprising of our native woodland shrubs and flowers – honeysuckle, germander speedwell, stitchworts and the like – start to colonize the rides and clearings. Even conifer plantations can in their first few years play host to a surprising variety of species (including nightingales and nightjars) that are adapted to the open or shrubby zones of natural woodland.[48] Plantations provide, in effect, a protective scaffolding inside which more natural woodland communities can grow up. They can never 'catch up' with a wood that may have been evolving over several thousand years, but they are likely to be a good deal richer than the cultivated land. The one feature which is common to *all* woods – and which, with one important exception, makes the planting of trees something which will usually improve the natural interest of a place – is their *comparative* stability. By the standards of the modern countryside, even a spruce plantation run on a thirty-year rotation is a positive oasis of permanence.

But the exception is a serious one, the more so because it includes most of the situations in which afforestation is currently taking place. Nothing but good can come of the planting of woods amongst, say, intensive arable fields, new housing estates and industrial spoil-tips. They add variety to the landscape and to the lives of the people who live nearby. But land values in such areas are usually prohibitively high, and economic pressures have pushed large-scale woodland planting towards regions where the land is of little attraction either for agriculture or for development – for instance sandy heaths and upland moors. Unfortunately such areas are often of great natural interest precisely because they have so far escaped 'improvement'. Very few of their characteristic natural features can survive the imposition of a short-rotation plantation. Nor is it just commercial plantations that can be misplaced, literally, in this way. I know a small hardwood copse that was planted, by public subscription and with the very best of intentions, on one of the last stretches of open downland in the central Chilterns.

It is an area, ironically, that has to have its burgeoning scrub and young trees regularly cleared by hand if the down and its magnificent colonies of orchids are to survive at all.

There is one more reservation we must make. There is, I believe, a widespread tendency to regard new plantations as *replacements* for old woods, and to ignore the destruction of ancient parks and coppices provided it is matched – tree for tree, as it were – by similarly energetic planting. I hope I have shown by now that no such easy comparability exists. Many of the features we associate with woodland – spring flowers, mosses and lichens, a variety of tree shapes, for example – are dependent on the age and history of the wood and cannot be expected to appear of their own accord. Even birds, which as a group do not suffer from the inflexibility and immobility of plants and often move into young plantations in considerable numbers, always find a more congenial range of habitats in the complex structure of natural woods. In a study in Abernethy Forest of the bird populations of naturally-regenerating native pinewoods and Forestry Commission plantations of the same tree species, Ian Newton and Dorian Moss found that the more natural woodland carried nearly three times the number of breeding pairs (of a dozen species) as the same area of plantation.[49] There were fewer mature trees in the regenerating woods, but a much greater *variety* of habitats, including dead stumps, tree-free glades and a dense shrub layer of juniper, heather and bilberry. The plantation, on the other hand, though relatively mature (it was planted in 1932), had very little diversity. All the trees were of the same age, forming a dense canopy that permitted only a sparse ground cover.

From a nature conservation point of view, then, the desirability of a new wood depends as much on what it has replaced as on what it may become. And at no time can it ever become a substitute for an existing wood. Plantations should rather be looked on – and valued, possibly – as a new kind of woodland, an addition to the existing range.

With these qualifications in mind, we can begin to suggest principles for the establishment and management of plantations which will be of most benefit to wildlife. These are really implicit in the way that woods 'work' and they will apply to all plantations – old or new, commercial or amenity. The most fundamental principle is that a commitment to use and keep land as woodland is far more important than the planting of the trees themselves. New woods will always spring up almost anywhere where the ground is free from disturbance – along railway embankments, for instance – and they are arguably more interesting, begun naturally in this way, than if they had been planted. Unfortunately this often happens on sites where woody growth is not wanted, and the trees rarely survive beyond their teens. But self-sown saplings are so frequently cleared from areas where they are doing no harm (and sometimes where trees are positively wanted) that I think they are often not *recognized* as embryonic woods. For some reason we use the word 'scrub' (which is simply a derivation from 'shrub') disparagingly, as if nature ought to be subject to the same discipline as herbaceous borders. But the 'plantation mentality' that I discussed earlier may be more than a misplaced extension of the gardener's concern with tidiness. I think we cherish an arrogant belief that woods are the supreme demonstration of how much cleverer man is at creating landscapes than nature. Seen in this light, the planting of trees, with the appearance of instant miniaturized woodland which this gives a piece of ground, may be more important symbolically than ecologically. The trees become monuments to the dedication of the ground to woodland.

Whether they are started by planting or natural regeneration, new woods are best established close to existing woods, so that there are opportunities for colonization by woodland plants and animals. Colonization will also happen more readily if the planted tree species are those that would be native to the site; this will also, as a bonus, produce a wood that blends more naturally with the surrounding landscape. Once the wood is established, management should be introduced gradually and kept at as low an intensity as is practicable. The felling of trees in small patches on a long rotation, for example, or a policy of continuous selection of individual mature trees is greatly to be preferred to large-scale clear-felling.

It takes very little effort to encourage internal diversity in the wood by keeping rides and glades open, damp hollows undrained and steep slopes unplanted. The expense of disciplining areas like these usually outweighs any possible return. In fact the whole business of excessive tidying – clearing undergrowth and chopping down innocuous columns of ivy, for instance – is as much an affront to economic sense as to the potential wildness of the wood.

One of the most helpful contributions commercial foresters could make towards nature conservation (and quite possibly to their own budgets) would be to show a little more magnanimity to dead wood. This is a major component of natural forest, and its name (Kilvert's 'fallow wood' is much more expressive) hardly does justice to its variety. 'Dead wood' is very far from being a single, simple material. It includes twigs, logs, trunks, stumps – all of which can either be dry, damp or crumbling, attached to the tree or fallen to the ground; branches scorched by lightning or splintered by gales; hollows, rot holes and chambers excavated by beetles; bark strippings and sawdust. The whole ensemble plays host to more than 1000 different insects and other small animals and to many hundreds of fungi.

Finally, in this or that corner of a wood, there may be the option of taking under-management to its logical conclusion and doing absolutely nothing. I have touched on this possibility already, and on the difficulties and tactical dangers of embarking on 'non-intervention' as a policy. As an option, it is by no means as easy as it appears, especially where the wood as a whole is being run principally as a commercial venture. It is not just that the majority of foresters regard unmanaged growth as a gauntlet thrown down before their skills; many seem to believe that woodland as a habitat cannot *survive* without their assistance. The romance and habit of tree-planting seem to have obscured the fact that mature deciduous woodland is still the plant cover which would cloak most areas of land in Britain, if they were only left to themselves for long enough. To be fair, this hypothetical New Wildwood might contain a degree of scrub and dead timber that would be intolerable to a commercial forester. Yet ecologically it would continue to be self-renewing woodland. The difficulty is predicting the kind of woodland which might result. In fact it may be wrong to be thinking in terms of a 'result' – in the sense of a fixed, stable, climax community. The woodlands that do have this character (ancient coppices and high forest) are, with few exceptions, communities which have been 'frozen' by human intervention at a particular point in their development. What evidence we have of the primordial forest before man imposed regular management on it suggests that its only consistent feature was deciduousness. In any one place its composition and structure were constantly shifting, responding to long-term changes in rainfall and temperature, and to internal cycles in which, for example, a period of dominance by long-lived shade-bearing trees was followed by several generations of short-lived rapid growers. We can still see this happening today. In many areas on the chalk hills of southern England, for instance, where the beechwoods are badly affected by fungal disorders, there has been a great increase in ash. Ashwoods may not be as dramatic architecturally as beechwoods, but they are every bit as natural as an intermediate type on these soils. And their ground flora will probably become much richer once it is free of the heavy shade cast by the beeches. What may be lost, of course, are those plants and animals which depend exclusively on beech.

It is the possibility of this kind of change in species composition that makes some conservationists share the commercial forester's suspicion of unmanaged woods. We have already seen that in the modern countryside many plants and animals are confined to certain kinds of wood, or to isolated fragments of woodland. In these circumstances a surrender of management may well lead to local extinctions (as in parts of Epping Forest: see pages 173–174). Yet I have argued earlier that the maintenance of species and communities can only be one aspect of conservation; there is also the conservation – which here means the toleration – of natural *processes*, which includes the natural succession of types of woodland. In cases where this policy is not likely to lead to extinctions it ought to be amongst the aims of any conservation programme.

The best existing examples of near-natural woodland development can be seen in the native pinewoods of central Scotland and in many parts of the New Forest. In the Black Wood of Rannoch, for instance, the Forestry Commission and the NCC are collaborating in an experiment to increase the area of natural Scots pine forest. An area of existing wood and open moor has been fenced to minimize grazing and has been declared a non-disturbance zone. In other zones trees are being grown from local sources of seed. Apart from producing an area which catches something of the true wilderness quality of the northern forests, the undisturbed, unselected zones will also help to conserve the genetic variety of the native Scots pine. With plantations of North American pine in Sutherland currently being devastated by pine beauty moths, which seem to have little impact on native trees, this could have real economic as well as scientific importance.

The pattern of regeneration and succession in the New Forest is rather different. For a long time it was believed that the ancient beechwoods and oakwoods were not being replaced because seedlings were being grazed out by ponies and cattle. Then George Peterken and Colin Tubbs found that new woodlets were regenerating and would 'get away' whenever the grazing and browsing pressures slackened for a period.[50] This might only happen once a century, but this is more than enough to replace woods whose individual trees are many hundreds of years old. The new generation of woods is very varied, with holly, birch and hawthorn mixed up with some oak and beech, and they often spring up far away from the 'parent' wood, out on the open heath, or where a large tree has fallen and opened the canopy. The most distinctive are the little round groves, known locally as 'hats' or 'holms', in which beech and oak are growing up under the protection of dense thickets of holly.

Woods clearly need space if they are to evolve in this way – and the New Forest has plenty of that: 9500 acres (3800 hectares) of unenclosed woodland in a total area of over 70,000 acres (28,000 hectares). Yet 'non-intervention' is a management option for *any* wood. On sites where the loss of this or that species is not critical, and where there are no real resources or obvious directions for management, it may be a better short-term policy than half-hearted tinkering. Unless they are subject to exceptional pressures, sites like this can be left alone indefinitely in the confidence that they will continue to be woodland of some kind.

2
Agriculture

The trees from Redbourn to Hempstead are very fine; oaks, ashes and beeches. Some of the finest of each sort, and the very finest ashes I ever saw in my life. They are in great numbers, and make the fields look most beautiful. No villainous things of the *fir-tribe* offend the eye here. The custom is in this part of Hertfordshire (and I am told it continues into Bedfordshire) to leave a *border* round the ploughed part of the fields to bear grass and to make hay from, so that, the grass being now made into hay, every corn field has a close mowed grass walk about ten feet wide all round it, between the corn and the hedge. This is most beautiful! The hedges are now full of shepherd's rose, honeysuckles, and all sorts of wild flowers; so that you are upon a grass walk, with this most beautiful of all flower gardens and shrubberies on your one hand, and with the corn on the other. And thus you go from field to field (on foot or on horseback), the sort of corn, the sort of underwood and timber, the shape and size of the fields, the height of the hedge-rows, the height of the trees, all continually varying. Talk of *pleasure-grounds* indeed! What that man ever invented, under the name of pleasure-grounds, can equal these fields in Hertfordshire?

WILLIAM COBBETT, *Rural Rides* (1822)

Forestry, even in its most intensive forms, tends to work in comparatively long cycles, and this is one of the chief reasons why woodland generally provides a more congenial habitat for wildlife than farmland. Agriculture, on the other hand, is characterized by frequent disturbance and cultivation. It is curious then that the kind of landscape described above by Cobbett is probably closer to our image of 'natural' countryside than any kind of woodland. It is not hard to understand the appeal this scene had for Cobbett, and still has for us 150 years later. It was not just an example of good and ingenious husbandry but a working model of the idealized relationship between man and the land. It was all there: the country in good heart, tamed and ordered, yet a delightful wildness at the edge of things.

It is so tempting to take accounts like this out of context, to see in them proof that there really was a Golden Age in the countryside. Yet it is precisely such pastoral stereotypes that have obscured the real and often troubled history of the farming landscape. Cobbett's importance as a documenter of the ninteenth-century countryside is precisely his attention to *particulars*. Just a short while before his midsummer's day idyll in Hertfordshire, he had been a few score miles to the north, in the Cambridgeshire fens:

The land just about here does seem to be really bad. The face of the country is naked. The few scrubbed trees that now and then meet the eye, and even the quick-sets, are covered with a yellow moss. All is bleak and comfortless; and, just on the most dreary part of this dreary scene stands, almost opportunely, 'Caxton Gibbet', tendering its one friendly arm to the passers-by. It has recently been fresh-painted, and written on in conspicuous characters, for the benefit, I suppose, of those who cannot exist under the thought of wheat at four shillings a bushel.

In the 1820s, in fact, England was in a state of agricultural turmoil. A run of bad harvests, a shortage of imported grain resulting from the blockades of the Napoleonic Wars, attempts by desperate landowners to protect their incomes by a series of inept Corn Laws, had all combined to cause wild oscillations in the price of wheat. The rural population – which had increased greatly in the wake of the first wave of eighteenth-century agricultural improvements – found itself faced first with unemployment and then with a rise in the price of bread that together pushed many families to the verge of starvation. The eastern counties that Cobbett was touring that summer had been, just a couple of years previously, the scene of the 'bread-or-blood riots'. And behind this crisis another, more permanent, revolution was under way: the tide of parliamentary enclosure, which was robbing agricultural labourers of what little independence and marginal income they used to obtain from common lands. By 1830, 300,000 people out of the 686,000 families of rural workers were on poor relief, and the rick burnings of

Captain Swing had begun.[51]

This is not to say that those Hertfordshire 'pleasure-grounds' were an illusion (though Cobbett would never have suggested, as we might be tempted to, that they were also pleasure-grounds for the men who worked in them). The point is that such pockets of harmony existed inside a framework of continuous upheaval, which was inevitably reflected in the patterns of the landscape. At no time in recent history has the working countryside been free of the tensions between capital and labour, between wage rates and food prices, between the lure of intimate contact with the soil and the convenience of machines, between the 'pull' of nature (which anyone who has worked the land has felt, tugging in many different ways) and the 'push' of progress.

It is a very similar set of conflicts and problems that is transforming the farming landscape today. The burdens of taxation, the rise in farm rents, the drift of workers away from the land, the control of food prices and the increasingly complex structure of international agricultural policies are making farmers take every opportunity to maximize productivity and profit from their land. We have to remember these economic pressures when we are considering the conflicts between agriculture and conservation. There is as great a temptation to idealize the *intentions* of modern agricultural progress, to see it as a selfless effort to feed a hungry world, as there is to invoke a mythical ancient landscape where agriculture and nature were in timeless harmony.

But, as I said, those Hertfordshire fields were not a mirage. They were part of a working farm, and they show that conditions can exist where agriculture and conservation are compatible. It is important, then, to identify the characteristics of a landscape that made such compatibility possible.

It was, to begin with, diverse rather than specialized. It exploited the variety thrown up by nature rather than ignoring or overriding it and, when it relied on natural renewal, preserved the continuity that we have seen is so vital to conservation. It also prefigured our modern concept of multiple use in having an abundance of social and economic uses for all its components. Before the days of weedkillers, for instance, there could scarcely have been a better way of cashing in on the naturally grassy and flowery – what today we could call weedy – edges of a field than to cut them for hay. The 'grass walk' that resulted also provided a track round the corn for the harvesters to work from. Ash was the most useful farm timber and was encouraged to grow where it was most accessible and least obstructive – in the hedges. The remainder of the hedge was cut regularly to keep it stockproof and to prevent its shrubs invading the field, but, whilst there was still a call for the trimmings for firewood and small timber, it could be looked on as a kind of linear coppice, a *productive* component, not a drain on labour. There was even room, amongst all this, for a tourist on horseback.

Cobbett's ride has a particular meaning for me, as the route he took lies only a few miles from the corner of the Chilterns where I have lived for most of my life. The road from Redbourn to Hemel Hempstead is still a pleasant one and, if you are glancing at it from a car rather than a horse, it does not seem to differ much from Cobbett's description. It is still arable country for the most part, with ash trees on the field borders (and still no 'villainous' firs) and shepherd's roses in what is left of the hedgerows. But when you look more closely you see how much the requirements of modern farming techniques have transformed the intimate details of the landscape. None of the ashes could be called 'fine'. Most are either about sixty years old or very young saplings, and whole generations between and beyond these are missing. Since there is little need for timber or firewood on the farms, most of the copses have gone as well, and many of the hedges have been grubbed out to make the working of the combines smoother. The corn (now chiefly barley) is manured by artificial fertilizers, not animals, so there is no need for 'grass walks' and the hay they produced. Where a field is growing hay, it is usually a 'ley', ploughed and reseeded every few years, and you will be lucky to see a single wild flower amongst the planted grasses that crowd to the very edge of the road. And so, as 'you go from field to field . . . the sort of corn, the sort of underwood and timber, the shape and size of the fields, the height of the hedge-rows, the height of the trees' are not 'continually varying', but continuously uniform.

Yet the whole area, at first sight, does seem to have much in common with what we imagine to be the traditional farming landscape, and this suggests to me that we should be careful about the way in which we use that term 'landscape', and avoid confusing it with superficial 'scenery'.

The hen harrier was one of the most widespread birds of prey of the open fields and wastes of the pre-enclosure landscape. In **The Shepherd's Calendar,** *John Clare marvelled at the sight of these pale birds floating over the harvest fields near the Northamptonshire fens:*

> *A hugh blue bird will often swim*
> *Along the wheat when skys grow dim*
> *Wi' clouds – slow as the gales of spring*
> *In motion wi' dark shadowed wing*
> *Beneath the coming storm it sails.*

Up until the nineteenth century they were recorded as breeding on Newton Common (now absorbed into Carlisle city) and on Newcastle Town Moor. In 1933 Desmond Nethersole-Thomson referred to their nesting 'within living memory in what are now the tram-lined streets of Bournemouth'.

Like many other predators at the top of the food chain their fortunes have reflected almost every change in the countryside over the last century and a half. They declined rapidly as the heaths and fens were drained and enclosed.

They were driven almost to the point of extinction during the Victorian period under the combined onslaught of keepers and collectors. They recovered slightly in the early decades of this century, as a result of a let-up in keepering pressures and the spread of young forestry plantations, but the real expansion in their populations only began in the 1950s (see page 190). They are now completely protected at all times of the year, and though they are still illegally persecuted on grouse-moors, their southwards spread continues. It is a reasonable certainty that, keepers permitting, they will be nesting in East Anglia by the end of the 1980s.

(Field Sketches by Donald Watson)

Two recent additions to the British breeding list.

The collared dove (above) began spreading across Europe from the Near East in the 1930s and first nested in Britain in 1955. Finding a comparatively vacant niche in the fringes of towns and villages where there were supplies of grain (mills, farmyards, garden hen-runs, etc.), it colonized the whole country very rapidly, and by the end of the 1970s its population was probably in excess of 100,000 pairs.

Cetti's warbler (left) first definitely bred in Kent in 1972. Since then it has spread across southern England (showing a particular liking for the scrubby edges of flooded gravel pits) and in the summer of 1977 there were estimated to be more than 150 breeding pairs (see page 47).

Still-life with lichens, in Dartington Hall Gardens, Devon. Henry Moore's reclining figure is a fascinating demonstration of the sensitivity of these plants. There are quite distinct communities on different parts of the statue: moisture-loving under the armpits, shade-tolerant on the back, and nitrogen-loving on the head and knee, which are used by birds as perches (see page 52).

NCC workers in Kent engaged on the very agreeable task of surveying old meadows, a project in which they earned a wealth of goodwill and assistance from the public (see pages 153–154).

Oak standards in Hayley Wood, Cambridgeshire (see page 71). The great variety in shape and branch-patterning is characteristic of 'wild' oak populations.

Another kind of 'wild' wood: Glen Tanar NNR in Aberdeenshire, a relic of the natural pinewoods that once extended over much of the central Highlands. The rich variety of habitats – juniper and bilberry scrub, the mix of young, mature and dying trees – contrasts strikingly with the uniformity of pine plantations (see page 106).

One of the ancient pollard oaks in Moccas Park (overleaf) which Francis
Kilvert described in his diary (see page 100). 'No human hand set those
oaks,' he wrote. 'They look as if they had been at the beginning and making
of the world, and they will probably see its end.' Luckily human hands are
now setting a new generation of oaks in Moccas, from the acorns of those
gnarled, low-browed, knock-kneed . . . misshapen oak men'.

Deer parks – old landscapes, new roles. Moccas Park, Herefordshire (above), one of our finest remaining private deer parks, scarcely changed since the middle ages. Bradgate Park in Leicestershire (right), owned and managed as a country park by the city and county councils of Leicester, also has a history dating back more than 900 years. It has retained almost all the elements of the traditional deer park – ancient pollards, grazed grasslands, enclosed coppices – and in addition enables up to a million visitors each year to experience a medieval landscape at close quarters (see page 101).

We are all apt to gloss over these different ways of viewing the living features of the countryside, and farmers are no exception. When the Countryside Commission introduced a new phrase to the conservationist vocabulary with the publication of its report *New Agricultural Landscapes* (sceneries, in my sense – but I have made the point and will try not to labour it), it reported that farmers were aware that the landscapes they were creating were not to everyone's taste, but that they were divided about whether this was any of their business.[52] Most of those interviewed accepted that they had a responsibility towards the landscape and social duties which went beyond the mere production of food, though this must always be their prime concern. But there were wide divergences of opinion about whether landscapes should simply be accepted as by-products of whatever farming style happened to be current. These differences, understandably, seemed to be related to the degree of change that had already occurred in a farmer's home county. In the comparatively unaltered, mixed farming areas of Herefordshire and Warwickshire, for instance, there was strong opposition to the idea that the landscape should simply be accepted as a by-product of agriculture. In the intensive arable regions of East Anglia the predominant opinion was that, since farmers had been the prime shapers of landscapes in the past, the public must learn to accept those they were creating at present. Attitudes varied from 'I like trees, but on someone else's land' to 'I don't like trees and, if you do, don't come to the fens, go elsewhere'. If there was one implicit assumption shared by all the farmers – regardless of whether they felt the landscape *mattered* – it was that somehow, somewhere, on somebody's land, interesting and agreeable landscapes would continue to be created. Is this perhaps just another version of that deep-rooted belief which we examined at the start of this book, that nature can, by definition, take care of itself, provided the land is kept 'green'? The Countryside Commission's own conclu-

Ant-hills are a feature of ancient parkland, and of unimproved grasslands of all kinds. These are in a derelict orchard in Wyre Forest NNR. They will not be touched, but the NCC is replacing some of the dying fruit trees with traditional varieties, like the celebrated 'Warwickshire Drooper' plum.

sions, stated in its accompanying discussion paper, were as follows:

The Commission accept the inevitability of further large-scale changes in the appearance of farmed lowlands but also seek to encourage the creation of new agricultural landscapes, different from, but not necessarily less interesting than, the old. These new landscapes would differ critically from those which are already evolving because there would be a conscious input of new features; they would not, in other words, be the accidental product of modern farming.[53]

There is no doubt that some of the changes are inevitable, and that there is scope for creating new and imaginative semi-natural scenery on farmland. It might indeed be just as visually attractive as the old. But how would it rate as *landscape* in the special sense I suggested earlier, as a continually developing product of natural and human change? We have seen in our look at woodlands one case where the superficial architecture of a community is not a reliable guide to its variety and liveliness: trees, by themselves, do not make a wood. Would the new agricultural sceneries similarly fail to provide the richness and detail of the old agricultural landscapes? Does accepting 'the inevitability of further large-scale changes in the *appearance*' (my italics) of farmland mean that we must also be willing to say goodbye to our cowslips and dragonflies, to our barn owls and butterflies? A few cosmetically sited tree clumps could never make up for that kind of loss.

If our wildlife is of any importance at all the answer to this question is critical. Farmland, for all its manifestly man-made character, is not an unimportant habitat, peripheral to the needs of wildlife. It occupies 80 per cent of our land-surface and provides food and living quarters for the bulk of our wild plant and animal populations. Changes in agriculture therefore have the profoundest implications for their survival. What is remarkable is that a wildlife that succeeded in surviving – relatively intact – alongside an increasingly intensive agriculture for at least 3000 years should seem to be in such peril from the advances of the last thirty. It suggests that we need to look at the impact of different agricultural practices in closer detail and to beware of mistaking grass for a meadow as much as trees for a wood.

FARM HISTORY

Farmland, unlike woodland, is of course not a naturally occurring habitat, but a whole collection of habitats – some entirely *un*natural. It is dominated by fields of one kind or another, but includes functional elements such as hedges, ponds, copses and shelter belts, and 'incidentals' like rivers and bogs which play no real role in the working of the farm. It is a description of the *use* of the land rather than of its biological characteristics. Yet in spite of this it is difficult to discuss the wildlife of farmland without reference to the ecology of 'natural' habitats. The very earliest farms, for instance, were really little more than extended clearings in the forest and could be regarded as examples of wood-pasture which included areas of particularly disturbed ground. ('Field' is a derivation from the Old English *feld*, that is a felled area.)

The fully developed farm, whose basic structure survived with only minor adaptations for most of the historical period up until the last half of the eighteenth century, was still modelled on these Iron Age woodland settlements. It had three major components: an area of cultivated land for arable crops; various kinds of grassland, some cut for hay, others continuously pastured; and common and wasteland, which included the remains of the uncleared Wildwood, fens, marshes and bogs and, in the uplands, the higher reaches of the hills.

The variations on this basic pattern were immense, both historically and geographically. As with woodlands, they developed out of an interplay of climate, geology, local tradition and the external pressures of economics and politics. In central and parts of southern England, for example, the most common pattern was based on the open field system. Around the village stretched two, or more usually three, large open fields. Arable crops were rotated round them so that in any year two were producing crops whilst the third lay fallow. Each field was divided into strips which were held and cultivated separately by the villagers, but after harvest the stubble was grazed in common. (The unploughed headlands of the open field were also sometimes grazed by tethered animals.) The hay meadows usually occupied the most fertile soils in the river flood-plains. These were either divided into permanent strips like the arable fields or shared out afresh each year by some system of lot. In either case they were usually grazed in common after the hay harvest. Permanent pasture (wooded or otherwise) lay on the less productive soils. It was nearly always common land, and often merged with the 'waste of the manor'.

On heavier soils (in the central Devon valleys and the boulder-clay of west Suffolk, for example) where large-scale woodland clearance happened comparatively late, the open field stage was often missed out and a freehold enclosure landscape was formed by *assarting* – that is by carving small fields directly out of the surrounding forest and leaving strips of wood as hedges and boundary markers.

In the upland zones, where the soils were generally poorer, the agricultural emphasis was always more pastoral, and the richer valley lands that would have been meadow in the lowlands may have been used for arable crops, though by no means exclusively so. In much of Wales it was the custom for the population to move with their flocks in summer from the winter-grazed *hendre* in the valley, to the *hafod* pastures on the hills. Grazing here – and even more so on the damp acid soils of the Scottish Highlands – tended to produce a heathy pasture, with a vegetation resembling the ground flora of the woodland that had previously occupied the site (just as forest clearance and grazing in the lowlands produced swards that were analogous in their composition to the flora of woodland clearings).

Some local enterprises produced quite new habitats. In Cornwall and parts of the Lake District, Celtic farmers created fields in areas that were still covered by glacial debris. They cleared countless numbers of stones from the ground and used them to build massive boundary walls around soil that had been opened to the light for the first time since the Ice Age. In river valleys in Hampshire and Wiltshire and in some parts of the Midland plain, complex irrigation systems were constructed to produce water meadows, in which flooding could be precisely controlled to produce springs of grass at the time they were most needed.

In all these ways the progress of traditional agriculture capitalized on, extended, and in some cases enriched naturally occurring habitats. Ecologically, it amounted to a kind of time travel. The great increase in the extent of open land provided a range of habitats that had not existed to such a degree since the period immediately after the Ice Age, and species adapted to disturbed or well-lit situations were able to spread out from the small enclaves on cliffs and screes and river banks where they had been confined during the long reign of climax forest.

The changes which have revolutionized agricultural practice since the beginning of the nineteenth century, and which have become critical since the Second World War, make up a pattern observed in every other sphere of life. They are characterized by increasing specialization and mechanization, and by movements towards large homogeneous units at the expense of small diverse ones. Ownership has tended to become distant and institutional, rather than local and intimate. Yet paradoxically the impact of technology has tended to reinforce large-scale regional differences. Although the ways and means are now available for converting upland moors into barley fields and draining valley pastures until they will grow carrots (and there is no shortage of ambitious farmers ready to try), it is the opportunities opened up by refrigeration and long-distance transport that have had the greatest effect on the national farming pattern. Crops are now produced not so much where they are needed but where they can be most effectively grown. So, by and large, we have a series of regional monocultures based on crude geographical divisions: grain on the dry flats of East Anglia, vegetables on the fenland loams, sheep on the hills, dairy and beef in the wet south-west where grass grows so well.

These changes in practice have been accompanied by equally dramatic shifts in working and social relationships in the countryside. 80 per cent of the land surface in Britain is now farmed by less than 2½ per cent of the national work force. In the first half of the eighteenth century, before the full impact of the Industrial Revolution and the Enclosure Acts, the position was quite different. Half the national work force was employed on the land in some way or another, and the majority of the people concerned had a holding in the land by 'leasing' strips in the open field and by the possession of an extensive and thoroughly exercised system of common rights over more than 10 million acres of heath, moor and wasteland.

The ecological effects of present-day modernization present a pattern similar to that which has occurred during the development of forestry. Almost all farmland is now cultivated (in the sense of being ploughed or chemically treated) and even 'permanent' pasture is ploughed and reseeded every few years to maintain its productivity; so habitats with long histories of unchanged status are becoming scarce. Those that do remain are shrunk and isolated, and the less mobile plants and animals have become stranded, with little hope of being naturally replenished from outside populations.

The internal diversity of farms – the cluster of orchards, paddocks, barns, coverts, ricks and dykes (even scarecrows, which have an ecology all of their own!) that was the product of a mixed, locally self-sufficient agriculture – has been smoothed out. So have the 'fringes', where one kind of farmed habitat merged into another; and the fragments that remain are likely to be subject to increasing pressure as land is taken out of agriculture for housing and industrial development. It was precisely these marginal habitats, which were either outside the intensively cultivated heartlands, or not contributing much to them, that gave farmlands such a variety of wildlife. Even a habitat as fundamentally unnatural as a drystone wall can support a whole community: lichens and mosses growing on the stone itself, flowering plants in the pockets of humus built up from their dead remains, insects feeding on these and fed on in their turn by birds like wheatears, which may even find a nest site where a stone has slipped out. If the wall is replaced by a barbed wire fence, the whole system is wiped out at a stroke.

If a farmer fills in his ponds and replaces his ditches with underground drainage, all the plants and animals which depend on aquatic habitats will disappear. At its simplest level, it is a matter of living space. Yet, even where there is space, the sheer restlessness of modern farming eliminates the more sensitive species which, like the plants of primary woodlands, are dependent on long-established, settled conditions. In its appraisal *Nature Conservation and Agriculture* the NCC sought to estimate what would happen to the wildlife of farmland under a policy of total modernization.[54] If farms were to have all their old pasture converted to grass leys, if all fields – arable and pasture alike – were sprayed with weedkillers and artificial fertilizers, and ponds and ditches similarly treated or filled in, and if all hedges and headlands and field trees were cleared, the farming landscape would lose 80 per cent of its birds and all its butterflies. There would be no dragonflies and only half a dozen mammal species capable of surviving in the open grasslands and arable prairies. Such a complete transformation is, of course, highly improbable, if only because it would be monumentally expensive. But the movement towards this hypothetical barren landscape is ominously clear. In Huntingdonshire, for instance, the number of ponds in Kimbolton parish has halved since 1890; in three parishes the hedgerow has been reduced to one-fifth of its 1850 length, and, throughout the county, the average number of trees per acre has fallen from fifty-nine to twelve since 1947. In Dorset, the area of unimproved chalk downland has been reduced by nine-tenths since 1811, and heathland by four-fifths over the same period.

These transformations have already happened, and there is little point in bemoaning them. The important thing is that we recognize the trends – and their implications – and adapt our countryside policies accordingly. There is no reason at all why modern intensive agriculture should *necessarily* be the overriding agent in the shaping of the landscape (particularly as so many of its policies are determined by very temporary economic and political structures). One of the ironies of scientific farming is that the technological sophistication which currently makes it so damaging to wildlife could equally well generate ways of *reducing* its impact. Single-cell protein synthesis and organic waste recycling, for example, could eventually take a good deal of food production out of the countryside altogether. In the more immediate future we may well see movements back towards smaller farms and towards a greater concentration on vegetable crops. What matters is that the direction in which agriculture does develop takes proper account of all the other legitimate demands we have upon the countryside. We can no longer afford – in any sense of the word – persistently to relegate these to second place.

Such a considered and frugal approach to the use of our land will need give and take on both sides. Conservationists must constantly remind themselves that the world does need to grow more food and that farmers have as much right to try to improve their standard of living as the rest of us. And farmers must realize that the pressures on the earth's diminishing natural resources are too great for us to accept any longer the kind of attitude to the land expressed by one of their number in *The Countryman* in 1979:

All other weeds such as couch grass, chickweed, fat hen and charlock can be killed by continual spraying, but not the dreaded curse – wild oats . . . so what can the corn grower do? The best advice is to adopt a scorched earth policy: spray the ground in autumn and before planting, spray again in the spring, and rogue the corn before combining. In view of this, you will readily understand why we were angry when our local authority in Herefordshire decided to refrain from spraying the verges last summer in order to cut back on expenditure; so that while we were fighting the menace of the wild oats in our fields, the plants were thriving on the other side of the hedge.[53]

It is the proprietorial tone of this – unconscious, I'm sure – which is worrying. Although it may not be our business to question the wisdom and economics of 'scorched earth' policies on already cultivated land, it is surely not unreasonable to ask for wild plants to be spared in the verges if we are to lose them in the fields.

Yet we can see here that there are, broadly, two approaches to the reconciliation of nature conservation with modern agriculture. Either we physically separate the areas where they are carried out, or we modify the intensity of farming techniques so that they are no longer so destructive of natural life. They can be complementary approaches, of course, and any comprehensive conservation policy will need to have elements of both. And, between them, we can see any number of possible options: increasingly intensive farming on those areas already heavily cultivated combined with equally intensive protection of the few remaining wild areas; some modification of intensive farming (encouraged by grants and compensation) so that existing natural features are retained and new ones created; an extension of the idea of multiple-use over much greater areas of agricultural land; accepting wild areas as a 'pay at the gate' crop (and if this seems like a waste of productive land, we should remember how many of our crops – like hops – are already 'recreational'); and so on.

All of these options involve finding viable ways of maintaining – and paying for – features of the farming landscape that in current terms are mostly anachronistic, and in some senses 'useless', relics. In this chapter I have tried to identify these features, to examine how they were created and sustained by traditional practices, and how they are threatened by current developments. I have looked at what might be the minimum ecological requirements for their survival, and in what ways these might be met, in practice, inside the framework of modern agriculture. The rather special case of the landscape of supplementary, low-intensity agriculture, the relics of the common lands and wastes, I will be examining in the chapter on recreation, as this is the land-use they are increasingly moving towards.

COVER

Many small primary woods – perhaps the majority – lie within the province of farms, but the woody cover most characteristic of the agricultural landscape is the hedge. Hedges still seem to us as quintessentially a part of the English scene as they did to Cobbett – home of our favourite flowers and birds, and an adornment to the dullest of fields. They are nature on a human scale, wild but not overpowering, enclosing without oppressing. It is no wonder that their widespread destruction over the post-war period (at its peak the rate of loss of hedgerows was reckoned to be 5000 miles a year) became one of the rallying points of the nature conservation movement. It was not just that the hedge was perhaps our most familiar and intimate wildlife habitat; the sight of those straggling rows of shoulder-to-shoulder shrubs going down before the bulldozers also became an exact symbol of the transformation of the whole countryside. What had seemed like a landscape modelled on the needs of humans and other living creatures was being reshaped, appropriated, to meet the demands of a machine-based agriculture.

Between 1946 and 1963 we lost something like 85,000 miles (130,000 kilometres) of hedge, perhaps 15 per cent of the total length in England and Wales.[56] The rate has slowed down now, probably to 2000 miles (3200 kilometres) a year, and here and there we are beginning to see the planting of new farm hedges for perhaps the first time this century. It is worth pausing a while to consider the reasons for this easing, as it may help us to assess the impact of hedgerow clearance more dispassionately. Pessimists will say that fewer hedgerows are being grubbed up because there are not many left to attack, optimists that conservationist arguments about the importance of hedges are at last being listened to. There are elements of truth in both these points of view, and somewhere between them we might be able to formulate a realist's explanation of hedgerow clearance which would be more utilitarian than either. Clearance was not done for its own sake but because hedges had outlived their usefulness and become a positive obstacle to modern agricultural techniques. On most farms they have been removed to the point where they cease to be an obstacle, and where the expense of further grubbing-out is likely to exceed the savings in ground space and management costs. Rates of clearance on different kinds of farm have consequently been widely different and have depended on the character of the local hedges and on the contribution, for better or worse, that they make to the overall economy of the farm. In purely dairy-farming areas a well-kept hedge is still an asset, providing a stockproof barrier as well as a shelter for the cattle, and clearance has been small. In some of the arable prairies of East Anglia, where combine harvesters work six abreast, hedges are regarded as obstructions and have been extensively removed.

The national average figures of clearance tend to obscure these regional differences, and with them the essentially functional nature of hedges. Like most of the other features of our semi-natural landscape, hedges were created – or adapted out of natural landscape features – to do a job. Some of the earliest marked the course of manorial and parish boundaries. In its most primitive form a boundary hedge was simply a strip of woodland left standing between two fields cleared of trees. Later, it might have started with the scrubby growth forming along rows of hurdles, or have been deliberately planted. In regions where trees were scarce, as on the poor soils of Cornwall and west Wales, it was often a wall of gorse-covered turves flanked by the ditch from which these had been dug. Yet a hedge rarely had just a single function. If it marked a visible estate boundary for humans, it could also serve as a physical barrier for stock. And if – as was the case across most of lowland Britain – it was formed from trees and bushes, it could also provide a supply of wood. Earlier I described the hedge as a 'linear coppice'. It would have been more accurate to say a 'coppice with standards', for every thirty yards or so an oak or ash would be allowed to grow into a timber tree, usually by promotion from a promising shoot in the bush layer – exactly as would be done in a wood. Both underwood and timber were harvested and used, in their seasons, as part of the management of the hedge.

Until Max Hooper's work on hedge-dating, all kinds of hedges were widely believed to be products of the enclosure Acts, and therefore ephemeral additions to the landscape that were not worth a backward glance. Hedges are certainly associated with enclosure; that is what they are about. What was not properly understood even twenty years ago was the degree of enclosing that went on prior to the Parliamentary enactments of the eighteenth and nineteenth centuries. Oliver Rackham has estimated that one half of the hedged and walled landscape of England dates back to between the Bronze Age and the seventeenth century.[33]

There is a great deal of difference between the natural richness of these ancient hedges and the Enclosure Acts hedges, which are never more than 200 years old. Max Hooper's now celebrated formula linking the number of woody species in a thirty-yard stretch of hedge to its age in centuries needs to be used with care, but its underlying principle – that the older a hedge is the more species of tree and shrub it contains – holds true in most circumstances.[56] And the richer the variety of shrubs the greater the variety of insects and birds which will be able to use the hedge for food and shelter. Those hedges which were formed directly out of relict strips of the Wildwood can carry with them sensitive woodland flowers like bluebell and woodruff and early purple orchid.

Hedges dating from the last two centuries were almost invariably planted, usually with just one or two species (hawthorn, blackthorn and elm were the commonest), and have flowers associated with them which are more typical either of the fields they border or of secondary woodland. They have one other feature in common with plantation woodland. They were *imposed* on the landscape, often with great geometric orderliness and with little regard for the natural contours or character of the soil. Ancient hedges, like the estate boundaries or trackways they often follow, are frequently associated with natural boundaries – springlines, valley bottoms and scarps, for example. They not only look more fitting as a result, but are more open to colonization by the rich mix of plants and animals that occur in these transitional zones. They are 'developed' habitats, as against the 'designed' strips of the nineteenth-century planners.

I have borrowed this distinction between design and development from Felix Paturi's book *Nature, Mother of Invention*, where he uses it to distinguish between the inflexible and often ill-adapted technologies imposed by man on the natural world (and on himself) and the more tentative and gradual ways plants evolve, testing out, as it were, new forms and ideas for compatability with their environment:

. . . the products of development have already stood the test by developing. Designs can be mistaken; developments cannot . . . developments follow on environmental conditions, as though they could not progress more quickly than these conditions. Their products will always be adapted to the environment. They will not outstrip it and therefore force it to adapt itself to them. Designs have other time standards. They can be speeded up almost at will.[57]

Paturi uses this distinction to describe two contrasting styles of change in living systems, and in so doing suggests a principle by which we can evaluate the desirability, in conservation terms, of *processes* in man-made environments comparable to the distinctions between primary and secondary habitats (as in woodlands). (The distinction could also be used retrospectively to classify existing secondary communities. We have already discussed how minimally-managed plantations – 'developed' habitats – are more naturally interesting than 'designed' plantations.)

In this sense, ancient, developed hedges have a continuity and 'grain' that is not possessed by the nineteenth-century planners' hedges, and they can seem as integral a part of the landscape as a river or a hill. And by and large they are still the most secure. It is the newer, 'internal' hedges which have proved a greater obstruction to mechanized farming, and which also make up the larger proportion of hedges removed in the post-war years. Hedges along roadsides or farm boundaries are less of an obstacle and have suffered less by comparison. I think they are also the higher conservation priority, and not just because they are richer ecologically. Unlike the new hedges, which are normally just a scenic feature, a grid of thin lines in the distance, these boundary hedges often run alongside lanes and footpaths, and are perhaps the most intimate and familiar features of our whole countryside. They have the best of every season: the spring flowering shrubs, crab apple and may and dog-rose; fruits and nuts to pick in autumn; and the bright skeins of bryony and ivy and old man's beard in the winter – all at arm's length, and seeming in more than one sense to be outside the private domain of the farm.

And the oldest could, in practice, no more be re-created than a primary wood. Max Hooper has shown that, in areas with little or no woodland, many plant species that need settled, sheltered conditions, or scrubby growth for support, are absolutely confined to mature hedges.[58] If these are removed at the rate that young hedges are going, then, by the year 2000 A.D., as many as thirty species – including crab apple, wayfaring tree, climbers like honeysuckle and hop, and bankside herbs like scented violet and periwinkle – could be lost from many parishes.

Ideally, of course, all hedges are worth saving, as a new hedge could one day become an old one; and even the emaciated wisps to which many internal quicksets have been reduced are some kind of uncultivated oasis. (Something like 10 million birds are reckoned to breed in our remaining 600,000 miles of hedge, and many of these nest in the newer hedges. They are often found in surprisingly high densities, because their territories can extend outwards, at right angles to the hedge.) Yet it would be unreasonable of us to expect to save every hedge. Hedges are a liability to most farmers, and many of the arguments that have been raised about their agricultural importance give only one side of the story. Their value as windbreaks is cancelled out, in most places, by the fact that they also cut out the sun. For every beneficial insect-eating bird they harbour, a farmer could point out what he regards as a pest or a weed.

Yet there are good agricultural, as well as conservation, arguments in favour of the retention of *boundary* hedges. Properly maintained, they are still immeasurably better barriers to stock and people than any kind of fence. And the raised banks they usually stand on form ideal refuges for the insects that play such a crucial role in the pollination of cultivated flowering crops, particularly clover and fruit trees.[59]

Yet that 'proper maintenance' is the snag. The problem with boundary hedges is not so much that they interfere with the efficient running of farm machinery but that the cost of their upkeep may simply be too high. And, if they are not adequately managed, they are not only likely to lose a good deal of their natural diversity but to encroach on the adjoining field or road. So in practice the choice usually comes down to finding an economic way of managing the hedge or losing it altogether. Since our overriding aim must be to prevent the hedge being grubbed out, we may have to accept the use of rather violent machines like the flail mower.

The most efficient way of maintaining a hedge mechanically so that it retains its attractiveness and natural interest is to use some variant of 'A-shaping' where, ideally, the hedge is trimmed with just two sweeps of the flail cutter. The initial reduction of an overgrown hedge to this shape is not a pretty business; yet, ironically, the drastic and random pruning that flailing gives to shrubs often encourages them to shoot more densely than usual, and a mature, mechanically managed, A-hedge is as good a wildlife habitat as one laid manually in the traditional way. It is tightly bushy, broad at the base, and an almost totally secure nesting site for scrub birds. It is by no means the only case where modern technology has proved the saving of an ancient organic contrivance.

Unfortunately, mechanical management may exact a price of another kind. If it is carried out for maximum economy, the cutter must be able to sweep back and forth along the hedge with the minimum of interruption, and this may mean sacrificing potential new timber trees actually growing in the hedge. It does not take much to save them – simply lifting the cutter near standing trees and promising shoots and hand-trimming round their trunks – but to a hard-pressed farmer this may be regarded as an extravagant waste of time. Yet in the long term the overall costs of establishing wayside trees by other means – planting up on road verges for example – may prove even greater. Too many roads are currently fringed with the dead spikes of saplings planted in well-meaning attempts to replace more mature trees destroyed or dying in the hedge. Conditions are not on the side of new plantings on sites like this. The young trees are easy victims for vandals or careless highway maintenance men. They suffer badly in their first few years from lack of water, particularly if they are near deep roadside drainage ditches which have taken the water-table below the level of their roots. They need continuous care and attention until they are established, and this is not usually something which can be guaranteed by local authorities which have already had to pare their road maintenance programmes to the bone. A promoted hedgerow shoot is not only fully established – its stool and root system may be literally hundreds of years old – but physically protected by the surrounding hedge. Establishing trees in this way is nearly always successful and will produce specimens which reflect the genetic variety of the hedge itself. And, if it were done as part of a rotational system of wayside management (also the most economical approach), it would help create something of an age structure in the network of hedges. There could be stretches representing every stage of succession – dense scrub, newly trimmed lengths of hedge and verge carrying selectively promoted saplings, and blocks of mature trees and stools. (The requirements of safety near roads and footpaths mean that wayside hedges would also be ideal situations to experiment with the creation of new pollards.)

I think it would be difficult to overemphasize the importance of re-establishing field and hedgerow trees as part of a continuous programme. It will not be long before it becomes very obvious that, between the late nineteenth century, when farms grew their own timber, and the widespread amenity plantings of the seventies, nearly 100 years passed during which there was no economic or social 'use' for farm trees, and so virtually no new specimens established. Despite the current wave of planting this means that mature trees are now one of the most rapidly declining features of our landscape. Just how fast they are going is difficult to assess. The last full census was carried out by the Forestry Commission in 1951, and the catastrophic history of our treescape since then has made this document of no more than historical value.[60] A quarter of our hedges – including the trees that stood in them – have been grubbed out. By 1978 half of our 25 million elms were dead or dying of Dutch elm disease. An uncounted number of other farm trees are succumbing to water starvation and a seemingly never-ending list of new diseases, affecting oak, beech, crab apple, whitebeam. . . .

The most detailed study of tree loss at a local level has been done in Norfolk, where in 1976 the County Council carried out a remarkably sophisticated survey which it is hoped will act as a spur and a model to other counties.[61] By sampling 200 representative plots the Planning Department estimated the county's population of farm and hedgerow trees to be about 634,000. 34 per cent of these were oak, 27 per cent elm and 21 per cent ash. No other species exceeded 3 per cent of the total. The condition and age of the trees in the sample plots were also recorded and, by correlating these figures with such factors as trends in hedgerow clearance and incidence of disease, the Planning Department was able to predict that, over the next twenty-five years, the loss of trees was likely to be about 8000 a year. This means that, allowing for natural mortality and thinning, 40,000 young trees will have to be established every year to make good the losses. It is pleasant to be able to report that Norfolk County Council has succeeded in getting roughly twice this number planted in the county's farmland each year since the publication of the survey. Oak has been the preferred tree in most cases, but a much wider variety of species has been planted than currently exists, and in a wider variety of situations. Many are in the marginal sites recommended by the Countryside Commission as the foundation of the 'new agricultural landscapes' – in field corners, in uncultivable hollows and as screens for farm buildings and so on. These are greatly to be welcomed in a treeless countryside and may, with time, become as scenically attractive as the hedgerow trees of the earlier farming system. But their value in the natural scheme of things may depend on how we come to use them once they have been planted. In the traditional landscape each element was doing a job – and quite often a number of jobs – in the place most suited for it. This not only produced that 'rightness' of appearance that is always a sign of good functional design, but helped preserve the crucial factor of continuity. If we wish our new treescapes to be similarly attractive and rich, we may need to think more carefully about their long-term function. For whose benefit are we planting them? What aims will guide the management of the trees once they begin to mature? How will we ensure continuity?

FIELD

Yet the futures of boundary hedges, field corner coverts, silo screens, and so on are really the least of the conservation worries raised by modern agriculture. They are, quite literally, peripheral problems, and with money and goodwill some sort of solution will be found for them. It is the farmland itself, the open fields, the productive 90 per cent of the surface area of the agricultural landscape, that is under the greatest pressure. The sum total of this land – arable fields, hay plots, water meadows, sheep walks on the northern uplands and southern downs, dairy pastures, and rough grazing on heath and moorland, saltmarsh and fen – accounts for almost the complete range of open habitats in the countryside. Whilst they were farmed in traditional ways they provided ideal conditions for an immense range of wildlife.

It would be wrong to infer from this that the pattern of traditional agriculture was itself static and immutable. The stresses of poverty and the profit-motive, of political change and war, of technical innovation and of an unstable climate, placed the business of growing food in a state of continuous flux. But it is possible to see an underlying direction in the pattern of change and to pick out a number of principles common to traditional farming techniques which have now largely been superseded

In this hypothetical ancient field system changes, when they did occur, tended to be slow and short-lived. Without the technology (and perhaps our contemporary arrogance) utterly to overrule nature, the pattern of farming was determined by such factors as the character of local soils and rainfall, by the slope of one field and the liability of another to flooding. These were, to a degree, constants – facts of nature – and as a result the plant and animal communities of the traditional field evolved slowly as a compromise between natural colonization and the demands of human agriculture. They might not be the same plants and animals that would occur if the field was abandoned by agriculture (which would usually result in its reverting to woodland), but I do not think it improper to use the word 'natural' about them. Some, like the grasses in rough pasture, were the actual bread and butter of the agricultural process itself, whilst the insects, say, that lived on them were incidental cohabitants. But both were successfully adapted associates of a regular pattern of land-use. Continuous tight grazing by sheep, for instance, favoured mat-like herbs and fine grasses, and produced the characteristically springy turf of chalk downland. Grazing by cattle (which are more selective feeders and 'tear' the vegetation rather than nibbling it) produced a more varied and tufted sward. Meadows allowed to grow hay gave taller plants an advantage, particularly those that flower and set their seed before haymaking. Arable fields were characteristically the habitat of annual weeds adapted to disturbance, like poppies and forget-me-nots, and ground-nesting birds like partridges.

The second difference is that the traditional fieldscape invariably had some kind of margin or 'fringe'. It might be no more than a hedge, or a rough encircling strip like the 'grass walk' that ran round Cobbett's fields. It might be a much greater expanse of fen or bog. These ragged edges were a literal and figurative expression of the *physicality* of traditional farming practices. Whilst the land was still worked by human and animal muscle-power it was not worth breaking your back to try and gain a few extra cultivated crops from these marginal lands. It was better to take from them the products they gave up freely and naturally – a few rabbits for the pot, reed for thatching, turves for the fire. They could always be cultivated in hard times and until then kept as reserve land. For wildlife, too, they were reserves, more natural than the cropped fields, and places where the course of growth and selection could proceed relatively unhindered.

Although there were periodic drifts away from this pattern of a diverse, low-intensity agriculture in which crops and techniques were determined largely by natural factors, it was not until the nineteenth century that the changes reached a critical, concerted pitch. During this period we can see the rise of a powerful new class of entrepreneurial landowners who were in a position to finance and co-ordinate three crucial changes: the appropriation and enclosure of large areas of common land and waste by parliamentary enactment; the introduction of new techniques for the cultivation and drainage of the marginal 'fringes'; and the injection into the previously self-sufficient farming cycle of energy sources from outside, particularly coal for threshing machines, processed feed and artificial fertilizers:

Until the nineteenth century, the production cycle on a mixed farm holding had been almost closed: it produced wheat, barley, meat and some wool for sale, and hay, roots and clovers and rotation grasses for consumption by the livestock which manured the land and pulled the plough and which, in turn, ensured larger grain yields.[62]

The availability of 'fuel' produced externally broke this cycle, and meant that there was no longer any need for the diversity of habitats that developed alongside traditional mixed farming. The way was open for specialized farming, and for the eventual development of monocultural holdings.

Such changes have accelerated again since the Second World War. Yet it is not so much change and increased cultivation in themselves that make modern agricultural techniques so incompatible with wildlife; in the past, as we have seen, these processes often heightened the natural diversity of farmland by increasing the variety of open habitats. It is their use in new combinations, in new situations, and at unprecedented levels of intensity which is the real threat, and which makes it necessary for us to look at these techniques in much greater detail, and at where they 'break' with natural processes. Conservation on farmland must also, of course, be concerned with the protection of the remaining unimproved agricultural sites – chiefly old pastures and meadows, undrained grazing marshes and upland moors. But these make up such a small proportion of existing farmland that site protection cannot play the same role here as it does in, say, woodland conservation. So I will be concentrating in the rest of this section on four basic farming practices: ploughing, burning, fertilization and drainage. I shall examine the impact of their current intensive forms on the wildlife that in part, at least, they once helped sustain, and try to identify areas where there can be compromises with the needs of nature conservation.*

PLOUGHING

The ploughing of the ground is the most ancient of all organized cultivation practices. Some historians have suggested that the use of the plough – a simple enough device in itself, but one which implied a certain sophistication in measurement techniques, planning for the future, and agreement about land-use – marked the crucial turning point in the evolution of settled agricultural civilizations, as against the looser and more nomadic societies associated with pasturing and slash-and-burn crop-growing.

Areas of regularly disturbed ground are rather scarce in nature and confined to such habitats as seashores, scree slopes and river beaches. Ploughed fields share a few annual herbs with these places, but their wildlife is dominated by opportunist scavengers, ground-nesting birds with short breeding seasons, and those familiar weeds that have become particularly adapted

---

* I have deliberately not touched on the use of pesticides, partly because it is a very complex subject, exhaustively documented elsewhere,[63] but also because, on this question, there is really no compromise possible. It is the *purpose* of pesticides to kill wild organisms and, until such time as there are efficient, economic and ecologically preferable substitutes, the most nature conservationists can hope to achieve is a vigilant watch over the safety and conditions of use of such chemicals, and to ensure that they do not kill more than they are intended to.

to the arable cycle. Since settled farming is invariably associated with trade, many of these are of foreign origin, and arrived here as impurities in seed stock from countries where naturally open habitats are more widespread. Poppies, scarlet pimpernel, fumitory and cornflower probably all first came to us this way, mixed up with the seed-corn of early settlers from the Mediterranean.

All these adaptable species added to the natural diversity and attractiveness of the agricultural landscape. But they are a relatively small number compared to those species dependent on settled conditions. The impact of ploughing is therefore closely connected with its scale, with the area of land currently being used as arable.

The current trend towards expanding cereal production (chiefly for animal feed rather than direct human consumption) has been especially evident on the chalk, where it has resulted in the destruction of large areas of downland and the immense variety of colourful flowers and butterflies they supported. There is nothing new in the conversion of these sheep pastures to cereal. In Wiltshire, for instance, there was widespread cultivation of downland during the population explosion of the thirteenth century and again during the corn shortages of the Napoleonic wars. But, equally, there were movements back to grass during the early sixteenth century, when the price of wool was high, and during the latter years of the nineteenth, when the country was flooded by cheap grain from America. During these periods of reversion the downland sward (and its attendant insects) was built up again by colonization from uncultivated grassland nearby; and in the absence of documentary evidence it is often hard to tell a stretch of 'secondary' grassland, ploughed up in the nineteenth century (or even briefly during the Second World War), from an area which might conceivably never have been disturbed. In this sense chalk grassland communities may be re-creatable in a way that an ancient wood is not.

Figure 3. Reduction and fragmentation of heathland and downland in Dorset since the 1800s. Condensed and simplified from A. Carys Jones, The Conservation of Chalk Downland in Dorset.[65] Maps provided by Furzebrook Research Station of the Institute of Terrestrial Ecology.

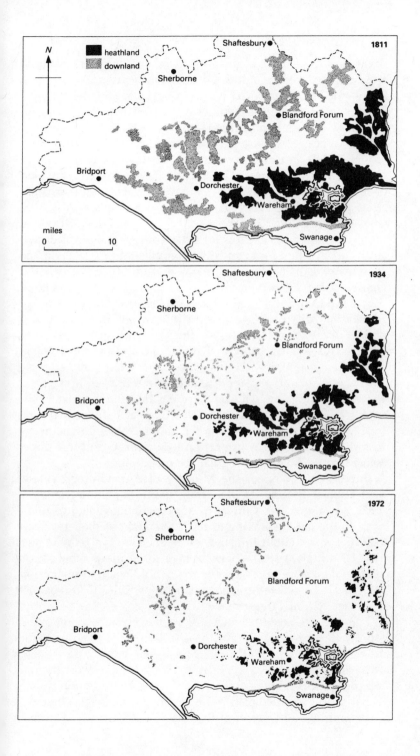

Yet in practice there is now little likelihood of a rich turf being re-established. When cultivated downland is returned to grass today, the turf is restored by the sowing of commercial seed mixtures and the suppression of other plants by herbicides. In any case, the remaining fragments of old downland are too small and scattered to serve as sources for recolonization. The ploughs have moved into areas that would have been thought impossible thirty years ago – winched up one-in-two gradients, trundled along the shelves of Celtic strip lynchets, and threaded along the winding valley bottoms of steep combes. A Nature Conservancy survey in 1966 showed that only 107,000 out of the 3¼ million acres of England's chalk soils remained as downland.[64] Carys Jones's detailed historical study in 1972 on the changes in Dorset (which contains a total acreage of exposed chalk soils of 236,880 acres) showed a drop in the acreage of downland from 69,910 acres in the First Edition of the Ordnance Survey in 1811, to 19,284 acres in 1934 during the Land Utilisation Survey, to 8212 acres in the Open Country Survey of 1967.[65] This was probably a slight underestimate, but the loss in the five years between this survey and Carys Jones's own – 2542 acres – is not, and represented a drop of over 30 per cent. Parallel with this overall loss there has been an increase in the number of fragments of down, and a great reduction in their average size. Two-thirds of the remaining Dorset fragments are less than fifty acres in extent, and they are mostly on slopes which are too steep or irregular for ploughing.

But, as it happened, the Ministry of Agriculture, Fisheries and Food withdrew its ploughing grants for the lowlands in 1972, and the greatest threat to our remaining chalk downland is from the aerial spraying of fertilizers and weedkillers. There are now, throughout England, probably less than 100,000 acres (40,500 hectares) left. What we have to decide is whether the marginal increase in production that would result from 'improving' these, by whatever means, is really worth the loss of such a unique national treasure.

Nor are the costs of such intensive reclamations measured purely in terms of wild flowers and butterflies. The footpaths which are ploughed up can be restored. But the few tractor drivers who are killed every year trying to take their ploughs up precipitous slopes cannot. And the soil on these slopes, once it has been disturbed, can be decidedly mortal itself. There was a striking demonstration of this in 1978 at Barnsley Warren in

Gloucestershire. The south-facing slope of this steep limestone valley has a wonderfully rich sward which, as far as is known, has never been ploughed or chemically treated, and which carries Britain's largest population of Pasque flowers. The opposite side of the valley (in another ownership) had been ploughed a short while before and reseeded with a commercial grass mixture. The centuries-old network of root-fibres that knitted turf and soil together was completely destroyed, and the heavy rainfalls of the winter of 1977/8 (helped by cattle-trampling) washed away most of the new grass and a good deal of the topsoil. Even by late spring, the area still had the look of a moto-cross track. Just 100 yards away the undisturbed grassland was as lush as ever. Nothing could have demonstrated more forcibly that, even in agricultural terms, intensive methods are not always the most productive.

Downland is by no means the only kind of pasture to have gone under the plough. Heathland has been another major target, from the Cornish coast to upland heather moors in the north of Scotland. In Exmoor 12,000 acres (4900 hectares) were lost to agriculture and forestry between 1947 and 1976. By 1978, when Lord Porchester recommended that the appropriation of moorland for intensive agriculture should cease, up to 150 acres (sixty hectares) were still being ploughed up annually.[66] In the Breckland of East Anglia, the area of open heath has been reduced from 54,000 acres (22,000 hectares) to 19,000 acres (7500 hectares) since 1880, partly as a result of coniferization, but also because of the extensive conversion of sheep walks and rabbit warrens to arable. Even mountain pastures are not immune. In Radnor Forest, Powys, a tract of sub-montane heath and grassland, parts of which lie over 2000 feet above sea level, has been ploughed and reseeded with commercial grasses.

This type of conversion, where the *function* of the land is retained as pasture but the grass is treated as a transient crop, is the most deceptive of all, for at a superficial glance it simply replaces one kind of green field with another. As scenery, old and improved pastures are scarcely distinguishable, and the distinction between them has not attracted much attention from those concerned with the 'new agricultural landscapes'. Yet intensive ley grasslands are no more hospitable to wildlife than the large arable prairies. Already one-sixth of the 6½ million hectares (16 million acres) of grassland in England and Wales is ploughed and reseeded more than once every five years, and this proportion would be much higher if we excluded rough upland grazing.

The purely agricultural value of ploughing up old grassland, cultivating it for a few years and then reseeding (often with seed swept from the hayloft, which would have been very rich in species) was recognized as early as the sixteenth century. But it was not until just before the last war, when scientifically balanced seed mixtures and artificial fertilizers had reached an advanced state of sophistication, that the idea of ley farming as a *system* became widely adopted. In 1939 the Government introduced its grant systems for the ploughing up of old grassland, and a few months later Sir George Stapledon published his influential book *The Plough-up Policy and Ley Farming*.[67]

In recent years, high market prices and attractive subsidies for milk and beef have encouraged farmers to move into intensive grass production even in the uplands. In Forsinard, in the remote heart of Sutherland, the Highlands and Islands Development Board is backing a private landowner in what it has described as the most ambitious programme of land conversion ever undertaken in the north of Scotland. The programme is monumental and will eventually involve the transformation of 20,000 acres (8000 hectares) of moorland. First a forage harvester will strip off all the existing heather and other vegetation. The ground will then be levelled and rotavated, spread with fertilizer, rotavated again and finally sown with grass or winter barley.

It would be wrong to suggest that all upland moors are of great importance to wildlife. Some are the result of forest clearance on poor soils that have gradually had their nutrients leached away and have no great variety of plant or animal life. Nor must we forget the rather special needs of the human communities of the uplands, which are badly in need of new development initiatives if they are not to collapse altogether. But our uplands contain some unique peatland systems, many of which are natural and *not* the result of forest clearance. And even the newer moorlands are amongst the dwindling number of places in Britain that can, without too much exaggeration, be called wildernesses. It is still possible to find a measure of solitude in them and a wildlife which, though thinly spread, includes birds as evocative of lonely places as greenshank and hen harrier. Given the investment of work and public money which will be involved in 'reclamations' of the kind proposed at Forsinard, it has to be asked whether this kind of development really is the most efficient use of the land, and whether a pattern based on a labour-intensive mixed economy – incorporating carefully sited forestry and tourism, for example – might not make a more exciting and thrifty use of the area's human and natural resources.

BURNING

If ploughing was the foundation of settled agriculture, burning was the basic clearance technique of earlier nomadic societies, and has probably always played some kind of role in the farming of Britain's wilder fringes. In these areas of high rainfall and acid soils, heather and its relatives tend to dominate the plant cover after forest clearance, just as grasses do in more hospitable conditions. But neither moorland nor grassland can be maintained unless there is some external factor which prevents the regeneration of trees. Historically the most significant of such factors has been grazing by domestic animals. This may have been supplemented by occasional burning, particularly in sheltered areas where uncontrolled heather can grow into large, woody and unnutritious bushes. Yet Professor C. H. Gimingham, in his extensive study *Ecology of Heathlands*, suggests that the practice only became common in many areas of upland Britain at the beginning of the nineteenth century, when the natural productivity of the heather moors began to drop.[68] By this time, for instance, sheep had almost entirely replaced cattle in the Scottish Highlands, which, since the clearances 100 years before, had been stocked at densities which the natural growth of food plants could not support. Their feeding habits tended to aggravate the degenerative effects of overstocking. Sheep are selective grazers, and in pastures dominated by heather tend to go for grasses and young shoots and ignore old woody growth and bracken. In these circumstances burning kept the older – and economically useless – growth down and encouraged the sprouting of nutritious young shoots.

Once its advantage became clear, rotational burning became the standard technique for managing heather pasture and soon generated an unexpected by-product in the institution of the organized grouse shoot. Red grouse (which also feed on young heather shoots) began to increase substantially in areas managed by burning, and landowners were quick to realize the potential value of letting the sporting rights on their grazing land. Pasturing and grouse-rearing are more or less compatible, but, as the returns on hill sheep began to decline in the latter half of the nineteenth century, and recreational access to the uplands to improve because of the extension of the rail network, so the management of the moors was increasingly biased towards the needs of the grouse.

There are presently not far short of 3 million acres (1,200,000 hectares) of grouse moor in Britain, the bulk of which is in Scotland. The customary management system is a rotation in which patches of heather are burnt off every ten to twelve years. This provides a range of stands of different ages and structure, from the young shoots which spring in the recently burnt areas and provide the birds' food, to the denser old clumps which are used as cover and nest sites.

The management of moorland for grouse has at least preserved a considerable expanse of a habitat that, given present trends, might otherwise be in danger of going under the plough. The practice of 'muirburn' has also guaranteed the survival of the heather itself, which is the backbone of the whole heathland ecosystem. Yet from a conservationist viewpoint there are disadvantages in relying on intensive burning as the exclusive, or even the chief, technique for managing heather. Even when carried out on a rotational basis it results in what to all intents and purposes is a heather monoculture. Large numbers of less mobile creatures are destroyed by the fire itself (even though they can recolonize from unburnt patches) and the average number of plant species, including lichens and mosses, is only half that of areas never subjected to burning. Unbroken sweeps of heather do of course have their own specialities, particularly in the south of England, where they are the haunts of scarce insects and reptiles; and when the ling is in flower in late summer they provide an unequalled spectacle through their sheer expanse of colour. Yet we have to set this against the attractiveness and natural variety of less intensively burnt heathlands. Round Loch Maree, for instance, the oldest heather is chest high and still flourishing. It grows in an intimate mixture with native pine and juniper, and is a habitat where even wild cats can live unmolested by keepers. In the New Forest the heathlands merge with orchid-rich bogs and grasslands in the valleys. Dartford warblers nest in the denser gorse, and hobbies in isolated clumps of pines.

There may also be more far-reaching disadvantages in the encouragement of a uniform heather cover. Like all monocultures it is prone to disease and infestations by insects such as the heather-beetle. And in areas of high rainfall and wind exposure, repeated burning – even when properly controlled – may produce a gradual but serious degeneration in the overall productivity and diversity of the habitat. D. N. McVean and J. Lockie, in their study *Ecology and Land Use in Upland Scotland*, point out that the geographical conditions which normally favour the growth of heather in the north and west of Britain also make burning one of the least appropriate management techniques.[69] The poorly drained peaty soils are prone to take-over by rough and unpalatable plants like mat-grass and cotton-grass, whose root systems are comparatively invulnerable to fire. And where regeneration is slow, the high rainfall tends to encourage erosion of the soil. Often this is severe enough to lead to the formation of 'hags', islands of peat separated by deep fissures that penetrate right down to the underlying rocks. These hags are themselves highly unstable and liable to break up and be washed away entirely. Consequently the end result of imprudent burning can be the destruction not just of the heather but of the peat itself.

McVean and Lockie make out a convincing case for a much more varied pattern of land-use on upland heather moors, in which grazing, recreation, forestry, water catchment, and wild-life conservation in its own right are all given a role, in a mosaic of specialized patches or, wherever possible, complementing each other over the same area of ground. Heather moors are resilient enough to support a wide range of different uses – provided that degenerative management techniques like burning are kept in their proper place. I think it is worth recording that, on parts of Moor House National Nature Reserve in the northern Pennines, a rich mixed-age heather cover has been maintained without resort to burning at all. Light grazing is used to help produce a patchwork of old and new growth, but the factor which contributes most towards structural variety is simply the contouring of the ground. The heather grows lushly in sheltered gullies and short on exposed scarps. In places where complicated changes in topography are compressed into a small area, you can find all kinds and stages of growth apparently emerging from single, hugely extended, plants.

Before it became a National Nature Reserve, many of Moor House's 10,000 acres (4000 hectares) were managed specifically to produce grouse – a far cry from the varied communities that are encouraged at present. It is cheering therefore – though not without its ironies – that the 'productivity' of birds under this regime is just as high as on the heather monocultures and grouse 'farms' of Scotland.

Since the Second World War, burning has also become a common practice in arable areas. The burning of straw and stubble after harvest is often justified as a way of clearing the field of weeds and infestations. But its rapid spread in recent years is chiefly an economic phenomenon, related to changes in both the internal structure of modern farms and the more specialized national pattern of agriculture. The areas where most straw is now produced (the arable East and the Midlands, for instance) are precisely the areas where it is least needed. The costs of harvesting, storing and transporting it to stock-raising areas far outweigh the price it can command. Like the majority of simple, bulky materials, straw is only economical when it is produced on the spot.

What long-term effect burning-off may have on the structure and fertility of the soil is difficult to tell. Although the minerals in the resulting ash are more quickly released than they would be from unburnt plant material, a good deal of the ash is lost as smoke. No doubt a good number of the animals that live in the top-soil (and which are important in maintaining its natural fertility) are also lost. But farmers are, at present, in complete agreement about the economic and agricultural desirability of straw-burning and, until there is concrete evidence to challenge this view, we must concentrate on the incidental effects of uncontrolled field fires on the surrounding countryside. The code of practice which has been drawn up by the National Farmers' Union, and which recommends, for example, that a six-foot-wide fire-break should be ploughed round a field before it is burnt, is voluntary and is by no means respected by all farmers. Hedges and field trees are so frequently consumed along with the stubble that it is sometimes hard to believe that this is wholly accidental, particularly when the burning of the hedge is followed smartly by its grubbing out. In dry weather much larger areas of nearby countryside may be at risk. In September 1972, for instance, fifteen acres (six hectares) of reedbed in Fingringhoe Wick Nature Reserve in Essex were destroyed when a straw fire got out of control.

FERTILIZERS

When agriculture was less intensive and individual farms relatively self-sufficient, the stubble was grazed or ploughed back into the field and the straw used for cattle-bedding. Both by-products thus had most of their goodness returned eventually to the soil. We have seen how the breaking of this cycle by the adoption of artificial fertilizers (especially by-products of the expanding chemical and steel industries) marked a crucial turning point in nineteenth-century agricultural history. Today farmers are applying nitrogenous fertilizers to grasslands at twenty times the pre-war rate. It may seem odd that a growth-promoter can be inimical to wildlife: what is good for one plant should be good for others, you would think. Yet artificial fertilizers are now one of the most destructive influences on the natural diversity of our grasslands. On one site in Wiltshire, for instance, where a three-year cycle of aerial top-dressing was begun in 1967, the average number of plant species per square metre dropped from thirty-three to twenty-one by 1975.[70]

The reason that organic manures do not have this effect appears to be their much more complex chemical and physical structure. The nitrogen and phosphorus are 'bound up' in them and slowly released over a matter of months. The active ingredients of most artificial fertilizers, on the other hand, are available immediately, and are taken up by those plants that can make quickest use of them. In most agricultural situations this means the grasses – especially fast-growing, aggressive species like rye-grass, which can rapidly smother the slower-growing herbs.

As is the case with a growing list of intensive agricultural practices, the marginal returns of increasing fertilizer application are beginning to be outweighed by escalating costs and other disadvantages. Amongst the plants that are suppressed by dense rye-grass growth are the pea-flowers, including the clovers (which are plentiful in 'natural' grasslands as well as sown leys). Clovers are natural fertilizers. They not only raise nitrogen levels in the soil free of charge by 'fixing' atmospheric nitrogen in their root systems, but are also now believed to be a more nutritious cattle food than grass. 'Bag nitrogen', on the other hand, is highly energy-consumptive, expensive, inefficient (that twenty-fold increase in application has only been accompanied by a doubling of stocking rates over the same period) and wasteful.[71] It is not possible to measure exactly how much of this nitrogen is taken up by plants, and how much is lost by leaching and evaporation. The high nitrate levels in watercourses are probably as much a result of sewage and industrial effluent as of run-off from the fields, but their effect is always the same, producing a thick scum of algae that smothers more sensitive water-plants and suffocates fish. The unnatural levels in ground water supplies, though, can be directly attributed to intensive agriculture. The nitrate levels in domestic water are sometimes so high that treatment plants cannot cope with them, and in parts of Lincolnshire, for instance, there have been a number of occasions recently when babies have had to be given specially treated water in bottles.

There is no doubt that, in agricultural terms, intensive fertilizer application does increase production and benefit the farmer. But if we look at it in a broader social context and take into account human health, the necessity of making more frugal use of our resources and the need to conserve freshwater life, it begins to look less attractive. Yet again, the kind of policies which are desirable for the conservation of nature, pure and simple, may be indicators of those we need to follow for the wider conservation of our quality of life.

DRAINAGE

In prehistoric times, continuously wet habitats – marshes, fens, bogs, lakes, streams and rivers – accounted for most of the low-lying land that was not wooded. Although moisture is essential to the growth of all plants, no conventional British food crop will flourish in waterlogged ground. So, undrained, many wetlands represented a frustrating loss of potentially productive agricultural land. The problem was that removing water from the ground was a good deal more difficult than removing trees. It was not really until sophisticated Dutch techniques were introduced to the East Anglian fens in the seventeenth century that any serious large-scale drainage was carried out in this country. Even then the practice was slow to spread and relied on what could be achieved by gravity-feed and windmills. As late as the beginning of the nineteenth century the feature of the agricultural landscape that would probably impress us most, were we able to see it, would be its all-pervading wetness. Much lowland grazing was under water for the latter part of the winter. All farms and villages had ponds, which were as vital for stock as wells were for people. They were also likely to have a stretch of common fen, where villagers had the right to cut sedge and dig peat (which incidentally kept the surface of the fen from drying out and so maintained suitable conditions for species of wet habitats). The rivers were fuller and more luxuriantly bordered, and springs and small streams abounded. Even where extensive drainage had been carried out – as for instance on Romney Marsh in Kent – the intricate system of dykes and ditches represented a kind of linear, 'stretched-out' fen, and was populated with the plants and insects and birds that had inhabited the more extensive wetlands that preceded it. Early drainage works broke up and redistributed the wetlands more than drying them out entirely. The only species really to suffer were those which depended on large areas of secluded marsh. Chris Newbold, who has special responsibility for freshwater habitats in the NCC has described what the wildlife of one of these great fens might have been like:

In the early nineteenth century the Oxford clay scarp of southern Huntingdonshire was heavily wooded and some of the woods merged into the vast reed beds of Whittlesey Mere. In the summer, bittern would boom, marsh harriers would be seen silently quartering their hunting ground, while buzzards and red kites, both woodland species, would circle in the rising warm air currents along the scarp. Sparrowhawk and hobby, nesting in the woodland, would prey upon the tits and warblers in the reeds, or, in the case of the hobby, the rich invertebrate fauna which must have existed. Wildfowl – gadwall, mallard, teal, pintail, shoveler, tufted duck and pochard – were also abundant; indeed Ramsey, a market town on the edge of the mere, was famous for the sale of wildfowl.

Most of the birds have now disappeared from this area. . . . The loss of some of these species is undoubtedly due to shooting and to clearance of woodland but the disappearance of many species came about with the drainage of Whittlesey Mere in the mid-nineteenth century. Other fens in East Anglia suffered the same fate, and a flat, hedgeless, almost treeless, but highly fertile farmland remains.[72]

The aim of modern drainage is to keep water on the move, and ideally to reduce wet*lands* to a minimum. Farmers regard water which hangs about in the soil or on the top of fields as a nuisance. They want to shift it out rapidly when the ground is waterlogged and move it back in during periods of drought. Industrial and domestic water consumers (who now use more than 45,500 million litres a day – one-sixth of the entire daily rainfall in Britain) similarly want quick and easy *access* to water. We are consequently seeing the evolution of a kind of water 'grid' for the smooth and rapid shunting of water back and forth between agricultural land and the main river systems (and even between different river systems).

So freshwater habitats on the farm are undergoing the pattern of regimentation that is becoming so familiar in all natural habitats. In form the remaining rivers, streams and ditches are being converted to what are essentially canals: wide, deep, straight, hard-edged channels, with a relatively slow current but capable of moving a great deal of water. These would not be particularly hospitable habitats at the best of times, but the intensity with which they are managed to ensure that there is no impediment to their carrying capacity means that very little natural life has time to settle down in them. Beyond this, the pervasive quality of water as a medium means that the changes brought about by drainage improvement schemes are rarely contained, in the way that those resulting from, say, ploughing are.

The chain reaction can begin with the most modest of works, perhaps with the laying of percolated pipes under a stretch of permanent pasture by means of mole ploughing. The wildlife of the field itself is the first to suffer. The water content of the

Corncrake singing in a Hebridean hay meadow (above right). *Corncrakes have not been able to survive the development of intensive grassland management techniques, particularly the current fashion for early, mechanized cutting. Only in the remote north-west, where hay is still cut late in the breeding season – and often still by hand – have they survived in any numbers (see page 150).*

(Alan McGregor)

Feeding time at the Wildfowl Trust's reserve at Welney in the Ouse Washes (see page 161) (right). *River flood-plains (often cut for hay or summer-grazed) are another declining agricultural habitat. Luckily, more than half the area of the Washes is now owned or leased by conservation bodies and has become an outstanding example of a multiple-use wetland.*

Woodwalton Fen NNR – a relic of much larger areas of fenland that once existed in eastern England. Like the Ouse Washes, it is a multiple-use habitat, and is grazed in parts by the NCC's own herd of Galloway cattle. There are also plans to use it to 'hold' flood-water in winter (see page 143).

The blue-tailed damselfly, Ischnera elegans, depends for most of its life-cycle on the kind of wetlands – fens, ponds, sluggish streams – that are rapidly being drained away from the farming lundscape.

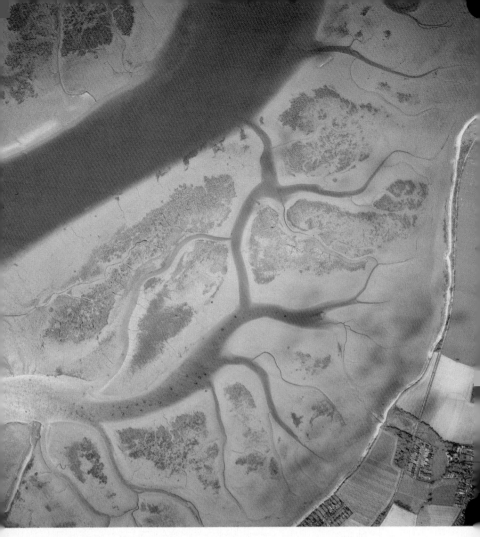

An aerial photograph of Langstone Harbour, Hampshire, in 'false colour' to highlight different vegetation types and geographical features. The intricate mosaic of creeks, flats and marsh that make up natural estuaries is very clear (see page 146).

soil drops drastically, and any plants that depend on damp conditions will soon disappear. Marshy corners, which may have supported sedges and rushes and herbs like marsh marigold, become indistinguishable from the rest of the field. The whole pasture may become dry enough to be ploughed and converted to arable.

To accommodate the extra flow of water from the field, the ditches into which it runs will be widened and straightened. Reeds, meadowsweet, loosestrife and other plants which may have clustered along the shallow edges will be scraped off with a drag-line excavator, which will also change the irregular cross-section of the ditch into a deep V. For good measure herbicides may be sprayed on the water to kill off waterweeds. This treatment may be repeated every two or three years, which means that there is no time for plants to recolonize the waterside – assuming, that is, that there are any points along the steep banks where they could find a roothold. Warblers, dragonflies and water voles, which may have lived in the ditch vegetation, will also vanish.

Meanwhile, the carrying capacity of the farm's ditches will have increased so much that the water-table in surrounding fields will start to drop. Natural ponds will dry out. Oaks in the hedgerow may start to develop stag-heads as their roots are deprived of moisture. To accommodate the flow from the drainage system, the nearest stream or river is now dealt with in much the same way as the ditches themselves. Willows and alders are grubbed out to give the excavating machinery room to manoeuvre. Silt dredged from the bottom of the river is dumped on what remains of the bankside vegetation, and the insect life which provides food for fish and birds has nowhere to breed. The marvellous, complex irregularities that give natural rivers their charm and variety – the meanders and rapids, the pools, eddies, backwaters, shallows, cattle wallows – begin to be levelled out. Otters lose their holts. Kingfishers are unable to find nest sites in the levelled banks. Many water animals begin to decline as their food plants are ripped out and as the

The cornflower or corn-bottle: once a familiar arable weed (see pages 19 and 132), now very scarce as a result of new seed-cleaning techniques and the regular use of herbicides.

water (probably already polluted by sewage) becomes increasingly contaminated by the fertilizer and weedkillers so efficiently drained off the fields. Fish consequently begin to suffer in their turn – but are likely to be declining anyway because the weedy shallows and gravel beds in which they spawn have vanished. Herons, dependent on fish and frogs, have to move away. . . .

The desiccation of a whole landscape, piece by piece, is one of the most graphic demonstrations of the interdependence of living things, and it is likely to happen wherever intensive drainage is carried out. Some wetland habitats – reedbeds and ponds, for instance – can be fairly quickly re-created where there is sufficient water about. We can see this in the speed with which flooded gravel-pits are colonized by quite rich communities of water birds and plants. But even these simple wetland habitats depend, by definition, on the presence of *water*, which it is the business of land drainage to remove. And, though they have their own attractions, they cannot be looked on as substitutes for wetlands whose physical features and living communities have evolved over many centuries and which are no more re-creatable than ancient woods. The remarkable raised peat-bogs of west Wales, for example, (two of which are safeguarded as National Nature Reserves) have been growing continuously for many thousands of years. Their structure is dependent not just on thousands of years of growth, but on a unique *sequence* of years. The layers of peat that are the foundation of their living surface have also preserved a record of the plants and animals that lived on them in the past, and even – like the growth rings of a tree – of changes in climate.

We can see the contrast between new and 'ancient' wetland features most clearly in estuaries, which invariably contain examples of both. Because of the physical disturbance they are subject to from tides and floods, estuarine marshlands are intrinsically 'mobile' habitats. Existing stretches are repeatedly washed away, and new ones laid down. This wear and tear is part of the natural experience of these marshes, and they have developed a very effective self-repairing system. In the rich silt that is washed down to them by the river, microscopic algae grow in very large numbers and, because of a mechanism evolved for their own protection, are able to begin the process of stabilizing new land. In order to avoid drying out between tides (and to help bury and protect themselves *during* tides) these diatoms secrete a mucus from their outer sheaths. This binds them not only to each other, but to the solid particles in the mud, producing something that could be called a 'living glue'. Except in extreme weather conditions (or if the water is badly polluted) this binds the silt together sufficiently securely for it to be colonized by larger plants, which in turn catch and bind down yet more silt. So the level of the land begins to rise and saltmarshes to form along the muddy edges of the channels.

To this extent, estuarine saltmarsh is self-renewing. But the estuary as a total *system* is not, and its natural interest depends on much more basic geographical features. Estuaries which have been allowed to develop naturally over many centuries are, characteristically, wide, gently-sloping deltas, scalloped with a jumble of creeks and bays. These can all be destroyed by dredging and drainage schemes, and especially by barrages which 'hold in' the water and dampen out tidal effects. Although a certain amount of immature marsh may form on the seaward side of a barrage or new sea-wall, it is unlikely to have the extent and variety of older, more natural marsh.[73]

The geographical *position* of the estuary is important too, particularly for migrating or wintering waders and wildfowl. The Wash, for instance, is an internationally important wintering site, and supports up to 180,000 birds at any one time. 32,000 acres (13,000 hectares) of marsh in the Wash have already been reclaimed by land drainage since the sixteenth century and, if more is lost, these birds will have to find new wintering quarters. Yet the pressure on all estuarine sites – from industry and bunded reservoir schemes as well as agricultural development – is such that they would quite literally have nowhere to go to.

You would think it were just such rich, irreplaceable but vulnerable sites that were in the minds of the drafters of the Countryside Act of 1968 when they stated that 'every Minister, government department and public body shall have regard to the desirability of conserving the natural beauty and amenity of the countryside' including its flora and fauna, and of the 1973 Water Act, under which Water Authorities were similarly required to 'have regard to the desirability of conserving flora and fauna'. Yet land drainage for agricultural purposes is eligible for large grants of public money. Both individual farmers and Internal Drainage Boards (autonomous bodies which represent small groups of neighbouring landowners) can claim government grants of up to 50 per cent for under-drainage, construction or improvement of field ditches and the like. Together, they have responsibility for 80,000 miles of dyke and watercourse in Britain, which control the water level in seven million acres (1973 figures) of farmland.

Larger-scale works, which involve river management or have implications for flood control, are, in England and Wales, the responsibility of the Water Authorities, which, if they can establish the agricultural desirability of a project, can petition for grants of up to 80 per cent from the Government. It was inevitable that the Water Authorities' dual obligations to facilitate land drainage and 'have regard to the desirability' of conservation would one day prove to be incompatible on a major site. Such a confrontation happened in 1978, over Amberley Wild Brooks in West Sussex.

The Wild Brooks are an area of grazing marsh, roughly 900 acres (350 hectares) in extent, which forms part of the flood plain of the River Arun. They are bounded by sandstone hills to the north, and by clay beds and the South Downs chalks to the south. Since the late eighteenth century they have been used for cattle-grazing, hay-making and peat-digging, and even now their management is sympathetic and conservative. The chief man-made addition to the landscape is an intricate system of dykes, which are normally cleared once every seven years.

The great variety of soil and water types, the layers of peat and alluvial silt, the miles of unpolluted ditch in every stage of development from open water to dense fen, and the long history of restrained yet diverse management have meant that the Wild Brooks have an outstandingly rich assemblage of plants and animals. The communities of water-plants in the dykes themselves are probably not equalled in any other comparable area of wetland in Britain. Eighty-six species occur, which represent 56 per cent of the entire British aquatic flora. The list includes all five British duckweeds, all three native species of water-milfoil, five of the six species of watercress, six out of the seven species of water-dropwort, and fourteen out of the twenty-one pondweeds.

Water rails, redshank and seventeen species of dragonfly (nearly half the British list) also breed in the dykes, and in winter the flooded meadows are visited by large flocks of

Bewick's swans. All these factors combine to make the Wild Brooks a place of unique charm and fascination, an oasis of wild marshland amongst the dry southland hills.

Following flooding in the notably wet winter of 1974/75 opinions were expressed by farmers and others to the Southern Water Authority that drainage works carried out in 1968 were not adequate. Accordingly the Authority prepared a major pumped drainage scheme for 700 acres. It was a comprehensive and ambitious project, likely to cost nearly £340,000, and the Southern Water Authority applied to the Ministry of Agriculture Fisheries and Food (MAFF) for the high level of grant-aid (in this case £245,000) for which such schemes are normally automatically eligible. But the outcry from local and national conservation bodies was so great that the Minister took the unusual step of calling a public inquiry in March 1978. The essence of the case against drainage – that it would represent the destruction with public funds of what was publicly recognized as a unique natural monument – was concisely put in the evidence given by Norman Moore, the NCC's chief advisory officer:

This is a test case. . . . If we lose Amberley we show that all statements about conserving wildlife on farmland are a sham. If conservation is not paramount in this case, no site can be considered safe. Britain has taken a lead in the European Wetlands Campaign. If it became known that we sacrificed this outstanding wetland for the sake of a minute increase in national food production, Britain would lose credibility among the nations who rightly expect us to take a lead in the matter of rational use of natural resources.

As a result of the evidence given by the NCC and other groups – notably the Sussex Trust, the Council for the Protection of Rural England and the Amberley Society, who produced a formidable critique of the cost-effectiveness of the projected schemes – the minister declined the Water Authority's application for grant-aid. He accepted instead the inspector's conclusion that 'Amberley Wild Brooks constitute a very important site in respect of unique natural history features, and that the probable agricultural benefit of the proposed scheme in relation to its cost is questionable and could not compensate for the loss which would occur to the flora and fauna including wildfowl or to the uniquely valuable peat deposit on the site.' The precise terms of this decision have considerable implications for nature conservation. They acknowledge, first, the idea that natural communities can legitimately be described as irreplaceable and, secondly, that excessively expensive marginal improvements in agricultural productivity may in such circumstances represent an overall *loss* to the community which is paying for them. It remains to be seen whether this precedent is followed in the similar inquiries which are bound to follow – for instance over the future of parts of the Somerset Levels where, in July 1979, the Ministry of Agriculture announced its intention to grant-aid a land drainage scheme over 2500 acres (1000 hectares) of West Sedgemoor.[74]

MEADOWS

If we were looking for a species to act as an indicator of the whole gamut of modern agricultural change, we could do worse than choose the rook, which during the year makes use of just about every declining feature of the farming landscape from timber trees for nesting to the seed in unburnt stubble. Between 1945 and 1977 the population of rooks in Britain fell from 1,413,000 pairs to 907,700 pairs (a reduction of 43 per cent).[75] But, if we were to look for an indicator *habitat*, the feature of farms most sensitive to the combined pressures of ploughing, drainage and chemical dressing, I think it would have to be the traditional hay meadow. I must stress the word 'traditional'. Any field growing grass is liable to be called a meadow, and there is no shortage of these. There are even a scattering that are still pleasantly coloured with buttercups and moon daisies. But was there really once some kind of hayfield vastly richer than this? I must admit that, until I had actually seen one, I wondered whether such places ever really existed outside our stubbornly romantic rural fantasies. My first encounter, when it finally happened on a dull day in north Oxfordshire, put paid to any such doubts. It was one of those experiences that was the more vivid for being, in many ways, so unexpected: a stroll across flowerless pasture, a gap in a hedge, and then, suddenly, this brilliant field lapped with layers of colour and movement – yellow hay-rattle, red betony, purple knapweeds and orchids, the swaying cream umbels of pepper-saxifrage, and butterflies so dense and vibrant above the flowers that it was hard to tell them from the heat-haze. On the far side of the meadow they had started cutting the hay, and the air was full of the heavy smell of new-mown grass and the sharper scents of meadowsweet and burnet.

I had, quite certainly, not seen anything like this in my life-time. Yet, so indelible is the impression of these flowery meadows on our folk memory, that every detail was familiar to me. Hay-plots like this were once as important and character-istic a feature of the village agricultural system as the open field and the coppice wood. They were usually sited on low-lying land, which was prone to flooding and not suitable for spring grazing, but which produced as a result a heavy crop of grass in summer which was cut to provide winter feed. In fact Domes-day Book defines meadows as grasslands managed in this way, and restricts the term 'pasture' to land available for grazing throughout the year. It also makes it clear that meadow was regarded as the most valuable of all kinds of open land, and frequently rated at three times the value of arable. Until the development of artificial feeds and improved grass strains, unbroken swards continued to be regarded as a vital capital resource, to the extent that tenancy agreements often contained covenants prohibiting their ploughing-up. It was not until these covenants were annulled by Parliament in May 1939 that trad-itional, undisturbed meadowland began to vanish on a large scale from the countryside.

It is their long history of regular and gentle management that makes surviving ancient hay-plots probably the richest and most attractive of all grassland habitats. 'Laid up' for hay – and therefore ungrazed – between March and July, they can support not just all the usual plants of unimproved pasture, but species which rely on flowering and setting seed during the early sum-mer. Some of the richest remaining meadows carry more than 100 different species, including cowslip, betony, saw-wort, wild daffodil, hay-rattle, pignut, meadow-rue, various buttercups, half a dozen species of orchid and, just occasionally, flowers like fritillary and great burnet which are now virtually extinct in other habitats. Collections of such species are indicators of long-established, conservative hay-making in the same way that wood anemone, archangel and the like are indicators of ancient woodland. Yet, as with primary woodland, no two meadows are precisely alike. Their flora is influenced by how close they lie to the water-table, by the acidity or alkalinity of the soil, and by the style and timing of their management. On calcareous soils in central Wales there are meadows which carry waxy-coloured mixtures of globeflower and greater butterfly-orchid.

On similar soils on the limestone rocks of Upper Teesdale and Westmorland you may see more vivid purple mottlings of wood cranesbill and melancholy thistle and, in the damper corners, pink clusters of bird's-eye primrose. In the Midlands there are a few meadows which still carry meadow saffron, known locally as naked ladies from its habit of producing rosy mauve flowers well after the poisonous leaves have died down. These meadows are traditionally cut late, but before the flowers appear.

Meadows on the alluvial flood-plains of large rivers are often as good for birds as they are for flowers. Redshank and snipe nest in them, and large flocks of wildfowl use them for feeding when they lie under water during the winter months. Along the Thames, these flood-meadows are also the traditional site of the snakeshead fritillary, which seems to benefit from regular manuring by silt. Yet the fritillary's bulbs only live for about ten years, and depend on the freedom to flower and seed which is guaranteed by a long-term commitment to hay production. The largest population of fritillaries in Britain is at North Meadow National Nature Reserve in Wiltshire (see page 34), where it is possible to see the influence of the finer details of management. North Meadow is what is known as 'Lammas Land'. Its forty-four hectares (109 acres) are divided into parcels, or 'lots', which can be bought for their hay crop. (Most of the lots – which are marked out in the meadow by ancient stones – are now owned by the NCC.) The meadow is laid up for hay on the 13 February each year until the cut some time in July. But, on old Lammas Day, 12 August, it becomes the common pasture of the Borough of Cricklade, and any resident of the town may put on it up to ten head of horses or cattle, or (after 12 September) twenty head of sheep. As far as is known, this system of land tenure has continued unchanged for the past 800 years, and the continual slight shifts in the pattern and concentration of grazing which accompany it have produced a very varied mosaic of grassland communities. But its most important consequence has been the survival of the meadow itself. As we shall see in the next chapter, the existence of common rights is one of the most effective stabilizers of land-use, since it prohibits any one commoner obstructing the rights of the others (by ploughing, for example).

Without such customary safeguards, old meadows would have very little to protect them. Their uniquely rich mixture of plants – moisture-lovers, broadleaved herbs sensitive to weed-killers, slow-growing perennials, plants that flower in the early spring as well as those that bloom in autumn – is vulnerable at every point to the armoury of modern grassland management. The losses have been dramatic. In 1965, for instance, M. E. Ball inspected thirty sites in Lincolnshire where green-winged orchid (a fairly reliable indicator of ancient grasslands) had occurred during the previous thirty years.[76] He found that over half had already been converted to arable fields or leys, and most of the rest treated or 'improved' in some way. The orchid could only be found in five of its original sites. And, in 1971, when Chris Fuller organized the Nature Conservancy survey of ancient meadows and pastures in the south-west Midlands, he was only able to find 584 acres divided amongst sixty-nine different sites.[77] This was the total muster for the entire area of the three old counties of Herefordshire, Worcestershire and Warwickshire after four years' intensive searching. Even during the course of the survey, four sites totalling thirty-two acres were lost to the plough.

The results of the survey painted a depressing picture of the comprehensiveness of post-war agricultural changes. Nor did they hold out much hope for the future. A good deal of the meadowland that had survived was owned or occupied by older farmers suspicious of 'new-fangled' methods, and it was likely to vanish when the farms changed ownership. But there were one or two reasons for optimism. A small but significant number of the remaining meadows were not part of the conventional agricultural structure at all. They were scattered about in churchyards, old orchards and private paddocks. A few were even discovered attached to pubs, a relic of the time when inns had to provide feed for dray and coach horses. And parallel with this (though not necessarily connected with it commercially) there was clearly a growing extra-agricultural market for 'sweet' hay, particularly amongst the owners of pedigree animals and racehorses, who were prepared to pay quite high prices for it. (There is some scientific support for the belief that, weight for weight, herb-rich hay is more nutritious than the modern fast-growing grass mixtures.)

Another feature of the survey was the great amount of public interest and sympathy it aroused. The NCC had in fact anticipated this and had relied on public help for much of the preliminary fieldwork. In some ways this was a practical necessity.

Many of the meadows lay in the heartlands of remote farms and, being small, flat patches of grass, were extremely difficult to locate. Maps did not help, for they rarely distinguished between different kinds of grassland, and field-by-field elimination surveys would have involved expensive commitments of specialist staff and time. But, though old meadows might have been slipping away from sight and from the land, the one place they were demonstrably secure was in people's memories.

When the NCC's South-East Region mounted its own meadow survey in Kent, Surrey and Sussex in 1978, it decided to tap this reserve of public knowledge and goodwill to the fullest extent. A national press release was prepared, and 5000 leaflets headed 'Do you know where they are?' sent out to local societies, museums and papers. Within a few days the response had become quite literally overwhelming. An article had appeared in the *Daily Mirror* as a result of the press release, and for three days the survey team's phones rang non-stop. Hundreds of reports arrived from farmers and naturalists, pensioners and ramblers. The survey had unleashed a remarkable fund of nostalgia and affection. Some of the calls and letters were terse and to the point, but many were intimate descriptions of long-remembered walks, recounted plant by plant and field by field, and tinged often with a sense of real personal loss. Even if no ancient meadows had been discovered, the letters which accumulated in the South-East Region's office that summer would have amounted to a unique documentation of a nation's feeling for the landscape it had grown up with. As it happened, 286 sites had been identified by mid-August, of which more than half were worth recording in detail.

Yet, of all the letters, it was the short, scrawled, almost furtive note from a Sussex farmer which expressed most vividly the dilemma of those who had found that modern agriculture had broken their love of the land into apparently irreconcilable parts. It read simply: 'You may be interested to know that we have one meadow fitting the description given. An admission to bad farming but a field full of flowers and butterflies.'

ON THE MARGIN

Efficient farming or fields full of flowers and butterflies – it is a peculiarly contemporary choice, and one that is by no means inevitable. It may be that the next step forward for technological agriculture will be to find ways of simultaneously producing high crop yields and sustaining a rich wildlife. But for the moment it is that word 'admission' which is the most significant. One meadow had been 'badly' managed, but the farm, seemingly, had not fallen into economic ruin. Time and again we have seen how most of the naturally rich areas that remain on the farm are now confined to land that is agriculturally marginal in this sense. It is intrinsically low in productivity, and the investment needed to raise its output usually greatly exceeds the overall social benefits, and in some cases even the agricultural returns.

This land – hedges, ditches, corner spinneys, streams, steep escarpments – is also frequently *physically* marginal. In the West Wales Farm Park, Blaenbedw Isaf, near Cardigan, the NCC has laid out a one-and-a-half-mile demonstration walk, which runs unobtrusively round the perimeter of a 160-acre (sixty-five hectare) dairy farm. It passes a wooded gulley, steep unimproved pasture, marshy field corners and a newly-dug pond, and is designed to demonstrate to other farmers the features they could retain on their farms without compromising the productive areas. It is a happy coincidence that on the other side of the farm is a display, open to the public, of rare breeds of farm animals. At the most fundamental biological level the two projects have precisely the same end – the maintenance of the variety of life-forms. Yet the rare breeds are more obviously 'useful' both agriculturally and as a source of public entertainment. The question we have to answer now is: if wildlife is to be regarded as some kind of deliberate 'crop' on the farm, who are the customers, and what are the terms of trade?

3

Recreation

The cottagers produced from their little bits, in food, for themselves, and in things to be sold at market, more than any neighbouring farm of 200 acres. . . . I learnt to hate a system that could lead English gentlemen to disregard matters like these! That could induce them to tear up 'wastes' and sweep away occupiers like those I have described! Wastes indeed! Give a dog an ill name. Was Horton Heath a waste? Was it a 'waste' when a hundred, perhaps, of healthy boys and girls were playing there of a Sunday, instead of creeping about covered in filth in the alleys of a town?[78]

WILLIAM COBBETT, (*circa* 1830)

First, there is a confession of faith, that the people's claim upon the English countryside is paramount, with the ground for it; secondly, a demonstration of fact, that the people are not as yet ready to take up their claim without destroying that to which the claim is laid: thirdly, a conclusion, that the English countryside must be kept inviolate as a trust until such time as they *are* ready, and that it is the duty of the readers no less than of the writers of this book, together with such others as can be brought to realise their responsibility in the matter, to act in the interim as the people's trustees. . . .

PROFESSOR C. E. M. JOAD in *Britain and the Beast* (1938)[79]

One response to the question I posed at the end of the last chapter is that its basic premise is wrong, and that wildlife is not something to be 'traded' in this sense. It can be a *value* in a general sense, for 'future generations' or 'mankind' or even simply in its own right, but it is not *goods* to be regarded inside a framework of supply and demand. I have already discussed the unprofitableness of thinking about the conservation of wild-life 'for its own sake'. As a guiding principle it is either self-evident or a way of masking the human origins and social complexity of conservation decisions in the real world. But the idea that 'posterity' or a generalized 'mankind' are the proper beneficiaries of nature conservation deserves more serious consideration. As an ideological principle it can hardly be questioned. But what is odd is how frequently those who support it as a philosophical goal resist it as a practical one, and find its expression in *active* enjoyment by *particular* people altogether less attractive.

There is no need to spell out the reasons for these worries, and Professor Joad expresses them succinctly in his second premise above. What is striking is the hardening of our attitude towards them over the years. Before the war Joad was already defining a problem that we have come to think of as peculiar to the recreational pressures of the last decade or so. And, though we may find his tone patronizing, his generous 'confession of faith' does not often seem to be shared by those who share his worries. 100 years earlier Cobbett – a defender of farming interests – was concerned about the *attack* on popular involvement with, and enjoyment of, the land. We can partially explain these changes in attitude over the last century and a half in terms of a response to population expansion and movements, and to the consequent loss of familiarity with the countryside (so that rural recreation is seen, in effect, as an invasion by foreigners of a landscape whose ways they do not understand). But I find that I am suspicious of the underlying motives when I hear recreational pressure on the natural resources of the countryside compared to the effects of modern forestry and agriculture, and seen sometimes as a kind of trespass, *intrinsically* worse than anything a landowner might do. I have lived in the Chilterns and on the north Norfolk coast, both popular tourist areas, and I have seen the damage which can be done by large numbers of active people to fragile living communities. Yet I have never once seen these amount to the kind of transformations of landscapes that we have seen repeatedly result from intensive modern husbandry.

I imagine it will be clear by now that I regard the recreational use of the countryside not only as fully-fledged rural land-use in its own right, but as perhaps that new use for 'obsolete' landscape features that we have been searching for throughout this book. It would, of course, be entirely justifiable to say that nature conservation *itself* was just such a use – and, in Part

Three, Chapter 2, we will be looking at how this idea has found physical expression in the form of nature reserves (though we will also see that many of these are themselves 'recreational'). But I am not sure that, in its own terms, nature conservation can provide a sufficiently practical – and comprehensible – social and economic framework. Countryside recreation might, and I will be looking at its potential as a force for conserving natural features, and the problems posed when it becomes over-intensive.

The rise of recreation in the countryside seems to have been inextricably connected – as a kind of mirror image – with the attack on diversity that has been a consequence of the rise of intensive production techniques in both country and town over the last 150 years. So I would like to begin with an optimistic case history which spans this whole period, and which demonstrates the transformation of a destructive leisure use of a natural 'feature', to its use in a protective way by a smaller group of consumers, and finally to its popularization and enjoyment by a mass audience. In doing so, it has become a concern sufficiently commercial to underpin yet more widespread conservation activity.

'OPERATION OSPREY'

Up until the middle of the nineteenth century the osprey was comparatively widespread in Scotland. It had even nested, from time to time, in south-west England. Then, as with so many other large predatory birds (compare the hen harrier, pages 189–192) it began to fall victim to the combined assaults of Victorian naturalists and sportsmen (the chief recreational pressure groups of the time), with gamekeepers and gillies despatching the adult birds and collectors removing the eggs. The scarcer the bird became, the more its eggs and skins were prized, and by the end of the century the osprey was virtually extinct as a British breeding species. The last nesting record was in 1916, at the most famous of its traditional sites – the ruined castle in the middle of Loch an Eilein on Speyside.[80]

Then, in April 1955, a pair began building on top of a Scots pine near Loch Garten. With some poetic justice this site was only ten miles from the Loch an Eilein eyrie, and there was great excitement at the possibility that the bird was about to return as a British breeding species. But by the end of May the nest was deserted, and it is believed that egg-collectors were almost certainly responsible. The next year the birds returned and nested a few miles away in Rothiemurchus Forest. Again the eggs were robbed. When a pair returned to the original Loch Garten eyrie in 1958, the Royal Society for the Protection of Birds (RSPB) realized that the birds were plainly trying to re-establish themselves on Speyside and quickly mounted a wardening scheme.

Round-the-clock watches from a hide some hundreds of yards from the nest began from the moment the first egg was laid on 11 May. The night of 3 June, about halfway through the incubation period, was exceptionally dark and wet, and Philip Brown and Bert Axell were sharing the night-time shift. At 2.30 a.m. they heard the sitting osprey rise from the nest screaming in alarm, and through the glasses they could see the dim figure of a man climbing to the eyrie. The two wardens ran out across the bog towards the tree, but before they could reach it the figure had dropped to the ground and run off into the darkness. A single smashed egg lay beneath the tree. Since the normal clutch was three, there was still some hope that they might have interrupted the thief in time. The next day the osprey returned to the nest, but she was restless and never sat for more than a few minutes. The RSPB wardens became increasingly anxious that all was not well with her eggs, and when they climbed the tree to investigate, they found that the nest contained two hens' eggs crudely blotched with brown boot polish.

Up till then the ospreys' return had been a closely guarded secret, but news of the raid soon leaked out, and the cloak-and-dagger circumstances in which it had been carried out made the story headline news. This brought in its wake a wave of public interest and concern, but also the reasonable certainty that, next year, sympathy would be expressed in the shape of thousands of sightseers. The RSPB, faced with a difficult situation and a good deal of conflicting advice, made the very courageous decision to 'go public' with the Loch Garten site, and began planning what has come to be known as 'Operation Osprey'. With the full co-operation of the landowner, they obtained an Order under section 3 of the Protection of Birds Act 1954, designating 677 acres surrounding the tree a statutory bird sanctuary. This Order made it an offence for any unauthorized person to enter the area during the breeding season. At the same time, they recruited a team of voluntary wardens, built a public hide (equipped with a massive pair of binoculars converted from a tank gun-sight) and secured the whole area with a complex alarm system of trip-wires and hidden microphones.

On 2 August 1959 the first three osprey chicks successfully fledged on British soil this century flew from the Loch Garten eyrie. 14,000 people had visited the hide that summer, and almost every stage in the chicks' development was broadcast to the nation on BBC news bulletins. The ospreys' success that year was a total vindication of the RSPB's act of faith in the public.

Since then the Loch Garten eyrie has become a national institution, and between 1959 and 1978 over three-quarters of a million people went to watch these magnificent piebald birds, five feet from wing-tip to wing-tip, go about the business of raising their young. Egg-collectors breached the security network on a few occasions, but during this period a total of thirty-seven young ospreys fledged from this one nest alone. Meanwhile the osprey continues to spread through Scotland, and there are now at least a score of regular nesting sites. And their return to the most popular eyries in the first week of April is still regarded as one of the news events of the spring – only rivalled by the recent recolonization of the Lake District by golden eagles for the first time in 100 years.

It is worth considering the implications of Operation Osprey in some detail, for it has been one of the most consistently successful experiments in integrating conservation with recreation and has helped counteract the view that the public is necessarily a kind of pest species. The direct conservation importance of the Loch Garten operation was probably not very great. It is now clear that ospreys were recolonizing Scotland anyway, and would probably have done so successfully without the RSPB's help. There is even the possibility that the publicity given to the site and its elaborate security system actually increased its attraction to more adventurous egg-collectors. Yet any magnetic effects of that kind were certainly cancelled out by the way that the Loch Garten site diverted interest and public pressure from other unwardened eyries.

It was the impact of Operation Osprey on the public rather than on the birds that may have been its greatest contribution to conservation. For twenty years the ospreys have never been out of the public eye, and the saga of their changing fortunes, as they weathered the assaults of pesticides, egg-collectors and freak Highland storms, has generated an immense fund of public affection for them and for birds in general. Without this widespread sympathy the RSPB might not have been able, in 1976, to raise £290,000 to buy 1500 acres (600 hectares) of moor and wood around the site (including a substantial tract of native Scottish pinewood: as a reserve for the whole range of Highland wildlife.

It is also worth considering the nature of the experience of those three-quarters of a million people who have visited the Loch Garten site. Shepherded along a sheltered boardwalk to a rather confined hut, overlooked by wardens, separated from the birds not just by 200 yards of no-man's-land but by a considerable quantity of barbed wire, they had in effect voluntarily entered a situation where it was they, not the birds, who were in a cage. An encounter as 'set up' as this is no substitute for a chance meeting with an osprey, and some might even find the Loch Garten osprey show as artificial as the view from the Wildfowl Trust's centrally-heated hide in the Ouse Washes, which Colin Tubbs once christened 'swan *et lumière*'.[81] Yet it makes its own point about the qualities of wildness and responsibility. The RSPB, by turning the conventional wisdom of amenity planning on its head (normally it is humans that get first consideration, and wild things that are fenced in) has demonstrated that, with the right safeguards, conservation interests and public enjoyment can be not only compatible but mutually supportive.

IN THE EYE OF THE BEHOLDER?

Yet, on the larger canvas of rural land-use, recreation is often regarded as inimical to conservation, a pressure to be coped with rather than a customer whose needs are, by and large, what the conservationist is trying to supply. Perhaps I should define the sense in which I am using 'recreation' here. I am not concerned with leisure activities incidentally situated in the countryside. The conversion of a derelict market garden to a swimming pool or a sportsdrome represents a conversion of countryside into 'occupied' land, and such a complete loss to conservation that it is outside the scope of this book. I have confined the word here to those leisure activities which make use of living components of the countryside either directly or as a desirable backcloth. Even the list covered by such a limited definition would range from bird-watching, fishing, canoeing, landscape painting and rambling, to cricketing on the common, walking the dog, and picnicking by the roadside. It is a list one could extend indefinitely, and it would be foolhardy to become too idealistic about how discriminating leisure users of the countryside are about its specific natural qualities. Yet I do not think it would be too far-fetched to make one or two generalizations about their preferences – which are really *our* preferences, for all of us are on some occasions the general public loose in the countryside. We prefer open country to fenced, access to exclusion. We prefer variety to monotony, stability to change – or at least slow development to sudden transformation. We prefer (otherwise we would presumably have stayed in a town) living things to inanimate structures. We want the countryside to remain, to continue not just to *be*, but to be visitable, viewable and familiar. In this sense recreation is potentially the most *conservative* of all current rural land-uses, far more so than the increasingly unsettling pressures of forestry and farming. The angler wants a lake that contains fish, not one sterilized by industrial effluent or farm chemicals. The canoeist wants a river that has not been dried out by drainage or water extraction. The family out for a game of cricket want a stretch of turf on their local common, not a ploughed field. Pond-dipping children need ponds, and blackberriers need bramble patches. And, epistemological hair-splitting apart, can beauty-spots really be said to exist without appreciative visitors?

The point about all these activities is that they make *use* of the countryside, and in many instances reinvest its redundant components with new meanings – and some of its new components with old meanings; who in the 1950s could have foreseen that motorway verges would become refuges for our vanishing grassland flowers? Employment, as we have now seen time and again with woods and hedges and meadows, is the best guarantee of a habitat's survival.

I have deliberately not touched so far on the damaging effects of countryside recreation – the litter, the eroded downland picnic-sites, the wildfowl poisoned by lead shot, the trees ring-barked by ponies. Cumulatively they can be devastating and dispiriting and may demand considerable ingenuity and expense if they are to be adequately controlled. But they rarely destroy habitats irreversibly in the way that intensive forestry and agriculture can, and they seem to me more properly regarded as side-effects, accountable wear and tear. Even those that are unavoidable are rarely more serious in their long-term effects than the results of extracting tons of cut wood through the young flower shoots in a coppice, or flail-mowing an overgrown hedge. They are the price we may have to pay for conserving the *basic* character of a site.

This is a highly pragmatic argument in support of rural recreation. I am suggesting that land held, used or simply gazed upon for public enjoyment is that much less likely to undergo those drastic changes in character that are incompatible with nature conservation. I would personally like to go much further and regard the facilitation of public enjoyment of the countryside as one of the goals of a nature conservation policy. Conservation as we practise it is, after all, a human creation. Sometimes it may even be a human recreation. It is all too easy, confronted with coachloads of tourists in what you have come to regard as your personal territory, to forget that the original meaning of 'recreation' – creating over again, renewing, replenishing – is not so far removed from the meaning of 'conservation'. To renew the living fabric of the land so that it also replenishes the spirits of its human inhabitants seems to me as close as one can come to a single expression of the aims of a total conservation policy. If we think that this is putting too great a premium on our fickle affections, I think that we may paradoxically be underrating our *own* vulnerability. We are in the same rather leaky ecological boat as the other species we are trying to conserve, and if any of us are to survive we may need to respect and restore some of the ancient, affective bonds between us.

That much is a statement of faith, and it is small comfort to hard-working conservationists to have the public's sympathy if in practice this is so vague and ill-informed as to be irrelevant or actually counter-productive. Yet I think the evidence is that the priorities of conservationists and of the recreational public are not so far removed. Notions of meaning and beauty are engendered by familiarity, by the long cohabitation between man and nature that has created our most finely-grained habitats. I do not think it is a coincidence that areas like the Chiltern Hills, the Wye Valley, the Gower Peninsula, the Suffolk Coast and Heathlands – places which are sufficiently attractive and popular to be officially designated as Areas of Outstanding

Natural Beauty (AONB) – also contain most of the acreage of nature conservation importance in lowland England and Wales, just as the National Parks do in the uplands. Their natural interest and diversity – the pastel shades of downland grasses, a river set in a wooded gorge, massed drifts of spring flowers on the cliffs, a square mile of heather in full bloom – are a major part of what *makes* them attractive. (Interestingly the Country-side Act of 1968 actually subsumes natural interest under 'natural beauty'. Clause 49 (4) states: 'References in this Act to the conservation of the natural beauty of an area shall be construed as including references to the conservation of its flora, fauna and geological and physiographical features.') And when the public are making choices about where to spend their leisure time in the countryside it is precisely such naturally rich areas they pick out. They go not to the arable prairies of East Anglia, but to the Lake District and the ancient countryside of Dorset and Devon. And the landscapes on the postcards they send home are not the dull and geometric field-plans of the Parliamentary Enclosures, but the close-knit pattern of small meadows, ancient hedges, winding lanes, old trees and coppices that was brought to maturity in the middle ages and yet is still as humanly evocative as it is ecologically rich.

When D. Lowenthal and H. C. Prince reviewed English landscape tastes they found a clear preference for 'landscapes compartmented into small scenes furnished with belfried church towers, half-timbered cottages, rutted lanes, rookeried elms, lich gates and stiles', and that what is considered 'essentially English' is 'a calm and peaceful deer park with slow-moving streams and wide expanses of meadow-land studded with fine trees.'[82] It is, in its present form, the landscape of privilege. Yet, at a deeper level, it is an image of one of our basic ancestral habitats, the common wood-pasture (page 76) that bears, like so many of these examples, the unmistakable handprint of a long relationship between man and nature. Townspeople enjoying these landscapes are, in a sense, just returning home. If at times they appear to show indifference to their fate, it is often because of misunderstanding, but also, I believe, because of an understandable (if mistaken) scepticism that anything so ancient and thoroughly 'natural' could possibly be endangered.

The affection and the support, then, are quite plainly there. The question is how to translate them into a form of currency which can influence the owners and managers of land. There is no real problem when recreation is a land-use in its own right. If, for instance, an angling club buys a stretch of river, or a county council establishes a country park, some measure of stability is immediately introduced into the pattern of land-use. The chief task then is to devise management systems which will maintain the natural attractions of the place and minimize wear and tear.

But most countryside recreation is a *subsidiary* land-use – a collection of intangible gleanings from another person's working territory.[83] They are likely to be as nebulous as the 'air and exercise' to which the public have a right on certain commons, and as difficult to quantify as a 'view'. In this sense recreation, although it is a land-use, does not directly shape and manage the natural landscape in the way that forestry and agriculture do. Nor, at present, are there many incentives to landowners to pay attention to the non-material assets of their land. All too often their only harvest is the debris that recreational man leaves in his wake.

THE COMMONS

I shall be looking in the final section at ways in which recreation might be a force for directing and financing the management of the wider countryside in the future. Yet if increasing rural recreation is to be compatible with nature conservation we need to understand more about the *ecological* implications of what, at a stretch, could be looked on as the regular mass migration of a particularly vigorous variety of *Homo sapiens*. The outstanding example of the successful incorporation of large numbers of active people into the natural landscape is in the history of our common lands.

There are approximately 1½ million acres (400,000 hectares) of common land remaining in England and Wales. Many commons are of great natural interest and some are quite outstanding. We have already glanced at the New Forest, North Meadow, the Cotswold limestone pastures and north Pennine moorlands. Today many are used in some way for informal countryside recreation, yet this was not their original function. They were once (and in some cases still are) a vital element in the traditional rural economy. 'Common' is not so much a description of a particular type of land as of a particular system of land tenure. It refers to lands owned by one party over which others are entitled to exercise various rights, such as grazing or the cutting of firewood. In strict legal terms rights can only be said to exist if they have been specifically granted, and the origin of common rights is customarily attributed to the Norman feudal system, which produced the first extensive written evidence concerning them. Certainly it makes little sense to think in terms of common lands and rights in earlier times, when there was ample land for all purposes. In these circumstances rights over the land had no need of definition, and therefore could not legally be said to exist. But it is now generally accepted that the rights that began to be defined in the eleventh century represented the relics of a much wider network of unrecorded 'customary practice' (amounting probably to the communal ownership of land) which was largely destroyed by political and military force during the Norman Conquest. What remained – formalized into a system of specified rights over particular wastes – were largely those practices and areas of marginal land which the Normans felt it politically expedient to leave well alone. (The lands were usually of low productivity in conventional terms – upland grazing, lowland heaths and the like.)

Yet even within these limits the practice of commoning was extensive and intricate. As late as the end of the seventeenth century (when the first reasonably accurate figures for land-use in England and Wales are available) Gregory King estimated that there were still more than 20 million acres of pasture, meadow, forest, heath, moor, mountain and barren land amongst the country's 37 million acres.[84] Even if common rights were only exercised over half of these, it still means that in 1688 one quarter of the total area of England and Wales was common land in the strict sense.

The range of rights was immense, and there were no doubt some we shall never know about. But the four most important were *pasture* – the right to graze stock; *estovers* – the right to take underwood and pollarded branches, for firewood and the repair of fences; *pannage* – the right to graze pigs on fallen beechmast or acorns in woodland; and *turbary* – the right to dig peat or turf for use as fuel. There were also *piscary* – the right to take fish from another's water; *housebote* – the right to take larger pieces of timber for house-building or repairs; and a miscellany of rights to gorse, bracken, chalk, gravel, clay, rushes, reeds, nuts and herbs. On Cartmel Common in Lancashire the local people even had rights to slate and juniper berries. And, though commoners living close to the poverty line would not have had much time for recreation in our sense, there is no doubt that what little they did take was centred on the commons, which were often the sites of fairs, markets, prize-fights and children's games.

This extensive range of rights was matched by an equally comprehensive range of rules and controls, designed to prevent over-consumption. We can find frequent references, for instance, to restrictions on the number of beasts a commoner could put out to graze and on the size of branches that could be cut for fuel. On Cartmel Common, the digging of clay (for house-building) was prevented from damaging the pasture too severely by an Order in 1662 that any holes formed by digging should be filled up within ten days, so that the herbage could re-grow over them. Cartmel also had a 'bracken day' (21 September) before which the commoners were not permitted to cut fern for litter. The close-season for bracken and gorse on my home common at Berkhamsted in Hertfordshire ran between 1 June and 1 September. On 31 August the commoners would listen for the chimes of the parish church at midnight and then stake out their claims, like gold prospectors. An Order made in 1725 also specified the maximum size of bill-hook which could be used for cutting the furze (though another made the next year provided exceptions for those over the age of sixty or under fourteen!).

W. G. Hoskins and L. Dudley Stamp's book *The Common Lands of England and Wales* gives an enthralling overall picture of the history and working of the common lands system, but we really need to go to local documents to capture the intricacy, ingenuity and thrift of the system, and the respect for the land and for individual rights that it embodied.[84]

It is hard for us, with our contemporary suspicions of human pressure, to understand how such a patently busy local enterprise was able to support the rich wildlife that it clearly did, if we are to judge by what remains on those commons that are still economically functional. But we have to remember that without the benefit of their immense range of resources many local communities would not have been able to survive, or at least not at an acceptable standard of living. For the commoners it was vital that their commons were maintained and harvested in such a way that their resources were self-renewing. Secondly, the fact that rights over the land were held in common meant that no one person could change its character, or that of any of its constituent parts, without infringing the rights of others. (We have seen how this helped preserve North meadow: see page 152.) It could even restrict the activities of the lord of the manor, who was normally the *owner* of the common (though often a commoner, too). In Epping Forest, for example, it prevented the felling of still-productive pollards.[85] The trees themselves were the property of the landowner, but the commoners had rights to lop their branches, and the pollards could therefore only be felled for timber when they were dead and no longer producing usable wood. In the common woods at Selborne the commoners had rights of pasturage and pannage, and the landowner was not permitted to replant trees unless they were beech, whose mast was crucial for the commoners' pigs. (This rule was retained when the common was bought by the National Trust, and it has helped guarantee the survival of the traditional beech cover on Selborne Hanger.) Perhaps the most remarkable surviving example is the distribution of hay rights by lot, which still persists on Pixey and Yarnton Meads in Oxfordshire. The rights of certain villagers here are expressed by their ownership of a part or a whole of thirteen ancient cherry balls, inscribed with a curious collection of names, including Perry, Dunn, Rothe, William of Bladon, Water Geoffrey and Water Molley. At hay-cutting time, the balls were drawn from a bag, and the order in which they emerged determined which strips in the meadow each ball-owner could take hay from that summer. Early this century, R. H. Gretton was able to trace the custom back to at least the early middle ages.[86] There were twenty-six (twice thirteen) *villeins* recorded for the manor in Domesday, and their family names, as recorded in the Hundred Rolls two centuries later, are recognizable as the probable originals of the corrupted forms recorded on the balls today. Sadly, the ball-drawing ceremony itself, which was an outward and symbolic reminder of the antiquity and justice of the system, has been discontinued in the last few years. But conservationists now own shares in some of the balls, and this is likely to ensure the survival both of the underlying land-tenure system and of the rich grasslands it has supported for 1000 years.

Finally, the variety of different uses that co-existed on commons was reflected in the variety of habitats they sustained or, in some cases, created. Grazing kept heather and grassland open. Pollarding prolonged the life of trees. Small-scale diggings added ponds, pits, flashes and fens. Where a common lay close to the water-table or at a junction of soil types, all this subtle remodelling could produce remarkably compact mixtures of habitats. Some of the best examples of this occur in the string of commons in west Norfolk – stretching from Foulden Common in the south to Syderstone in the north – which ranges across the complex boundaries between the fens, the chalky sands in the centre of the county, and the Greensand ridge between. My own favourite is East Walton Common, which is still grazed, and on which you can walk along a switchback of chalk grassland ridges round a complex honeycomb of pits and hollows that, in their time, were no doubt dug for many reasons and many different materials. There are scarcely two the same today. They have evolved into reedbeds, ponds, orchid-rich sedge fens, acid pools fringed by patches of heather, miniaturized damp meadows, alder coppice and wetland scrub with guelder rose and wild currants.

In every common the pattern is unique – the outcome of particular local conditions and customs. In Redgrave Fen in Suffolk (no longer a common, but managed as a nature reserve by the Suffolk Trust), peat was dug in a very distinctive way. The diggings formed circular depressions of up to ten feet in diameter and three feet in depth, which were surrounded by hard uncut pathways on which the peat was stacked. These little pits are now flooded and the compacted paths overgrown, and a habitat has been created sufficiently idiosyncratic to be the only British locality for the great raft spider, *Dolomedes plantarius*.[87]

The intricate system of checks and balances which guaranteed the stability and natural richness of the traditional common can be seen most dramatically in our finest remaining example – the New Forest.[88] There was a certain element of chance in the survival of such a remarkably large fragment of ancient wasteland – it currently covers 145 square miles (375 square kilometres) – but its status as common land has been the most important safeguard. Its appropriation as a hunting estate by William the Conqueror was a fortuitous act which ensured that the land was not taken into more intensive agricultural use in the medieval period. But it would have been hard to improve in any case. Its sandy soils are very acid and are waterlogged in many places, and multiple-use for hunting, rough-grazing and wood production was by far the most efficient way to utilize its natural resources. During the centuries following afforestation, when the Crown gradually switched its interest from deer to timber, the defence of their respective interests by both landowner and commoners ensured that no drastic changes occurred in the character of the Forest. The Crown protected the woodland, which it continually attempted to extend. The commoners, represented by their animals, grazed the advancing woodland back, and kept the heaths and plains open. Today, the public, rightfully staking a claim in what is a national treasure, has become a third interested party. It has successfully prevented the Crown (now represented by the Forestry Commission) from converting the remaining ancient woodlands to conifer plantations and the commoners from draining the bogs and heaths. The result has been the preservation of a mosaic of wood, heath, bog and grassland that is probably the nearest approximation to an ancient wilderness in all the lowlands of western Europe. It is not the perfect solution for any single faction, but it is a good compromise for all of them and that is perhaps the best outcome we can hope for.

When we look at the workings of commons in this way, we can understand why they are such rich wildlife habitats. The slow, tentative, often quarrelsome, jostling for position between commoner and landowner, commoner and commoner, is reminiscent of the way animals work out their territorial claims over a piece of land. Even when check and balance deteriorated into deadlock and cussedness, at least it meant that the land was preserved from the rushed and often ill-considered transformations that have been the fate of a good deal of land in exclusively private ownership.

It would be wrong, nevertheless, to over-glamorize the common land system. The state of impenetrable muddle that prevailed on some commons meant that their exploitation eventually ran down as a result of the sheer frustration of both commoners and landowners. But it was the parliamentary enclosures of the eighteenth and nineteenth centuries that brought about the demise of the bulk of the lowland commons. It was not just that enclosure appropriated the wastelands themselves, but that it undermined the social and economic fabric of the communities which had lived with and from them. By the time of the Common Lands Census of 1873–4 only 2½ million acres of common land remained. Of all the agricultural changes of the last few centuries it was the enclosure of the commons that spelt the end of the old rural economy. The hundreds of miles of new quickset hedges that marked the progress of enclosure were more than just an indication of a new pattern of agricultural organization. They were symbols of the new barriers which had been created between men and the land.

At the height of the enclosures, Parliament itself began to realize the impact they were having on the rural poor and took measures to mitigate their worst effects. A number of enclosure awards made provision for the setting aside of small fuel allotments or cow-pastures in compensation for land that had been appropriated. But it was, ironically, the rapidly expanding population in the towns (augmented by the tides of dispossessed rural workers) that finally stemmed the attrition of the commons. In 1790 four out of five people in England and Wales lived in the country. Forty years later one in every two lived in towns. It was clear that the future importance of commons lay in the opportunities they offered for fresh air and exercise for the new urban poor. These were intangible harvests, and they had no historical basis as rights, but beginning in 1836 there was a succession of Acts which began to provide them with a legal foundation. The General Inclosure Act of 1845, for instance, laid down that the health, comfort and convenience of the local inhabitants should be taken into consideration before any enclosure was permitted, and that the commissioners could specify as a condition the setting aside of an area 'for the purpose of exercise and recreation for the inhabitants of the neighbourhood'.

And these were very much the terms under which the remaining lowland commons survived up until the Second World War. (Those in the uplands had suffered much less from enclosure and many are still agriculturally important.) During the war, considerable areas of common land were requisitioned for the war effort, and it was largely the problems involved in returning these to the commoners that caused the appointment of a Royal Commission on Common Land in 1955 'to recommend what changes are desirable in the law relating to common land in order to promote the benefit of those holding manorial and common rights, (and) the enjoyment of the public. . . '. The most important of the Commission's recommendations, that there should be a comprehensive register of common lands and rights, was quite quickly implemented though the investigation of contested claims is still not complete. But many recommendations which could have profound implications for the integration of nature conservation and recreation are still awaiting the Common Lands Act that should have followed the process of registration. The first is the recommendation that the practice of taking 'air and exercise' on commons, recognized as important as early as the beginning of the nineteenth century, should become a statutory public *right* on all commons:

315 The recognition of a universal right of public access on common land is moreover a guarantee of the continued inviolability of the land. In some schemes of management (particularly for reclamation or improvement as woodland, as described in paragraphs 360 to 365) a common or a part of a common might have to be fenced for a few years. Despite the details and maps in the Commons Register, it is conceivable that where no holders of common rights survived any active memory of the land as common might in time be lost. So long, however, as the existence of a right of access was recognized and the intention to restore it was known and recorded, then whatever temporary restrictions might be necessary, there would be no danger of the common becoming for all practical purposes alienated permanently. In a sense, the interest of the vanished commoners in keeping the land open would be bequeathed to the public by virtue of the latter's possession of a right of access.

316 The extension generally of the public right of access is indeed a prerequisite to our other recommendations. It is no innovation but rather the logical conclusion of the long process over the past century of widening and establishing more firmly the free access over common land which the public has enjoyed in fact, though not generally in law, for a much longer period.[89]

Just how important a statutory right of public access might be even in the safeguarding of scientifically valuable sites was demonstrated in 1979 by the case of Cliffe Marshes in Kent. This nationally important estuarine site is registered common land, but is, at the time of writing, the subject of a de-registration application by the Port of London Authority and Blue Circle Industries (who wish to build an oil-refinery access on it) on the grounds that, at the time of registration, no existing common *rights* were recorded.[90]

In order to ensure that a universal right of access would not lead to an abuse of the commons or obstruct the running of those that were still used agriculturally, the Commission also recommended the setting up of a local management group for each common, on which landowner, commoners and local residents, for instance, would be represented. The responsibilities of these groups would include drawing up management plans for the common and recommending bye-laws to control their recreational use.

The survival and servicing of our remaining commons is of fundamental importance for the future of both nature conservation and countryside recreation. And in the context of other areas of recreational countryside – country parks and the sea coast, for instance – their history is important as a metaphor of the security that use gives to a site and of the capacity of the land to absorb a multiplicity of different uses. But there is of course one fundamental respect in which the recreational public cannot 'stand in' for the vanished commoners, as the Royal Commission suggested. In the vast majority of cases they are not themselves *managing* the land which they come to enjoy. There is nearly always the need for a third party to keep the land naturally diverse, and therefore recreationally attractive. If we look at the state of much purely recreational countryside – at the rubbish-filled ponds, at the overgrown grasslands, at the intensive mowing and gardening in country parks – it is clear that the problems are due as much to inappropriate and insensitive management as to over-use by the public.

There is a striking example of this in Epping Forest. When the Forest was bought for the people of London by the Corporation of the City of London, the conservators were charged by the Epping Forest Act of 1878 to 'at all times as far as possible preserve the natural aspect of the Forest . . . protect the timber and other trees, pollards, shrubs, underwood, heather, gorse, turf and herbage. . . '. Unfortunately it was not properly understood at that time how much of this 'natural aspect' was the result of centuries of ancient human practice. Pollarding was prohibited and grazing allowed to run down. Oliver Rackham and Colin Ranson have shown how this has resulted in the decline of just about every natural feature specified in the Act.[85] The pollard hornbeams and beech, magnificent specimens though they are, have shaded out virtually all the woodland wild flowers and shrubs. The lack of grazing has caused the loss of the heather and the overrunning of the plains by scrub woodland. Soon, the old pollards will die and vanish as well, and Epping Forest will have nothing left but its timber trees. This may be an acceptable future, but it is hardly a substitute for the uniquely diverse community it was a century ago, which was much richer in nature conservation terms and, I suspect, a good deal more attractive as a recreational area. I personally believe that small-scale wood-cutting in such areas is one practice it might be possible to leave to the public. Firewood is one of the few traditional 'crops' that are acquiring a new relevance – part recreational, part economic – and, even when the wood is inexpertly cut, the practice is likely to do more good than harm to most wooded areas. Recently I was able to observe in some detail the effect of an extensive period of illegal cutting on a five-acre (two-hectare) common green on the Hertfordshire/Buckinghamshire border. A group of some twenty gipsies lived on the site for about two years, and during that period cut down for firewood some 200 small trees, mostly hawthorn and holly. The felling was fairly random, but was done cleanly and with a certain sense of logic – at waist height, with a chain saw, and very rarely on trees more than eight inches (twenty centimetres) in diameter. (Though, with what can only have been respect for their shape, some of the finer hawthorn were cut at about twelve feet above ground level, with the gipsies standing on top of their vans to use the saw, and creating in the process what must be some of the very few genuine hawthorn firewood pollards in the country!) This kind of haphazard assault is, I suppose, the nightmare of most woodland owners, and in this case was partly responsible for getting the gipsies evicted from the green. But the results two years later could, without exaggeration, be described as spectacular. All but fourteen of the 200 stools had sprouted abundant new shoots and there had been a massive regeneration of beech and oak seedlings on the now well-lit ground. Even sensitive woodland flowers like sanicle, goldilocks and ramsons have reappeared on the site. It would be an interesting experiment to grant permissive estover rights for a limited period in selected common woods – and maybe in some private ones – to see if the results turned out to be as encouraging as they were on this green.

But in most cases the management of the natural fabric of recreational areas will be the responsibility of professionals appointed by local authorities, conservators and so on. A report prepared for the Countryside Commission, *The Management of*

Grassland and Heathland in Country Parks, reported how successful some parks (particularly the increasing number which are
based on old wood-pastures and deer parks) have been in
replacing mowing with grazing or hay-cutting regimes.[91] Some
of the parks using these techniques have established herds of
rare cattle breeds to do the job, which has greatly increased
their attractiveness to the public and engendered, apparently,
a more respectful attitude in visitors.

The next step forward should be towards using similarly
frugal techniques in the management of the public themselves.
The principles of zoning and 'honeypotting', and 'trailing' the
public away from particularly sensitive areas are now well
understood, but it would be good to see them expressed in the
more imaginative use of 'natural' features. We could, for
instance, do with more moats and fewer fences, and 'reed
hedges' instead of concrete piles to protect river banks from
erosion. And I have not yet heard of anyone adopting Nan
Fairbrother's splendid idea of sunken hedges – planted in a
deep ditch and mown across the top. I have a feeling that they
might be the answer to the moto-cross bikes that are the bane
of areas lucky (or unlucky) enough to have sandy hollows.

'RE-CREATION'

And this, finally, brings us to the idea of *creating* entirely new
semi-natural habitats specifically for recreation.

Some new habitats – reservoirs, for example – have already
taken up this role as a by-product of their original function.
And, though they have neither the authenticity nor the specialized scientific interest of ancient habitats with truly natural
origins, they can acquire exciting 'natural' characteristics with
time. They are very close, both in status and role, to reproduc-
tions of works of art. So the canal echoes the river, the land-
scaped park the wood-pasture, the flooded pit the lake. (It has
been suggested that one of the answers to the intractable problems of the Norfolk Broads is to dig a complete new set – which
of course is how the originals were created, six centuries ago.)

There is scope, too, for the reclamation of industrial areas.
Professor Bradshaw of Liverpool University has shown just how
far the greening of abandoned quarries and slag heaps can go.[92]
And though a book concerned essentially with *rural* land-use is
no place to discuss the fascinating opportunities for nature con-

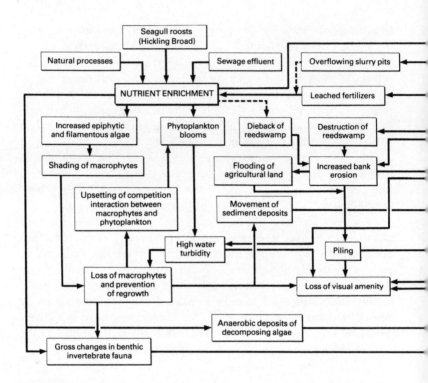

Figure 4. Proven and possible factors in the ecological deterioration of Broadland.

servation in the urban areas, it is clear that cities and industrial fringes, which have very few truly natural features and whose populations are deprived of contact with wild things, are ideal sites for such experiments. 'Bunny' Teagle's study in Birmingham for the NCC, an account of which appears in *The Endless Village*, has shown what a range of naturally rich wasteland – railway sidings, abandoned docks, car parks, building sites, rubbish tips – exists in the seams and margins of great cities.[93] Much could be done to enhance the interest of these places by regarding natural growth as a 'catch-crop' between more formal developments. Lyndis Cole has suggested, for instance, that disturbed city wasteland would be the ideal place for growing shows of the colourful arable weeds that are regarded as such a nuisance in the working countryside.[94]

Yet it is important that the tidying and management do not go too far. Although compromises have to be made in urban

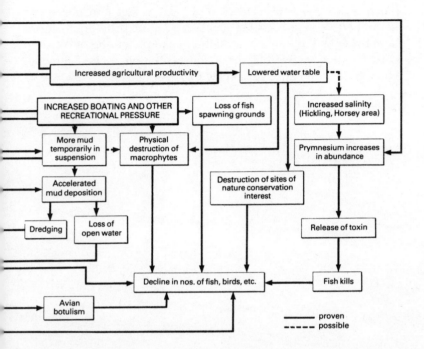

areas just as much as in the countryside and we must remember that untouched wasteland is by no means to everyone's recreational tastes, the natural potential of such sites can often best be realized by leaving them alone. The strange communities of ephemeral, opportunist and cosmopolitan plants and animals that spontaneously colonize urban wastelands are their truly 'natural' inhabitants and (as I explored in an earlier book, *The Unofficial Countryside*[95]) are what can make them places of such excitement and hope. No amount of human planning could have produced natural marvels like the sheets of rosebay willowherb that cloaked our bombed cities after the blitz, or the barn owl roost in a derelict East End gasworks, or the remarkable orchid colonies that have grown up on the lime-rich chemical tips near the old soda factories north of Manchester.[96] In an increasingly tidy and predictable world it is likely that people will want to experience this kind of wildness inside cities as much as in the countryside. If so, balancing a tolerance of natural succession with the creation of more orthodox recreational sites will become just another example of one of conservation's perennial problems – the resolution of free growth with the maintenance of specific kinds of habitat.

PART THREE
Policies and Priorities

In the preceding chapters I have tried to identify those features of rural land-use that have traditionally contributed towards the conservation of our wildlife, and those that are currently threatening it. Two quite clear patterns emerged. We saw that the uses of natural resources, provided they were at low intensities and not subject to sudden changes, not only tended to preserve natural communities by giving them social and economic functions, but frequently increased their diversity. In some cases (hay meadows, for instance) they could even be said to have created quite new habitats. Conversely, we saw that current trends in land management – which are encouraging a series of unstable monocultures – are destroying many 'obsolete' habitats and reducing the diversity of others.

Out of this contrast, a number of conservation priorities emerged: the preservation of those *ancient habitats* (primary woodland and raised bogs, for instance) which, once destroyed, can never be restored; the importance of maintaining *continuity* where change is inevitable; and the encouragement wherever possible of natural *diversity*.

We were also able to identify a fundamental process in natural systems which suggests ways of managing the countryside which are alternative to, or compromises with, its intensive economic exploitation. Natural systems work, by and large, by dispersing energy into a multiplicity of different outputs, as against the concentration of energy flow into single, specialized outputs which is characteristic of artificial, cultivated systems. The social corollary of this is the *multiple-use* of habitats. We also saw that one aspect of the diversity of natural systems is that their 'crops' are necessarily produced in the areas best suited for them, and that in a natural community as a whole there are always likely to be areas of intrinsically low productivity and 'fringes', where one habitat merges into another. The economic corollary of this is the idea of *marginal land*, which either is not naturally suited for intensive cultivation or is at the unstable edges of cultivated systems.

Finally, I suggested that meeting the immensely diverse human needs from the natural world was the goal of nature conservation, rather than an obstruction to it.

The goals, then, are the conservation of species, of irreplaceable habitats, of natural continuity and diversity, and of a 'natural aspect'. The *ecological* principles by which this might be achieved include the low-intensity multiple-use of land and the maintenance of marginal areas for their *optimum* rather than maximum outputs.

In the remaining chapters I want to look at ways of achieving these goals in practice. This is an altogether more difficult matter, as it involves complex questions of law, politics and economics, and the reconciliation of the needs of nature conservation with those of other land-uses (though one could argue that this emphasis should be reversed, and that other land-uses should be reconciled with nature conservation – or at least carried out inside a framework based on its principles). The rough outline of the policies we need is, in one way, *implicit* in our analysis of land-use in Part Two. Our surviving natural landscapes have been shaped and sustained by some thousands of years of specific human practices, and, if we wish to retain something of their traditional pattern, the ways we manage them will have to retain something of their original style. Yet the *organization* of these management policies has to take account of modern social and economic realities.

There are many factors involved. There is the application of the law, in the protection of individual organisms and specific sites, and, merging with this, various kinds of planning control over the use of the land. We need to inquire how relevant and effective such statutory measures are compared with more informal approaches, and look at the social organization of decision-making. Where is a national initiative most appropriate and where a local? What is the role of 'private enterprise' conservation as against governmental? How well do these different approaches supply the vital resources, both human and financial, that are necessary for any nature conservation to be viable? And, finally, what is the best balance between segregating land specifically, or chiefly, for nature conservation and modifying the ways we manage our land as a whole?

In the following chapters I shall be looking at the contribution made towards our principal conservation aims by three commonly-used approaches: first, the use of the law in the protection and conservation of particular species; secondly, the creation of nature reserves and the protection of specific natural sites; and thirdly, the idea of a more general policy for the management of the country's natural resources which takes the needs of nature conservation into account.

1

Species and Legislation

A capped Petrel . . . was once found by a boy in a furze bush near
Swaffham; it bit his hand, and he thereupon killed it, and made it into
a British bird.

Our Country's Birds (1890)

The use of the law in nature conservation is a contentious
matter. There are many people, I know, who regret the intrusion of any kind of legislation into our relationships with wildlife and see it as just one more constriction of the natural world's
'naturalness'. Yet, in cases where the destruction of wildlife
appears to be particularly wilful or gratuitous, we increasingly
expect the law to intervene as an instrument of protection.
Indeed the range of protective legislation which has entered the
statute books over the last century reflects an increase in our
care and concern for wild animals and plants which parallels
that for our own species. Yet a good deal of it is not quite as
protective as we may believe it to be, and if we probe a little
beneath its surface we can still find vestiges of that appropria-
tive attitude that put paid to the capped petrel on Swaffham
Common in 1850. By and large the law still makes rights of
property and ownership paramount over the well-being of
wildlife.

English law does not recognize an *absolute* right of property
in wild animals (or wild plants). Whilst it is still free and alive
an animal belongs to everybody – or, more correctly, to nobody.
But it can become property by being 'rendered into possession',
that is by being caught or killed. And from this moment it
belongs (since rights of property of another kind begin to be
involved) to the owner of the land on which it is taken (Blades
v. Higgs, 1865). (Wild plant crops – berries, mushrooms and
the like – remain the property of the picker, regardless of whose
land they are taken on.)

There are clearly two quite different ways of interpreting this statement of principle, depending on where you choose to see its chief emphasis. You may regard it either as a licence to 'render into possession' (and thus as a defence of the rights of individual people) or as an assertion of the idea that wildlife is not 'property' but a public, or common, asset. Both interpretations are legally valid, and they reflect two fundamental strands in our system of law: the *defence* of rights and freedoms (of property, privacy, life, etc) and the *control* of socially offensive or disruptive behaviour. Although in practice all laws contain elements of both approaches, they tend to lean towards one or the other. (Those governing larceny, for instance, are principally defensive of property rights, and the motoring laws principally concerned with maintaining social harmony.) There has been wildlife legislation of both kinds, but in general it has tended towards the defence of individual rights and to be concerned with who shall, and shall not, retain the right to 'render into possession'. It does not, that is, make certain actions against wildlife illegal *in themselves*, but only if performed by certain people in certain circumstances. Even the most advanced and comprehensive body of legislation (the Protection of Birds Acts) does not consider the killing or injuring of a species to be an offence if the person responsible can satisfy the courts that the act occurred as an 'incidental result of a lawful operation and could not reasonably have been avoided'.

There are good – or at least understandable – reasons why wildlife laws are seemingly short on absolute moral principles, and why they show an unusual degree of tolerance towards 'incidental' damage. Foremost amongst these, of course, is our need to defend our own welfare. There are many wild animals and plants which influence our well-being, either as sources of food or materials, or as major competitors for them, and any law which prohibited, absolutely, their 'rendering into possession' would be absurd and unreasonable.

In addition to being reasonable, the law needs to be fair and comprehensible, and not penalize people for actions which they cannot help committing simply by going about their daily business. In this respect, the complexity of the natural world makes it a very difficult system to make absolute laws about: most people have considerable difficulty in even discriminating between species. To take an extreme example, a law which gave blanket protection to all insects would clearly be unacceptable and unworkable, whatever we thought of it ethically. Apart from our need to control some insects deliberately, we would all become criminals every time we unwittingly squashed an ant on the lawn. On the other hand, a law which prohibited the wilful killing of specified and recognizable species *would* be practicable. (Indeed, two insects, the large blue butterfly and Essex emerald moth, have been protected in just such a way.)

These various constraints meant that legislation for the *protection* of wildlife was virtually non-existent until recently. Those laws that did affect the fortunes of wild creatures were concerned rather with the protection of the rights of various individuals to kill or take them, and found their clearest expression in the game and anti-poaching laws. These, if you like, were the legal expression of the traditional notion that the earth and its natural inhabitants were a form of *property*, to be disposed of as we wished. But, as Lewis Thomas has suggested, we have moved on two stages since then (see page 28), and the law reflects the current confusion in our attitudes toward the natural world – 'still believing in the new way but constrained by the facts of life to live in the old'. We are forced, in practice, to regard some wild creatures as little more than a rather troublesome form of matter. Yet we are beginning to talk in terms of 'animals' rights' as if they had a moral and legal status something like, say, human infants, who also need others to speak on their behalf. But we are not sure if this makes them simply *communal*, as against private, property or whether it begins to take them out of the realm of property altogether.

The ambivalence is clearest if we look at the status of game-birds, which are caught up in the legal assumptions of both the old and new thinking. A wintering bar-tailed godwit, for example, can find itself *simultaneously* in at least three contrasting (and by no means compatible) legal positions. It may be destroyed 'incidentally' (as if it were inanimate matter) in the course of lawful drainage works. Between 1 September and 31 January it may be shot and claimed (as if it were private property) by the owner of the land or anyone authorized by him (though if he shoots a rare *black-tailed* godwit by mistake – and the two species are easily confused in winter plumage – he may be guilty of an offence). And it may be rightfully enjoyed, without being harmed, by everyone else (as if it were a public asset).

As we look at the development of recent legislation we will see the tension between these various functions of the law, as it attempts to defend human rights *and* animal rights, and as it tries to balance the essentially moral aim of *protecting* life (of all kinds) with the more practical business of *conserving* species.

MAN AND OTHER PREDATORS

Although the protection of *habitats* is clearly at the root of nature conservation, it cannot by itself prevent the persecution of individual species in those habitats. Nor can it do much to protect highly mobile creatures – otters and eagles, for instance – whose territory is much greater than could be included in a protected site. There was a time when it was believed that the effects of deliberate killing were always insignificant by the side of habitat loss. But there is now strong evidence that, in the case of predatory animals at least, whose numbers are never large, determined hunting can have a disastrous effect on populations. (The studies described below also highlight some of the forces that have held back more effective legislation.)

In 1977, P. J. W. Langley and D. W. Yalden of the Zoology Department at Manchester University published an important paper on the factors that contributed to the decline of the polecat, pine marten and wild cat during the nineteenth century.[97] By a thorough examination of written records, they were able to trace when each of these three mammals became extinct in almost every county in Britain. In no case did the pattern of retreat seem to bear any relation to habitat changes, and certainly not to woodland clearance, which was the conventional explanation for the decline of these animals. The pine marten, for instance, the most tree-loving of all three, became extinct throughout most of the English lowlands between 1800 and 1850, just the period when the plantation system was beginning to extend England's woodland cover for the first time for three centuries. Its decline, however, did coincide with the enclosure Acts and with the rise of two of their nastier by-products – the sporting estate and the gamekeeper. Similarly, the decline of the wild cat in the uplands correlates with the spread of keepered grouse moors (see page 137) in the second half of the nineteenth century. All three species were classed as 'vermin' on sporting estates and came close to being exterminated in Britain in the early years of this century. They were probably only saved by the relaxation of keepering during the First World War. Their slow recovery in recent years has been helped by the spread of Forestry Commission plantations, but the recovery is as much a result of the Commission's tolerant attitude towards these animals as of the new woodland habitat it has provided. On many private estates they are still persecuted by gamekeepers (with or without the knowledge of their employers), often with vicious and illegal trapping devices. At no time – even though all three could still be regarded as scarce – has it been thought necessary to oppose the sporting lobby and bring in legislation to protect these mammals. (The reason usually given is that they are increasing in numbers and therefore in no need of protection.)

This is in striking contrast to our attitude towards predatory bird species. Although many of these are in a similar position (depressed in numbers yet slowly increasing), they are now all protected by law. Yet they are still illegally shot and poisoned in considerable numbers. (Potting rough-legged buzzards was a popular sport amongst some Norfolk keepers during the great influx of this species in the winter of 1973.) Their drastic decline up to the First World War correlates closely with phases of deliberate persecution.[98] It can be no coincidence that at the beginning of this century the only breeding site for common buzzards in the whole of lowland England was the New Forest. The one feature which distinguished this from many typical buzzard areas (such as the valleys of the Weald) was that it was not managed as a sporting reserve. Nor can it be an accident that the red kite found its last refuge in the remote wooded valleys of mid-Wales, where the raising of game has never been an important land-use. It is chastening to remember that in the fifteenth century the kites of London made such a contribution to public health by scavenging carrion in the streets that it was made a capital offence to kill one. This was the first piece of nature conservation legislation which was not solely concerned to protect hunting rights. Three centuries later the bounty was on the kites' heads, not their hunters'.

Donald Watson's masterly study of the hen harrier probably contains the most detailed account of the impact of hunting (and of laws to control it) on any single species.[99] The hen harrier was once a common and widespread bird, the classic large predator of the open wastelands of the pre-enclosure landscape. It was well enough known to have forty local names to its credit, and once plentiful enough for two Ayrshire estates to claim that their gamekeepers killed 351 between June 1850 and November 1854. The pattern of its eradication followed an almost identical course to that suffered by the carnivorous mammals. It was virtually extinct in the lowlands by 1865, and by the turn of the century had even vanished from the upland moors.

Collectors played a minor role in the pogrom compared to keepers, but were more revealing in their attitudes, whose dual standards strike a very familiar note. Nature was, by definition, enduring and inviolable. No action by a single, paltry individual could possibly destroy it. So if it was being destroyed, something – or someone – else must be responsible . . . . A. W. Crichton greatly enjoyed 'collecting' hen harriers and recounted his exploits in *A Naturalist's Ramble to the Orcades* (1869). On one occasion, having wounded but failed to collect a male harrier, he wrote: '. . . so, swallowing my disappointment as best I could, I then as humanely as possible consigned the youthful members of the family to a premature decease.' Just a few sentences previously he had written: 'Sad, indeed, is it to hear such melancholy comment . . . of the influence which thoughtless man is continuously and culpably exerting to thin the number of, if not exterminate from among us, the charming companions which the Creator has formed for our mutual enjoyment.'

Thirty years after this was written the hen harrier was extinct on the mainland of Britain. Crichton's hypocrisy is so astounding that one is tempted to forgive him on the grounds of diminished responsibility, to believe that he truly did not understand the impact of what he was doing. But his modern successors cannot be so easily excused. For the hen harrier has survived to be fought another day. A residual population clung on in the Orkneys and the Outer Hebrides, where there is little grouse-shooting and where the harrier's food preferences are shown by its local Gaelic name, *Clamhan luch* – mouse-hawk. At the end of the Second World War, it began slowly to recolonize the mainland, encouraged by the slackening of sporting activity and by an increase in the amount of suitable breeding habitat. The unburnt heather on the temporarily neglected grouse moors was very much to the harrier's taste, as were the young Forestry Commission conifer plantations. In 1954, when the entire British population was probably less than 100 pairs, the hen harrier was included in the First Schedule of the Protection of Birds Act 1954, which lists those birds protected by special penalties at all times. This was modified in the Act of 1967 (largely as a result of landowning and sporting pressures) so that licences could be obtained for the killing of First Schedule birds 'for the purpose of preventing serious damage to crops, vegetables, fruit, growing timber or any other form of property or to fisheries'.

In spite of the fact that grouse form only 11 per cent of all the bird prey eaten by harriers and that, being wild birds, they are not a 'crop' under the provisions of the 1967 amendment, sportsmen still occasionally invoke this mistaken interpretation of the law as a defence for killing harriers on the moor. Most often, though, no one bothers to look for such justifications. Harriers are shot because they are big, conspicuous predators, rather more skilled at hunting than the men in the butts, and because they occasionally upset the carefully marshalled drives of grouse that syndicates pay up to £2000 a day for. Almost exactly a century after Crichton's complaints, *Shooting Times* carried an article supporting this illegal shooting:

Let us take a case which is not as hypothetical as it may seem. An intelligent moorland keeper goes out of his way to protect nesting Peregrines on the border of his beat and is delighted to have Merlins nesting on his moor to the extent that he once came to fisticuffs with an egg-collector who tried to bribe him to obtain a fresh clutch of Merlin's eggs. But this same keeper does not welcome Hen Harriers. What would happen if I could catch him shooting a Hen Harrier and a successful prosecution resulted?

In the first place, the keeper would not be ostracised by the local population: he would be regarded as an unlucky martyr. Secondly, I would find myself ostracised locally and not one keeper in that district would ever confide in me again. Thirdly, it is more than probable that Peregrines and Merlins would never again nest on that moor. So that if anyone makes so bold as to tell me that I must never be reluctant in reporting any breach of the law I could, as a practical conservationist, only answer him really adequately by resorting to the use of a succinct but very vulgar five-letter word.

15 May 1971

Donald Watson, who quotes this article, deserves to have his own reply repeated:

In other words it seems that the keeper should decide for himself which parts of the law he will obey, and the above writer evidently considers that most people living in the neighbourhood of moorland shooting preserves regard prosecution for killing Hen Harriers as a form of victimisation. I am not sure whether he means to imply that as a result of such a prosecution the keeper would also destroy the Peregrines and Merlins, or that he would allow others to rob their nests or otherwise prevent them from breeding. Either way, it credits the keeper with a strangely vindictive attitude. To my mind, the most disturbing feature of the article is the implication that the law is somehow an impertinence on the moorlands of Britain.

And it is not just on the upland grouse moors that the law is wilfully flouted. In the seclusion of sporting estates throughout the land, owls, sparrowhawks, buzzards – any birds that might conceivably scrump a pheasant egg or chick – are still illegally killed by keepers, often with the tacit approval of their employers. (The RSPB is continually bringing successful prosecutions of keepers for such offences, though it is very difficult to prove that employers also have a legal responsibility.) There can be little doubt that, without persecution, the common buzzard – the least secretive of the larger birds of prey and therefore the easiest target – would now be recolonizing many more of its old haunts in lowland England.

CONSERVATION OR PROTECTION?

We need constantly to remind ourselves that this is *criminal* persecution, happening in the face of the most sophisticated, comprehensive and long-established of all our wildlife legislation. It is frightening to think of the state our bird-of-prey populations might be in if they were afforded no legal protection at all. Presumably they would be as artificially depressed as are those of polecats and pine martens which, along with frogs, butterflies, foxes, hedgehogs – there is scarcely an end to the list – we are all entitled to kill wherever and whenever we like.

It is not easy to pinpoint a single reason why the law regarding birds should (in its intentions if not always its effectiveness)

Waste ground under Spaghetti Junction, the kind of marginal land that occurs in both town and country. It is rapidly developing its own flora and fauna – including a scarce (and extremely large!) spider, Tegenaria agrestis (see page 176).

Agricultural landscapes: (above left) the traditional, medieval pattern, with a rich mix of small fields, old hedges, lanes and copses. (Left) the modern, with wild and uncultivated habitats now confined to narrow marginal strips, chiefly in wet valleys and on steep slopes.

Reed was once an important crop in many lowland areas, until the decline of thatching and the draining of wetlands. Now demand is on the increase again, and many reedbeds are being harvested according to traditional rotations, but often by the use (as above, in the Norfolk Broads) of modern equipment. Reedbeds need regular cutting if they are not to develop into woodland, and so an increasing number of wetland nature reserves are able to obtain an income from their normal management work (see page 242).

he RSPB, being a voluntary body supported by public subscription, has a
rticular responsibility to help its members enjoy the birds they have helped
rotect. This may entail a very delicate balancing of the interests of the birds
d their watchers.

Minsmere in Suffolk (above left) has been particularly successful in this
spect (see pages 207–213). The car park, for instance, has been very
fectively shielded from the vast area of reed swamp by natural scrub
owth.

The avocet (left) is one of the star attractions at Minsmere, and first bred
re in 1947.

The osprey (above) is another bird that the RSPB has very successfully
ld' to the public. Nearly a million people have visited the famous breeding
e at Loch Garten (see pages 158-161), and 'Operation Osprey' has
nerated a great fund of sympathy for all endangered birds.

(Above left) *Mallard in traditional decorative formation, not too far from London Wall. Since the water of the Thames has been cleaned up, fish and wildfowl have returned in large numbers.*

(Left) *The otter, arguably Britain's most popular mammal, but only protected from hunting in 1978. Other threats such as water-borne pesticides and river-bank management are not so easily controlled by law.*

(Above) *The Gothic setting of Britain's largest colony of greater horseshoe bats. The mansion, ordered by its new owner to be kept derelict for the sake of the bats, is probably our oddest nature reserve (see page 214).*

Ecological industry: (Above) *The interior of the rake factory in Whelnetham village, Suffolk, which makes use of some of the coppice wood from the Bradfield Woods (pages 74–75 and 246–247).*

(Left) *Fine potential timber trees Ham Street Woods NNR, grown from promoted coppice stools or local seed (Recently cut coppice stools are visib in the background.) (See pages 94–9*

be so much more advanced than that covering any of our other kinds of wildlife. As a group, birds have always seemed more harmless and – by virtue of the fact that they fly – more *public* than other kinds of creature. So perhaps the collecting mania of the Victorian naturalists and sportsmen appeared more flagrant in the case of birds than it did with other creatures. The very first of the Acts to protect birds – the Sea Birds Preservation Act 1869 – came into existence as a result of growing public revulsion against the slaughter of seabirds for their plumage, which was used to decorate ladies' hats. The Act secured a close season between 1 April and 1 August for about thirty species of seabird.

John Sheail, in his book *Nature in Trust*, has documented the progress of this and subsequent protective legislation up to the elegant Protection of Birds Acts (1954 and 1967).[100] The form of these Acts is unique amongst the various laws concerned with wildlife in being based upon a universally protective premise, to which certain exceptions are then made. *All* British birds, and their nests and eggs, are protected from killing, injury or theft, except in certain circumstances clearly defined by the Acts. In the case of a few birds (species like the wood pigeon which are customarily regarded as pests) the 1954 Act permits killing at all times by 'authorised persons', which normally means landowners and occupiers or their agents.[101] In the case of listed species which are rare or subject to special threat (and this schedule includes all but two of our fifteen breeding species of bird of prey), the 1967 Act's exceptions actually *extend* the protective powers and prohibit wilful disturbance while the bird is at the nest.[102]

The other feature in which the bird Acts are remarkable is that the one exception they do *not* provide is automatic immunity by virtue of land ownership (except in the case of scheduled 'pest' species). As the result of an Order made under the terms of the 1954 Act in 1963 (which took into account the terrible effect of the preceding winter and the fact that even common birds could quite suddenly become scarce) it became an offence to take a blackbird's egg even in your own garden. In this respect the Protection of Birds Acts make up the only body of legislation formally to recognize the concept that wild things are a common heritage and that gratuitous 'rendering into possession' is an act of theft from the whole community.

The bird protection lobby had nearly 100 years to refine the law to this simple but civilized formulation. Yet I think this may not be the only reason why the ideological foundation of the bird Acts differs so conspicuously from other, more recent, wildlife legislation. Their prototypes were concerned with *protection* as much as conservation, and this is still expressed in the names of the Acts. They were concerned not just to safeguard the population levels of endangered species but to counteract the brutalisation of the relationships between birds and men, whether the birds were rare or commonplace and whether the men were sportsmen, scientists, landowners or just concerned members of the public. They evolved in direct response to enterprises like those of the Yorkshire plumage-hunters who, after they had cut off the wings of the gulls, threw the birds back in the sea – still alive; to the catching of exhausted winter migrants with strings of baited hooks ('teagles') in the West Country; and to the attitudes summed up by the member of a Midlands natural history club who, on hearing that an osprey had been sighted over Tamworth, complained that 'someone who should have known better let it go'. Bird protection was as much concerned with the quality of human behaviour as with the quantity of birds and took into account those 'intangible harvests' that I touched on in the chapter on recreation.

Given these aims it was not surprising that the provisions of the 1954 Act should finally invade the sanctums of private property. What a person does to the birds on his own land may or may not be of conservation importance in the limited sense, but it most certainly impinges on the sensibilities of the public, and on what I think is a widely shared belief that wild creatures should not necessarily be regarded as part of the private property on which they live.

Considerations of this kind, though they have undoubtedly been important motivators, have not really found expression in other areas of wildlife legislation. This is partly because of pressures from interests which are hostile to nature conservation, and which are quick to pounce on anything resembling 'sentimentality' in conservationist arguments. But there has been a degree of emotional self-censorship as well. 'Feelings' are shunned in the sharp scientific discourse of modern ecological conservation – which I find rather sad, because a compassion for and a delight in the natural world are what turn people to act in its defence in the first place. The fact that such feelings are impossible to quantify does not make them irrelevant.

So, for the moment, cool rationality is the fashionable style;

and the voice we can hear behind the major pieces of wildlife legislation in the seventies (covering seals, badgers, wild plants and a few scarce animals including, recently, otters) is more dispassionate and, I believe, ultimately less powerful than that which energized the bird protection Acts 100 years ago and through them helped to begin the whole organized conservation movement.

THE NEW POACHERS?

The Badgers Act of 1973 was closest in its inspiration to the early bird Acts.[103] It was principally intended to prohibit badger digging, not long ago a favourite Sunday pastime in parts of the country – and maybe still so in some areas. (Poisoning had been illegal since 1911 in England and Wales and 1912 in Scotland.) The barbarity of badger digs almost defies belief. The setts were dug up, and the badgers twisted out with four-foot-long, steel-toothed tongs. Then, often with their jaws deliberately broken, their eyes put out and their back legs hobbled, they were tied in sacks and baited to death by terriers. Yet Peter Hardy, who piloted the Bill through the Commons, believes that digging was actually on the increase in the early seventies.[104] Over two-thirds of the 300 setts in Staffordshire (there were then about 12,000 setts in Britain) were dug out between 1970 and 1973.

The 1973 Act completely outlawed the use of badger tongs and put certain restrictions on the circumstances under which digging could take place. It also gave the Secretary of State powers to 'declare any area specified in the order to be an area of special protection for badgers'. And that is about it. The Act is widely thought to have made the haphazard digging for, and killing of, badgers illegal, and that is an advance of a kind. But in fact it puts virtually no restrictions on the killing of badgers by landowners. Section 7(1) states: 'Except within an area of special protection, an authorised person shall not be guilty of an offence under section 1(1) of this Act by reason of – (a) the killing or taking or attempted killing or taking of any badger, or (b) the injuring of any badger in the course of taking it, or attempting to take or kill it.' (An 'authorised' person is defined, as is usual in such Acts, as the owner or occupier of the land on which the action takes place, or any person authorized by him, and also any person authorized by a local authority, the

NCC or the relevant Agriculture Minister.) The landowner does not even have to have a reason for killing badgers unless his land happens to be inside an area of special protection, when he must be able to satisfy 'the court before whom he is charged that his action was necessary for the purpose of preventing serious damage to land, crops, poultry or any other form of property or for the purpose of preventing the spread of disease'.

In the event no such satisfaction has had to be given to a court, for as yet only one area of special protection has been declared. And ironically, a short while after the passing of the Act, another kind of special area was declared where the extermination of badgers by gassing could be carried out under supervision by officials of the Ministry of Agriculture, Fisheries and Food (MAFF). This was a result of the discovery that a small percentage of badgers in the West Country were infected by bovine tuberculosis. Bovine TB in cattle had continued to persist in scattered pockets of the country despite the MAFF's confident predictions that it would be eradicated by the end of the sixties, and in 1971 an unfortunate badger which had been killed by a motor car was found to be carrying the bacillus. The MAFF immediately began analysing badger carcasses and faeces (most of which were sent in by the public) and found that up to 20 per cent of samples from the West Country were infected.[105] And the pockets of worst infection did seem to correlate roughly with areas where herds were most persistently tuberculous. Similarly, when the MAFF monitored the results of destroying all badgers in trial areas, it discovered that even after several months there was no evidence of new infection in the herds (which was perhaps not surprising since all the tuberculous cattle were also destroyed as part of the operation, thus removing the chief focus of contagion).

It was this suggestive but largely circumstantial evidence which persuaded the MAFF that badgers were the chief carriers of bovine tuberculosis and 'responsible for the persistence of the disease in cattle herds'. In August 1975 the Badgers Act was amended to permit the gassing of badgers by qualified teams in areas approved by the MAFF. By 31 January 1978, more than 1000 setts had been gassed in Gloucestershire alone. But what was even more alarming than the scale of the controlled killing (which dwarfed that of the pre-1973 diggings) was the widespread massacre of uninfected and unimplicated badgers which followed in its wake. (I think 'wake' may be a more than usually

appropriate metaphor: law – be it good, bad, enabling or pro-
hibitive – does tend to send out rather choppy reverberative
waves from its central course.) Some farmers tried to flood out
setts on their land with cattle slurry – an action as foolish as it
was barbaric and one which, where cattle were already infected,
was the most likely way of infecting not only surviving badgers
but the ground itself. (The TB bacillus can remain viable in soil
for up to a year.) In some parts of the country the old pastime
of badger-digging was taken up with a new purposefulness –
within the law, usually, but quite against the spirit of the 1975
amendment. By the summer of 1978 the situation was sufficiently serious for the Consultative Panel on Badgers and Bovine Tuberculosis to issue a press release about the
misapplication of control measures:

The Consultative Panel on Badgers and Bovine Tuberculosis has
expressed concern at reports from field observers that badgers are
being destroyed in places remote from the problem areas in South
West England because of fear that they may infect cattle with bovine
tuberculosis. The Panel wishes to stress that, outside the problem
areas, there is no cause for concern on this score.

The Panel, which includes representatives of the NCC and a
number of well-known authorities on the badger, is convinced
that there is no reasonable doubt that, where badgers have TB
and live at high density, they can transmit the disease to cattle.
It also accepts the need to control tubercular badgers regardless
of the source of the infection. But its conclusions, and the
control programme based on them, have not received much
support from the conservation movement as a whole. The
opposition is not simply a response to the widespread misapplication of control measures. A number of independent vet-
erinary scientists have suggested that there are serious
shortcomings in the scientific evidence on which the eradication
programme is based.[106] They have pointed out, for instance,
that it is based largely on the fact that tuberculous cattle and
tuberculous badgers tend to occur in the same areas. No mechanism by which the disease passes from cattle to badger and
back again has been convincingly established in the field, and
the possibility that there may be a 'third party' responsible for
infecting both badgers and cattle has not been adequately
explored. Although the bacillus has been isolated from moles,
rats and foxes, the testing of other wild creatures as possible

carriers has so far been nothing like extensive enough (1344 samples from twenty-four species, as against 4468 from badgers).[105] Even the sampling techniques to estimate the prevalence of the disease in badgers have been statistically unsatisfactory, relying largely on road-accident carcasses voluntarily sent in by the public – which is hardly a random sampling. And only a minute number of the many thousands of gassed setts have subsequently been examined to see if they harbour the bacillus.

Nevertheless there is strong circumstantial evidence that the badger may be one carrier of the disease, and the gassing programme may be justified on the grounds of caution alone. Whether it can be justified as being 'for the badgers' own good' is another matter. I feel we could well do with more knowledge about the status of the disease amongst badgers themselves (and about the viability of less drastic remedies) before presuming to become arbiters of their well-being. In emotionally charged situations like this where disease and threats to livelihood are involved, there is always the risk that a convenient animal will be singled out as a sacrificial scapegoat, to deflect attention from more complex causes and even from plain bad husbandry (cf. the Orkney seals). It is reassuring, then, that in March 1978 the NCC commissioned a research programme to inquire into the incidence and behaviour of the TB bacillus in other species of wildlife.

With unfortunate irony, the clause which amended the Badgers Act to allow controlled poisoning was added on to the end of the Conservation of Wild Creatures and Wild Plants Act 1975 (which I will call the 1975 Act for short).[107] This Act was the outcome of decades of parliamentary and judicial wrangling and, though the preface defines it as 'An Act to provide for the protection and conservation of wild creatures and of plants growing wild. . .', its provisions are, to tell the truth, rather more restricted. It can control the deliberate destruction or collection of certain scarce wild creatures and plants, but not a great deal else. That, in the last quarter of the twentieth century, is as far as the consensus amongst the different factions would reach. Nevertheless it is an important first step, and it has had some significant effects – though perhaps not exactly the ones that were intended.

The 1975 Act is a curious hybrid in terms of the *styles* of legislation enacted in it. The early sections could be looked on as social control laws, modified by exceptions based on the defence of property. Section 4, for instance, states: 'if, save as may be permitted by or under this Act, any person, other than an authorised person, without reasonable excuse uproots any plant, he shall be guilty of an offence.' This is a bold, simple and comprehensive enactment, and though it is extensively qualified (excepting as usual, the owner or occupier of the land on which the plant grows, or any person acting on his authority), it does come close to the kind of statement of principle that underlies bird protection.

Sections 1, 2 and 5 (framed principally to combat the threat posed to certain rare species by collectors) have a similar shape. They prohibit the unauthorized killing, injuring, taking, possessing or selling of specified wild creatures and the unauthorized picking, uprooting or destruction of specified wild plants. The chief exception provided in the case of scarce creatures is that an authorized person shall not be guilty of an offence if he can satisfy a court 'that his action was necessary for the purpose of preventing serious damage to land, crops, poultry or any other form of property'. The six animals originally listed (in Schedule 1) included the greater horseshoe bat, the sand lizard and the large blue butterfly, all of which are scarce and to some degree endangered because of habitat destruction and collection.

The twenty-one plants listed in Schedule 2 are an interesting collection – including alpine gentian, blue heath, Cheddar pink, ghost orchid, Killarney fern, lady's slipper orchid, Teesdale sandwort and wild gladiolus. They are not the rarest plants in Britain, nor, in Red Data Book terms, the most threatened. Nor – though this is necessarily a subjective judgement – are they the most beautiful, popular or widely picked. If one was looking for a single quality possessed by all twenty-one it might be 'glamour' – which perhaps best suggests their combination of scarcity, reputation and allure. If this was a deliberate consideration it was politically very astute, recognizing as it does that in such difficult areas laws function more as propaganda than as checks on specific actions. The exceptions provided in the case of these scheduled plants cover 'picking, uprooting or destruction' which 'occurs as an incidental result, which could not reasonably have been avoided, of any operation which was carried out in accordance with good agricultural or forestry practice' – which unfortunately exempts many of the situations in which scarce plants are destroyed.

It is section 12 (which specifies the conditions under which other species can be added to the Schedules) which is the most contentious, and where the Act begins to veer away from a statement of common social principles. It states that the Nature Conservancy Council

at any time may, and five years after the passing of this Act and every five years thereafter shall, review the Schedules to this Act and shall advise the Secretary of State if any wild creature or plant has become so rare that its status as a British wild creature or plant is being endangered by any action designated as an offence under this Act and it should be included in Schedule 1 or 2 . . . or has become so common that its status is no longer endangered and it should be removed therefrom.

It is an exceptionally restrictive condition. It seems only to allow a species to be added to the protected list if it is already on the verge of national or regional extinction – a condition which we have already seen it is the aim of any sensible conservation policy to *forestall*. But even that is not sufficient qualification for protection. The wording implies that the threats to a species' national status must be of a specific kind – namely the deliberate destruction or collecting which the Act was principally designed to control. So if a plant or creature was threatened with extinction from another source – habitat loss or pollution, say – it seemed it could not be given protection under the Act.

It was a very literal reading of section 12 that made the addition of the otter to Schedule 1 such a difficult and stormy manoeuvre. Although otters are secretive, highly mobile creatures whose numbers are notoriously hard to estimate, it was clear by the end of the 1960s that they had become very scarce in England and Wales. A survey of otter hunting returns by the Mammal Society in 1968 suggested that there had been a drop in population of between 40 and 50 per cent. A more detailed local field survey by Rodney West in Suffolk estimated that between 1967 and 1972 there were, on average, only eighteen pairs in the county.[108] In Norfolk, between 1974 and 1975, there were thought to be only seventeen pairs.[109] (The 'carrying capacity' of Norfolk watercourses is believed to be at least three or four times this figure.)

When the 1975 Act became law it seemed an obvious move to try to add the otter to the list of creatures in Schedule 1. But the report prepared in 1977 by the Joint Otter Group set up by the NCC and the Society for the Promotion of Nature Conservation concluded that, because populations in Scotland were still quite high, 'the otter would not appear to be sufficiently endangered for it to be added to Schedule 1 of the Act on a national basis', and that where it had declined there was 'insufficient evidence that this is brought about by killing and taking'.[110] Indeed there were obviously a large number of other factors influencing otter populations, including water pollution, river-bank straightening, disturbance by boats, and toxic pesticides drained off farmland. A subsequent and much more detailed analysis of hunting records by Paul Chanin and Don Jefferies, published in 1978, pointed very suggestively to this last factor being the most significant cause of the decline.[111] Throughout much of England (and particularly the arable areas) there was a sudden and rapid decline in the number of kills beginning about 1957, just after the persistent and highly toxic seed-dressing dieldrin came into use (cf. the decline of the peregrine, pages 31–32).

Nevertheless it was clear that, whilst otter-hunting might not have been an important factor in initiating the otter's decline, it constituted a considerable threat now that the animal's numbers were so depleted. In the end this led to an important behind-the-scenes judgement that, if a creature or plant had been made sufficiently scarce *by whatever means*, it would *automatically* be endangered by deliberate destruction or collecting thereafter. Accordingly the otter was added to Schedule 1 in England and Wales at the beginning of 1978.

It is a sad reflection on the restrictive frame of reference of section 12 that the otter could equally well be taken off the Schedule, and therefore cease to be a protected creature, if its population begins to recover. And there can be little doubt that the otter-hunting lobby will press for such a removal in the event of a recovery. Although most hunts exercised a voluntary ban on *killing* otters (not on chasing them) after 1964, they are strongly opposed to any legal restrictions on their activities. What I find especially disturbing are the proprietorial terms in which this opposition is often couched. The hunts appear to consider that otters are their concern alone and that this exclusive relationship is created and confirmed by the intimate ritual of the chase. The Friends of the Earth's report, *The Declining Otter*, quotes a circular sent out by the Master of the Eastern Counties Otter Hounds:[112]

Dear Member
The going is tough, but that is nothing new in our daily lives. Of course our sport is affected like everything else, but if we really value it we will fight hard to preserve our pleasure. Hunting is one of those rare things that allows the British to express their freedom, which is why those who wish to sell us into bondage, encourage the uncommitted to attack it.

A Bill to outlaw otter hunting which was introduced to the Commons under the Ten Minute Rule in 1972 had been objected to on similar lines. Reginald Paget (the Member for Northampton) said: 'If you abolish otter hunting you abolish the one wide-ranging organisation which has an interest in preserving the otter.' In 1976, this 'wide-ranging organisation' consisted of nine active packs of hounds and eight inactive, and on hunting days the average number of supporters in the field was between fifty and 100 per pack. In the light of these figures I do not think it is unreasonable to ask just whose freedoms are being upheld and whose (apart from the otters') are being eroded when otters are wilfully hunted and killed. When a small minority claims prior property rights over the living assets of a whole society, it does rather cast the old felony of poaching in a new light.

LAW AS TEACHING

It is hard to estimate what direct contribution the 1975 Act has made towards the conservation of the species it lists. At the time of writing there has not been a single prosecution under the Act, and the difficulties involved in its enforcement probably mean that it has had little deterrent effect on committed collectors. But this may be of minor importance compared with the effect of its implicit principles on public opinion. If the 'reverberative' effects of its penultimate section (the amendment of the Badgers Act) have been unfortunate, those of the body of the Act have been almost entirely beneficent. They have, for example, given *status* to the plants in Schedule 2, to the extent that there have been cases of land developers being prepared to amend their legitimate works in order to avoid damaging particular plants. The most surprising unintended result of the Act is the sympathy it has elicited for bats. There are only two rare species mentioned in Schedule 1, but it is quite clear from the continuing flow of inquiries in the press and on radio that the Act is mistakenly believed to protect all species of bat, and that, though they may not always be welcome guests, the public is anxious not to disturb them 'illegally'.

The Act itself recognizes that education must accompany legislation, and section 13(1) says: 'A local authority shall take such steps as they consider expedient for bringing the effect of this Act to the attention of the public and in particular school-children.' But what we are seeing here is the law *itself* acting as an educative force. Law has always functioned in this way, as a distillation or parable of the form of ideal relationships. It will always be most forceful when its guidance is simple and fair, and weakest when it is involved and compromised. And this is why, for all its commendable side-effects, section 12 of the 1975 Act does seem to me an unsatisfactory enactment. There is no doubt that we need legislation of some kind to defend endangered species against specific threats. But there are risks in relating this legislation exclusively to 'endangeredness'. The only principle which section 12 expresses with any force is that value depends on scarcity – just as it does for any other kind of property. I do not believe that this is an expression of the way we, as a society, regard our wildlife heritage at present. I doubt if we would be happy, for instance, if our bird laws were revised so that they related degrees of protection to population levels. If they were we would still be 'hunting the wren' (one of Britain's commonest breeding birds) as well as culling seals. The fact that most of us seem to find both these practices morally offensive is, I think, a sign that we wish our wildlife legislation to move towards the expression of commonly-shared moral principles. As we have seen, it still largely regards wildlife as potential private property, so that anything can be done to it unless it is expressly forbidden. Within this coarse mesh of prohibition, collectors, sportsmen, agriculturalists, even unscrupulous scientists, have enthusiastically exercised their right to 'render into possession'. The current abuses of this right suggest that, in future, wildlife legislation should be based, as the Protection of Birds Acts are, on a general presumption *against* the destruction of life (and wildness) unless there are good reasons to the contrary. The law would thus represent the *commonableness* of wildlife and the public interest in and concern about its fate (and perhaps eventually become the guardian of wildlife's own 'rights'). It would provide a moral context in which the more practical business of land-use could be carried out.

As I write, a comprehensive Countryside and Wildlife Bill is being drafted, which takes account, amongst other matters, of new EEC directives on bird protection and the need to give legal protection to certain specified habitats. This is greatly to be welcomed, yet the one exception that will still almost certainly be retained is that vast area of 'incidental' damage that occurs in the course of 'good agricultural or forestry practice'. It is hard to imagine British law ever containing a provision like that in the US Endangered Species Act of 1973 which prohibits all federal departments from carrying out projects which would 'destroy or modify' the habitat of a notified species,[113] and which meant that a $116 million dam project on the Little Tennessee River was halted because of the threat it posed to the tiny snail-darter fish. For the immediate future, at least, the protection of specific habitats is still likely to be most effectively achieved by segregating them as 'reserves'.

2

Sites and Reservation

I know encaging is not the worst of our crimes against nature this century; and that with some danger-list species it has now become their only hope of survival. Indeed I have only to go back to the woodlands I knew as a boy in the 1930s to see the greater crime: how once common birds are now rarities, how glades once full of butterflies are now empty of them, sunlight without wings. Here, as in every other heavily farmed area in the world, the silences and motionless-nesses of a dead planet begin to steal up on us.

This guilt, which we must all share, makes it impossible to write of nature in 1970 except in terms of lamentation and sermon. I have very little hope for any form of real progress that is not broadly based on the pleasure principle. The archetypal human demand, when faced with change, has always been 'What's in it for me' – what new pleasure shall I get?' And this is the strongest argument for trying to change ordinary attitudes to nature from pseudo-scientific to the poetic, from the general to the personal.

JOHN FOWLES, 'The Blinded Eye' (1971)[114]

Faced with the fact that individual organisms cannot be pro-tected without in some way protecting the places in which they live (and that some natural communities *are* places) we come inevitably to the idea of the nature reserve – something about which our feelings are as mixed as they are about the law. In a world where the day-to-day management of the land has become increasingly antagonistic to living things, it seems an obvious and necessary step to set aside places dedicated to their interests. But what we are protecting in reserves are also – if we are honest – our *own* interests. What does this make of the physical and metaphorical fences, between man and nature, man and man, by which we define these places? Who are we trying to keep out? What, for that matter, are we trying to keep *in*? Do reserves truly conserve 'wildness' in a way that zoos do not? Are they public monuments or private laboratories?

The problems of definition, of exclusion and inclusion, make it important that we do not lose sight of these questions. Although the establishment of reserves is clearly a necessity, given the fate of so much unprotected land, I feel that there are dangers in regarding it as the chief *purpose* of a conservation policy. As we examine the contribution which reserves make, we must ask ourselves to what extent they deflect attention from our failure to maintain ecological standards in the world outside, and to what extent their existence perpetuates a damaging view of nature as being somehow separate from our ordinary affairs.

The first formal nature reserve (on Breydon Water, Norfolk) was established less than 100 years ago, but the idea of *sanctuary* – a place of privacy and safety, set apart specifically as a refuge – is very ancient, and very deep-rooted in its appeal. Yet 'nature sanctuary' is not a phrase we hear much these days. Maybe its hint of sanctity and romance has left it behind as part of the era when protection rather than conservation was the guiding principle of the preservation movement. I find the change of emphasis regrettable, for 'sanctuary' (like 'protection') suggests a concern for the quality and breadth of the relationships between man and wildlife that is not caught by its modern, no-nonsense successor 'nature reserve'.

In practice, of course, very few reserves are as impassively utilitarian as their name might suggest. If we were to include everything from National Nature Reserves to two-acre school corners, there are probably about 2000 in Britain, and together they make up a cross-section of our wildest and richest countryside. Whatever doubts we may have about some of the principles of reservation, we should be thankful that conservationists have had the foresight to isolate these places from at least some of the pressures of development.

Yet giving a piece of land reserve status does not mean that conflicts about its future are over. The very act of deciding that wildlife will be its principal, conscious 'crop' rather than an incidental by-product, means that a whole new range of choices and value judgements has to be made. What kinds of wildlife, precisely? Do we concentrate on building up the diversity of species and habitats, or on increasing the populations of the rarer inhabitants? Do we attempt to maintain the site's current character, or to restore (or at least imitate) some earlier, less altered condition? How much notice do we take of direct human demands on the reserve? It was, after all, a human decision that created it in the first place. The immensely varied – and occasionally incompatible – functions which a reserve can fulfil are apparent in the word itself, which has picked up any number of shades of meaning in common usage. 'Reserve' can imply restraint or limitation; then again something held over for future use, as in gold vaults and football teams. It appears in modifications like 'reservoir' and 'reservation' – which is what you make if you 'reserve' a place for your own or someone else's exclusive use, be it a theatre seat or a tribal retreat.

Most reserves have willy-nilly to function simultaneously as wildlife reservoirs and private estates, as well as meeting a host of more specialized demands on their ground space and inhabitants. Yet these purposes, being essentially artificial development programmes for the land, do not necessarily harmonize. They need to be orchestrated. The most celebrated, and one of the most complex, nature reserves in Britain is Minsmere in Suffolk, which was leased by the RSPB in 1948 and finally purchased for a quarter of a million pounds in 1977. It is by no means a typical reserve, but it does incorporate, inside a single unit, so many of the different functions which reserves can fulfil that it may serve as a usefully composite example.

Minsmere is a concentrated mix of the kinds of habitats that used to be found all along the sandy coastal belt of east Suffolk – shingle, reedswamp, alder and willow carr, heathland and oakwood – each kind forever attempting to change into one of the others. But then the area now occupied by the reserve has never been stable. Low-lying and adjacent to the sea, it has been at the mercy of the elements as well as natural succession. At the time of the Norman Conquest it was a wide estuarine haven surrounded by woodland. Throughout the middle ages it swung between swamp and open estuary, as the sea alternately sealed off the river mouth with shingle and then burst through again. By the seventeenth century most of the woodland had been cleared and sheep put out on the open heath. By the end of the eighteenth, shingle had permanently dammed the estuary and major drainage works were begun. Then in 1940 the whole area of grazing marsh was deliberately flooded as part of war-time coastal defence plans. As is the manner of

Just before this book was going to press in 1979, it was announced that the last known colony of large blue butterflies in south-west England had failed to produce any viable eggs, and that the butterfly was therefore almost certainly extinct in Britain.

The demise of the large blue illustrates very graphically the practical and philosophical problems involved in supporting a creature whose 'natural' environment has become obsolete. The large blue is a predominantly central European species and was probably never very common even in southern England. The larvae of the butterfly have an extraordinary life cycle, feeding on wild thyme for their first few weeks, and then being carried underground to feed on the grubs of a particular species of red ant. But it was not until the 1970s, during a long-term research project by the Institute of Terrestrial Ecology under the supervision of Jeremy Thomas, that it was realized just how exacting were the conditions under which suitable populations of thyme and red ants could flourish side by side. The massive reduction and fragmentation of unimproved grasslands and the decline in grazing by rabbits following myxomatosis (rabbit-grazed turf was ideal for the ants) combined to produce a situation in which there were very few areas which had the combination of conditions necessary for the survival of the caterpillars. By 1976 there were less than forty adult butterflies at the one remaining site.

The conservation of this residual population posed almost insuperable problems. The habitat had to be maintained in precisely the right state. Unfortunately, freak droughts in 1975 and 1976 were followed by poor weather during the emergence period in the next two years. By 1978 the butterflies were so few in numbers that it was felt necessary partially to enclose them, to protect them from hard weather conditions and to ensure that they met each other for mating. But, although twenty-two butterflies emerged in 1979 (as against only five in 1978), the efforts to save this last known population were to no avail.

These drawings (made on the site in 1978) were part of a larger series produced specially for this book by David Measures, who has pioneered the illustration of living butterflies in the field. They are a historic record of what may have been the last successfully-breeding large blues in Britain.

Large blue ♂
20th June 1978

It is very unusual
in the wild to see the
Large Blue open
except the ♀ after laying her eggs
stretches parts before resuming
activities.

In this instance it is likely
that the cooling from the
intermittent spraying with
water to keep it humid
is the cause.

very much the impression
of dark blacky inky blue
when he flies

closed
when settling they very often
have a little bit of the blue
forewing showing   the pair
not quite closed

He is a largish male
♂ males tend not to have
such large lozenge shaped
marks as the hen.

Some of the remaining fragments of the southern heathlands.

(Above left) Bratley Wood and Plain, New Forest, in winter. In most areas of Britain, heathland is a man-made landscape, and will progress to woodland unless some external factor keeps regenerating trees in check. In the New Forest, the balance between heath and woodland is maintained by grazing cattle and ponies. (A new patch of woodland, which will eventually replace the ageing beeches in the foreground, can be seen in the distance growing up under the cover of evergreen holly.)

(Left) Studland and Godlingston Heaths, Dorset. The Dorset heaths – which Thomas Hardy immortalized as 'Egdon' – are on what are regarded as the poorest soils in Europe, and in parts they may be entirely natural. What tree growth does occur is kept in check chiefly by fire, either deliberate or accidental. These heaths are a stronghold of the Dartford warbler and other scarce heathland animals.

(Above) Another declining heathland bird is the nightjar, photographed here in Surrey. Nightjars depend not only on heather for nesting, but on large flying insects for food, and have been badly hit by the destruction of heathland, by the loss of heather on what remains, and by our deteriorating summer climate.

Pine marten in north Scotland. These carnivorous mammals were driven virtually to the point of extinction by intense keepering at the end of the last century. They are now on the increase again, thanks largely to the tolerant attitude shown towards them in the Forestry Commission's conifer plantations. On private shooting estates, however, they are still persecuted by gamekeepers (see page 188).

wetland ecosystems, recolonization was rapid. By the end of the war Minsmere had returned to the vast mosaic of reed-swamp and brackish lagoons that it must have been for much of the middle ages. And, most significantly for its future, it was recolonized by a number of species of marshland birds – bittern, marsh harrier, bearded tit – that had come close to extinction in Britain because of loss of habitat and outright persecution. And in 1947 it and nearby Havergate Island were graced by the breeding of a bird that *had* been extinct in Britain between the middle of the last century and the 1940s – the avocet.

The safeguarding of the avocets was one of the RSPB's priorities when it leased a 1500-acre block of marsh and heath in 1948, and a good deal of the early management work was directed towards improving and extending their nesting habitat. This involved digging and maintaining an artificial system of shallow, brackish lagoons – an area of the reserve that has now become internationally famous as 'the Scrape'. But that was hardly a policy which could be followed over the whole reserve. What was to be done with the remaining 1000-odd acres? Minsmere had been many things in the past, and there was no obvious, single, historical state to return it to. In prehistoric times, for instance, much of the area would have been woodland, and if it was 'left to nature' it would, given the comparative security of the new sea defences, progress rapidly towards woodland again, with the reeds invading the lagoons, willows invading the reeds, birch invading the heath, and mixed forest finally swallowing the lot. That would have been a perfectly legitimate future for Minsmere, but not perhaps the most valuable.

The programme which was eventually evolved over the next two decades, and which Bert Axell has documented in his portrait of the reserve, is a model of the kind of approach that is now followed on many large nature reserves.[115] Essentially it is a policy of compressing into a single composite unit the range of habitats that once occurred in the surrounding countryside – an artificial compression, admittedly, but justified because of the fragmentation and disappearance of these habitats outside. It would have been unusual to find such an intimate mixture of wood, heath, reed and marsh occurring naturally in such a comparatively small area. But up till the mid-nineteenth century there would, at any one time, have been extensive stretches of all these habitats along the Suffolk coast. The reserve's aim is to preserve a representative collection of these habitats as a co-ordinated estate, extending and enriching each one as far as possible without compromising the integrity of the others. The Scrape, for instance, has had more lagoons excavated and more nest islands built, and it now supports some forty pairs of avocet and hundreds of pairs of common and sandwich terns. It has also been visited by a spectacular list of rare migrants. The reed is harvested on a rotational basis to prevent takeover by willow carr and, as well as housing abundant bearded tits and sedge, reed and grasshopper warblers, is one of the last British refuges of the marsh harrier. The heather is being encouraged to replace the rather sterile sweeps of bracken on the heaths, which, it is hoped, will lead to an increase in the number of breeding nightjars. The hazel is coppiced, which will help the nightingales. Most of the habitats, in fact, are managed according to traditional, conservative techniques. It is their highly condensed *mix* that is novel, and which makes nature reserve management really a new kind of land-use.

Beyond maintaining the basic structure of the reserve, though, there are few absolute principles to guide the management team. By and large they must rely on their own ecological instincts, as the dominant animals in the reserve community. How much reed can they allow to become senile, for instance, for the sake of insects with rather eccentric tastes in living quarters? (One species of wasp nests exclusively in cigar galls on old reed.) How much public pressure can they tolerate? Minsmere was bought by donations from RSPB members, and they have an entirely just and understandable desire to watch the birds they have helped protect. Yet if all the people who wished to visit the reserve were allowed to do so, they would find very few birds left to watch. (Minsmere sensibly limits its permits to a maximum of 200 a day – but has provided, as a compensation, a range of public hides on the beach, outside the reserve but overlooking the Scrape.)

Subjective value judgements are also inevitable in attitudes towards individual species, and in deciding whether they 'belong' in the reserve. As we have seen, there is no way in which a reserve can be an exact reconstruction of an identifiable historical habitat (which might necessitate, apart from anything else, the reintroduction of various insects and other animals lost to the site). Yet there is usually an unspoken assumption about the 'time zone' in which a reserve is operating. This is evident

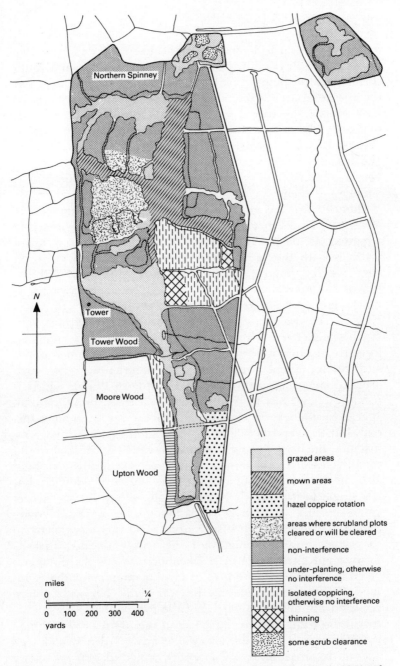

Figure 5. Map of management programme for Castor Hanglands National Nature Reserve, redrawn from an internal NCC document. (Compare Hatfield Forest, page 79.)

in attitudes towards naturalized plants like rhododendron. This grew wild in Britain about half a million years ago, and could therefore, stretching a point, be said to be a native plant. But on most reserves it is removed, either because qualifications for nativeness are restricted on theoretical grounds to those plants that arrived here of their own accord or, more practically, because it is an aggressive shrub and a poor habitat for birds and insects. At Minsmere, however, the rhododendron is not very aggressive, and patches have been left to provide colour, variety and shelter.

There is also the problem of what to do about species like stoats and crows that in the wider countryside are commonly regarded as pests. These were once despatched on many reserves with the same unquestioning haste as they are on keepered shooting estates. But there is a feeling now, I think, that as natural and integral parts of the food chain they have as much right to be there as any of the more delicate or scarce species. The problems begin when particularly rapacious individuals begin to erode the very species the reserve was intended to conserve. It is hard to be a pure non-interventionist under such circumstances, particularly when nature reserves are such artificial constructs anyway; and the rule of thumb which is usually followed is to try to maintain a stock of *all* 'natural' species on the reserve, to intervene if necessary to achieve this end, but to keep the killing to a minimum. At Minsmere, for instance, the black-headed gull colony, which unchecked would rapidly crowd out the terns and avocets, is kept down to about 100 pairs by injecting some of the eggs with formaldehyde. But the single kestrel which consumed all but two of the avocet chicks in 1977 was left alone. Although the warden, Jeremy Sorensen, was under pressure from some quarters quietly to assassinate the offending bird, he wisely decided that its extravagant tastes were in all likelihood 'just a phase', aggravated by an unusual shortage of small mammal prey that summer. As things turned out, he was right. No such pillage occurred the following year, and the avocets had a more successful breeding season. But, even if the kestrel had resumed its attacks, it is hard to believe that any warden would seek special dispensation to kill a legally protected bird in a place that calls itself a nature reserve. (In this case it could have sparked off a generation war: although the avocet is the symbol of the RSPB, the kestrel is the symbol of its junior branch, the

Young Ornithologists' Club!) Problems of this kind nearly always sort themselves out if some kind of stability and balance has been established on the reserve.

What is striking about Minsmere (and almost any other reserve we could have chosen) is how arbitrary this balance seems at first sight. Yet the details of management begin to make more sense when you consider them in the light of the functions and goals of the reserve. Reserves have been created variously for the protection of single species, for the enjoyment of the public, as centres of biological excellence, as open-air laboratories and classrooms, and as living museums of landscape types. There are even reserves dedicated principally to free natural *succession*, such as the Axmouth–Lyme Regis Undercliffs National Nature Reserve (see page 89). All of these are quite legitimate aims. Minsmere, through geographical serendipity and a history of good stewardship, has succeeded in covering almost the whole gamut of purposes which reserves can serve. But the horizons for most protected sites will necessarily be more limited and the sites will function better if the limitations are known and stated.

For all their diversity of aims and structure, I think it is possible to gather reserves into two categories (though I should stress that this is an arbitrary distinction itself). The first I will label 'sanctuaries'. They are informal, opportunist reserves, whose unpretentious aims are usually no more complex than providing a refuge for 'nature' in a very general sense, for people who wish to enjoy natural surroundings, or for a particular plant or creature which has become stranded in a hostile environment. For the other kind I will borrow the term 'living museums' which has been commonly used for them at least as far back as 1947 (see page 218). The analogy with museums is exact. These are carefully picked, delicately managed, *representative* – in all senses – examples of the classic natural and semi-natural communities in Britain.

SANCTUARIES

To my knowledge only one British reserve was established to safeguard a single *organism*, and that is the Hethel Old Thorn (an ancient 'meeting place' tree) in Norfolk. But there are a good number that have been established for the sake of a single *species*. The Suffolk Trust leases from the Forestry Commission a chalk-pit containing some 100-odd plants of the military orchid. The Gloucestershire Trust has an old stone-mine which was formerly the roost of a venerable and impressively fecund male greater horseshoe bat. Although this bat has died, the mine is still used as a roost. And there are doubtless some of his descendants amongst the vast colony of greater horseshoes (estimated at some 18 per cent of the British population) which inhabit a derelict four-storey mansion just a few miles away. This was purchased in 1978 by a sympathetic landowner, who requested that it should be left in its decrepit state for the sake of the bats.

Species which live in isolated colonies or eccentric habitats are the most appropriate subjects for 'single species' reserves, though keeping them in balance can be a precarious business. Mary Gilham described the experiences of the Glamorgan Naturalists' Trust with the fringed water lily in Broad Pool, Gower:

So small a pioneering stand of a plant so rare in western Britain was obviously worth saving, but the Trust was soon to learn that destroying a 'rare plant' can prove more difficult that conserving it. The water lily has lately been making successful conquests from small beginnings in various parts of South Wales. A few years after creating the Gower reserve the pool was well nigh choked with fringed water lily and the Trust was moving heaven and earth to try and keep it within bounds. Unfortunately there was less heaven than earth and, as one method after another failed, an intrepid band of volunteers waded in with hand tools and made some commendable inroads into the estimated two hundred and thirty tons of lily!

from *Everyman's Nature Reserve* (1972)[116]

Plants and creatures whose fortunes and preferences are less singular are usually best supported as part of the habitat they belong to. There are reserves in west Lancashire and Norfolk, for instance, in which natterjack toads are the star residents. But in both places they (and a good deal else) are conserved by maintaining the character of the whole habitat (in these cases dune systems). The majority of small sanctuaries are like this, a few acres of relict countryside, containing one or two particularly interesting or attractive inhabitants or patches of the kind of traditional, semi-natural habitats that we explored in Part Two. There are reserves based on coppices, canals, flooded gravel-pits, abandoned railway cuttings and watercress beds, roadside verges, steep downland banks and sometimes whole estates and farms. If there is an air of fortuitousness about this list (and occasionally about the reserves themselves) it is because the majority of them are owned or leased by voluntary bodies – particularly the Nature Conservation Trusts – whose income is largely restricted to donations and subscriptions from their members. With their limited finances, Trusts cannot always exercise a great deal of choice about what they acquire, and they often have to rely on land offered to them as gifts or which comes on the market at a price they can afford. A survey by the Society for the Promotion of Nature Conservation in 1977 established that some 50 per cent of Trust reserves were acquired 'passively' in this way.[117] Fortunately a low market price is usually an indication that land is agriculturally marginal, and so likely to possess a good deal of natural interest already. Even if it does not, acquiring reserve status immediately gives it more natural *potential* than most stretches of modern countryside. Yet the decision whether or not to take on responsibility for these 'opportunist' sites is a difficult one for a voluntary body. It has to balance the desirability of retaining resources for the possible purchase of more promising sites in the future with that of using them to protect sites which are certainly and immediately available. The RSPB's view of this dilemma is that 'Conservation bodies cannot possibly hope to acquire, as formal nature reserves, more than a token of the national land-mass so it is important to ensure that what they do select, purchase or lease and manage has the highest possible interest.'[118] Although only five County Trusts have reserve management programmes at the time of writing, there is a definite move in favour of them. The Brecknock Naturalists' Trust, for instance, drew up in 1968 a list of 110 sites representative of thirty different kinds of habitat in the county, and has based its reserve programme on the acquisition of as many of these sites as it can. By 1978 it had succeeded in designating thirteen of them as reserves.

But I believe there may be dangers in following preconceived acquisition programmes too rigidly. Some Trusts are already talking of disposing of reserves which are currently of no particular interest; and I have heard of others declining free offers of land because they feel they lack the resources to manage it. Yet land does not have to be actively managed to work as a reserve; there is always the alternative of simply leaving it alone.

The first and most important act of conservation management on any reserve is its *establishment* and the removal of insecurity and instability that this implies. Whether it is a twentieth-century slag-heap or a medieval coppice, its conservation prospects are a good deal rosier under a regime of assured neglect than under constant attention in the wrong hands.

The potentials of 'minimal management' are, as we have seen, clearest in urban and industrial areas, where the results of natural colonization and succession are often that much more exciting for developing from such unpromisingly barren beginnings. Eighty acres (thirty hectares) of the old Royal Arsenal at Woolwich, now an improbable wilderness of scrub-woodland, overgrown canals and crumbling ammunition silos, has been set aside as a nature reserve for Thamesmead. The Central Electricity Generating Board has created a number of educational reserves in the large areas of buffer-land that surround its power stations, for example at Hams Hall in the West Midlands.

Although the natural colonization of reserved sites can be a fascinating process in its own right, it is usually subject to some degree of human control, designed to speed its progress in some places and hold it back in others. Ponds are dug and trees planted. Some of the scrub may be cleared to encourage open grassland communities. Nest-boxes are built for birds and hides for humans. Except where the character of a site points unequivocally towards the maintenance of a single, scarce community – chalk downland, for instance – the aim of management on most sanctuaries is to increase the diversity of habitats, often to a degree that could never have existed 'naturally' on the site.

Specific human needs – for knowledge, inspiration, even pure entertainment – are frequently considered alongside those of wildlife. Steep Holm Island in the Bristol Channel, purchased by the Kenneth Allsop Memorial Trust in 1976, is actually advertised as 'an island nature reserve with unusual plants and a place for humans'.[119] One of the reasons for choosing this site as a memorial was precisely the challenge presented by its legacy of centuries of military dereliction. Its principal 'unusual plant' (and one of the reasons for the island's 'scientific interest') also has human connections. In Steep Holm's equable island climate, a small naturalized colony of the Mediterranean wild peony – the only one in Britain – has persisted since it was introduced as a medicinal herb by monks in the thirteenth century.

I suggested earlier that the idea of sanctuary is a very old one. Yet it begins to look as if *nature* sanctuaries are a rather special variation on this theme, and I think it is important that we understand what we are up to when we create them. The collection of ancient habitats they have preserved (and the quite new refuges created in them) are valuable remnants of a once much richer landscape and a contribution to the whole network of wildlife in these islands. But with the reserved estate of all the County Trusts, for instance, amounting to less than 40,000 hectares (99,000 acres), it would be wrong to over-estimate this contribution. I have a feeling that we are trying to do something more than conserve wildlife when we gather together to create sanctuaries. I have often wondered what a Third World anthropologist would make of it all – the planning, the fund-raising, the planting and building, the digging of ponds, the erecting of nest-barrels, the officiation by wardens, the following of ritual trails, the public gatherings and the private vigils. It would be hard not to see something sacramental in it, a kind of temple-building (albeit to some very fleshly and familiar spirits). We make these sanctuaries as acts of celebration and charitableness, and in that sense the gesture of creating them is as important as their effectiveness. We are preserving something in ourselves as much as in the outside world. Yet they are also paramountly places for reaching out and making *contact* with wildlife. In all these senses the business of conservation as practised in nature sanctuaries is more complicated than conserving natural features as an aspect of other activities on the land. It is a land-use in its own right, and its landscapes have a functional identity as specific as a golf-course or an airport – or a church.

'LIVING MUSEUMS'

Behind the idea of reservation there is also the desire to maintain *specific* sites which have a special significance because of their history and natural characteristics. There is no clear dividing line between these and more opportunist 'sanctuaries' of course. Many of the latter (like the National Trust's properties at Selborne) are unique national treasures; and all deliberately established reserves have some of the characteristics that I have suggested are distinctive of sanctuaries. Yet there is plainly a range of natural sites in Britain which have a different kind of status. They have, if you like, the quality of eminence. They have a long history of human interest and affection and often possess special and uncommon attributes. Many are very large, to the extent that, like the Lakes, they determine the character of whole regions.

When the idea of a national conservation strategy began to be seriously explored in the latter years of the Second World War, the preservation of these exceptional sites was regarded as the major priority. In the historic White Paper, *Conservation of Nature in England and Wales* (Cmd 7122, 1947), the Wild Life Conservation Special Committee compared site conservation to the activities of museums:

In the national museums the State has long recognised its responsibility for the collection and preservation of objects of artistic, scientific and cultural value. It has more recently recognised (and interpreted broadly) its responsibility for the protection, acquisition and custody of ancient monuments of historic and prehistoric importance. There is but a narrow gap between these and the reserves, which are both ancient monuments and living museums – a living embodiment of the past history of the land.[120]

The reasons why these special sites should be conserved were aesthetic, scientific, recreational and educational; but the principles on which they were to be selected would be largely dependent on their intrinsic biological interest and exceptionality. They would eventually form a series of National Nature Reserves, whose principal purposes, as suggested in Cmd 7122, would be:

. . . to preserve and maintain as part of the nation's natural heritage places which can be regarded as reservoirs for the main types of community and kinds of plants and animals represented in this country, both common and rare, typical and unusual, as well as places which contain physical features of special or outstanding interest. These places must be chosen so far as possible to enable comparisons to be made between primitive or relatively undisturbed communities and the modifications introduced by varying degrees of human interference; typical and atypical physical conditions; distinctive characteristics imposed on communities and species by differences in geographical position, physiography, climate, geology and soil, both within the main physical regions and in the transitional zones between them; the behaviour of species of communities living within and at the margins of their geographical distribution or their ecological tolerance. . . . Considered as a single system, the reserves should comprise as large a sample as possible of all the many different groups of living organisms, indigenous or established in this country as part of its natural flora and fauna; and within them the serious student, whatever his bent and whether he be professional or amateur, should be able to find a wealth of material and unfailing interest.

This statement, with its broad vision of a national natural heritage, and conversely its more specialized view of the parameters by which this should be selected and ways it was likely to be 'used', has been the single most important influence on the development of nature conservation in Britain. When, as a result of this report, the Nature Conservancy was formed and the National Parks and Access to the Countryside Act was passed in 1949, the establishment of nature reserves to safeguard such a series of specially important sites headed the list of the Conservancy's statutory obligations.[121] By 1973, when the Nature Conservancy Council replaced and took over the executive responsibilities of the previous Nature Conservancy, 135 National Nature Reserves had already been established by purchase, lease or management agreement. By the end of 1979 there were 165, covering 131,850 hectares of land throughout Great Britain.

The process of establishing these reserves has necessarily been somewhat haphazard, since it has to take place within a framework of political and economic constraints. But in the summer of 1977 *A Nature Conservation Review: The Selection of Biological Sites of National Importance to Nature Conservation in Britain* was published; it was, in effect, an argued inventory of the places which would represent a complete national series of 'key sites'.[122] It was the result of ten years' intensive field survey work and theoretical analysis under the guidance of the NCC's Chief Scientist, Derek Ratcliffe, and by any standards is a remarkable and inspiring document. Volume 2, which lists and describes the 735 selected sites, has been described without exaggeration as a 'Domesday Book of Britain's natural heritage'. It is a catalogue of such immense natural riches, and such seemingly inexhaustible variety, that it makes its case by sheer weight of evidence.

It would be irresponsible to try to summarize such a body of argument and example here. But its objectives and the principles which underpin them are really comparatively simple, and follow closely the guidelines set down in the 1947 White Paper. Under the six broad headings of coastlands, woodlands, lowland grasslands (with heath and scrub), open water, peatlands and uplands, the *Review* attempts to single out the best examples of the various kinds of community that occur in these formations. It recognizes that value judgements are inevitable in such a process and that the selection of key sites must in some way reflect the variety of human interest in the natural world as well as the variety of natural life itself. Consequently, the criteria for site selection – though closely argued and consistently applied – have an element of subjectivity about them. In essence they represent points where features intrinsic to sites 'meet' particular human interests and so become measures of quality:

As an example, *diversity* can be measured as an attribute, and as such has a neutral value; but because high diversity usually has more interest to biologists than low diversity, the actual value measured can be used as an index of quality in this respect.

Clearly a very large number of attributes have this dual quality. Broadly speaking, the ones used to measure priority in *A Nature Conservation Review* are: *size* – either of the site itself, or of the number of species of communities it contains, or of the populations of individual species; *fragility* – a reflection of how sensitive the habitat is to change (whether this is the result of an intrinsic instability or external pressures) and therefore of the degree of management and protection it needs if it is to be maintained in a desired state; *rarity* – which in this context chiefly relates to nationally scarce communities, habitats and groups of species (the presence of individual rare species being generally regarded as a bonus on sites selected for other reasons), and to the habitats of species at the limits of their climatic or geographical range; *typicality* – which sounds a self-contradictory criterion for choosing a special site, but really means a particularly good example of a classic regional 'type'.

The list of sites in Volume 2 includes, for instance, large areas such as the Cairngorms, the New Forest woods and heaths, and almost the entire twenty-five mile (forty-kilometre) complex of saltmarsh, shingle and sand-dunes that stretches along the north Norfolk coast between Holme and Salthouse. All these areas – though internally very diverse – have a long history of management and use as single units, and are composed of a collection of interdependent communities which are constantly shifting their mutual boundaries. Some river systems, including the Hampshire Avon and the Tweed, are also listed *in toto*, since it is impossible to conserve one part in isolation from the rest.

Other aquatic habitats on the list demonstrate the criterion of fragility, for instance several Scottish lochs which include unique geological features and whose plant and animal communities are particularly vulnerable to water pollution. Sensitivities of other kinds are partly behind the inclusion of 200 ancient woods and a number of limestone pavements in the north-west of England which are fragile in the very literal sense that many of them are being physically broken up to provide material for garden rockeries.

There are a handful of sites which are virtually 'one-offs'; for instance, a humid boxwood with naturally regenerating walnuts deep in the heart of Chequers; a tidal wood in the Fal estuary in Cornwall, where, at the March equinox, the sea creeps up amongst an incongruous mixture of saltmarsh, alder carr, oak trees and spring flowers; and at the other end of Britain, at Cape Wrath in Sutherland, a sand-dune system blown on to the *top* of a cliff. And then there are those 'typical' examples of, for instance, Chiltern beechwoods at Bradenham and seabird islands in the Shetlands.

Although you will hear quibbles about the merits of this or that site, there is no doubt that this inventory comes close to being a complete list of the prime sites of natural interest (and, incidentally, of beauty) in Britain. What we must now examine, then, is what *A Nature Conservation Review* is *not*.

SPECIAL SITES AND SPECIALIZED INTERESTS

To begin with, the *Review* is not a list of sites which, because of their exceptional natural interest, need to be 'reserved' in the sense of having their economic usefulness frozen. Though it would hardly make a serious dent in the economy of the country if it were: together the 735 sites cover about 2,300,000 acres (950,000 hectares), less than 4 per cent of the land surface of

Britain. Perhaps 70 per cent of this is uncultivated upland grazing or inter-tidal coastland, and a further 20 per cent may be of negligible agricultural value. In the majority of cases their natural interest will be best preserved if they continue to be farmed (and by that I mean the taking from them of some kind of harvest, be it wood, reed or grass) in traditional ways. If this was not the case, they would in all probability not have survived to be included in the *Review*.

Nor is it intended to be an exclusive list, an account of the *only* sites that are important. In this respect 4 per cent is clearly nothing like enough land to guarantee either the survival of our wildlife heritage or its 'availability' to the public.

But it does provide a list of the sites that would, in ideal circumstances, form the backbone of a complete series of National Nature Reserves. It is important that we understand the meaning of the word 'reserve' in this context, for it is more specific and specialized than the sense in which we have been using it so far in this chapter. The general purposes of a national series of reserves was, as we have seen, outlined at length in Cmd 7122 (page 218). In section 15 of the 1949 Act they were more precisely defined:

. . . the expression 'nature reserve' means land managed for the purpose –
(a) of providing, under suitable conditions and control, special opportunities for the study of, and research into, matters relating to the fauna and flora of Great Britain and the physical conditions in which they live, and for the study of geological and physiographical features of special interest in the area, or
(b) of preserving flora, fauna or geological or physiographical features of special interest in the area,
or for both those purposes.

Section 16 (1) of the same Act (as amended by the Nature Conservancy Council Act of 1973), empowers the NCC to enter into an agreement with every owner, lessee and occupier of any land, if it is land as to which it appears to the Council 'expedient in the national interest that it should be managed as a nature reserve, for securing that it shall be so managed'.[123]

There are two significant emphases in these enactments. First, the function of these reserves, and the criteria by which they are selected, are principally scientific ones. Secondly, reserves can be established by agreements about the *management* of land as much as by purchase, physical isolation and other territorial acts of reservation.

The same emphases appear in the provision for management agreements over Sites of Special Scientific Interest (SSSI), in section 15 of the Countryside Act 1968 (as amended in 1973).[124]

The NCC thus has a clear remit to base its site protection policy on what are principally scientific grounds. This is entirely acceptable, as these are often simply more precise expressions of qualities like antiquity and variety which we all value places for. And most of the sites themselves are 'popular' ones. Few people – whatever their point of view – would question the importance of places like the New Forest or Loch Lomond or the mountains of Snowdonia, or the priority which should be given to *irreplaceable* sites. But even if we restrict ourselves to these we are talking in terms of literally hundreds of thousands of places, beyond anything that could be taken care of by site protection as we understand it at present. Is there really an unshakable set of principles by which we can say one is more important than another? Scientifically, of course, there is. Inside agreed criteria, sites can be chosen which are the best examples of a habitat type. But what about those places which are not such good examples, or whose interest may lie outside the agreed criteria? You would think it was the business of the voluntary bodies to speak up for these, but increasingly (admittedly partly because of a lack of resources) they are behaving as if they were scientific research bodies, and are declining to consider, say, a particular woodland as a reserve because 'we already have such a community represented amongst our holdings'.

I think it is worth examining more closely that notion of 'special scientific interest' that underlies so many of these judgements. It would be pedantic to insist that, as it stands, the phrase is self-contradictory. (Science is a value-free, objective activity, so, strictly, one thing cannot be said to be more *scientifically* interesting than another.) The phrase is convenient shorthand for 'of particular interest to a special kind of scientist'. Interest is a function of the observer, not the object. So what *exactly* do we mean when we give higher status to the New Forest than to an ancient village spinney? We mean it is unique, certainly; that it is 'non-re-creatable' (but then so is the local copse); and that it is the finest example of a type of woodland defined by exact, but limited, criteria. It does not mean that the

Forest is an *intrinsically* more important piece of the world than the copse. By another set of criteria (those of the villagers for instance) the copse may be just as important. It all depends, in more than one sense, on your point of view.

That site protection inevitably involves the adoption of one value system or another seems to me its one drawback as a contribution to nature conservation. It obliges us to choose not just between sites, but between ways of *looking* at sites, which are based, in turn, on whole ideologies about the human value of the natural world. As we have seen, too many questions are begged, too much of value excluded, when these kinds of choice have to be made. As we go down the chain, from national to local, from objective description to personal meaning, from individual hedge to individual tree, so scientific criteria become less satisfactory as ways of assessing the value of places, and the formal procedures of site protection less practical as a way of conserving them. When we come down to a favourite old pollard willow, blown over in a stream, colonized for a few years by an improbable collection of birds and plants, and finally washed away, it would be an affront to its character to try to assess it purely in scientific terms, and absurd to think of it as a 'site'. Its short-lived fascination could only be secured inside a set of principles for managing the wider countryside which had room to consider the small place and the personal meaning.

Since we now recognize that these are the foundations on which a socially relevant conservation policy must be based, it seems to me regrettable that the 1949 Act implemented such a narrow range of the remarkably far-sighted recommendations of the various committees considering conservation at the end of the Second World War and reinforced the dichotomy between 'natural beauty' and 'scientific interest'. But there were understandable historical reasons. Science was enjoying a period of high prestige. The proposed system of National Parks, it was hoped, would protect considerable areas of scenically attractive countryside outside the nature reserves. And it was widely believed that the countryside as a whole would soon start to recover from the intensive cultivation of the war years. The Vice-Chairman of the Wild Life Conservation Special Committee himself (Professor, later Sir, Arthur Tansley) had written in 1945: 'It is scarcely probable that the extension of agriculture will go much further, for the limits of profitable agricultural land must have been reached in most places.' Tansley's views are of particular interest, since his seminal work *The British Islands and their Vegetation* (1939) was probably the most important influence on contemporary ideas about the classification of natural communities. And in 1949 he became the first Chairman of the Nature Conservancy. In a paper four years later, he pinpointed with great honesty the uneasy – dare I say unnatural – distancing between the 'two cultures' of nature conservation:

As I have already said, the Conservancy lays the greatest stress on the scientific value of nature conservation, in contrast to the 'amenity bodies', though it is difficult, or impossible, to keep the two interests strictly separate. When I am reporting on the merits of a proposed nature reserve, after describing the scientific importance of its flora and fauna, I often find it hard to resist bringing in the scenic beauty of the landscape or the attractiveness of the vegetation, though my allusions to these tend to take on an almost apologetic tone. It is as if I were trying to say, 'And of course the place really is beautiful as well, though perhaps I ought not to mention the fact.'[125]

How one wishes he had been able to drop his 'apologetic tone'! For, although the amenity organizations and the scientific conservation bodies often find themselves defending the same sites, their respective approaches remain as far apart as ever. Between those evasive generalizations of 'scenic beauty' and 'scientific importance' stretches a continuous range of natural qualities which are hard to define in the precise terms of planning designations. And, in an analogous rift, between the statutory Areas of Outstanding Natural Beauty and the scientifically-defined key sites, stretches what remains of the traditional British countryside, being transformed in ways that were not anticipated when the basic premises of a national conservation policy were being laid down. It must, I think, be obvious by now that site protection – especially when it is based on partial and specialized criteria – is neither an adequate nor a very appropriate approach to the conservation of the wider countryside and for meeting the vast range of local and personal interests attached to it. For that we need a quite different kind of approach, not imposed from above but worked out by a continuous process of debate and adjustment between all involved parties (and that means each of us) from the level of the local community up to the international.

3

Conservation and the Community: Towards a Land-Use Policy

That the land is a community is a basic concept of ecology, but that land is to be loved and respected is an extension of ethics. That land yields a cultural harvest is a fact long known, but latterly often forgotten. . . . We abuse the land because we regard it as a commodity belonging to us. When we see the land as a community to which we belong, we may begin to see it with love and respect. . . . A land ethic, then, reflects the existence of an ecological conscience, and this in turn reflects a conviction of individual responsibility for the health of the land. Health is the capacity of the land for self renewal. Conservation is our effort to understand and preserve this capacity.

ALDO LEOPOLD, *A Sand County Almanac* (1949)[126]

It is curious how often the figure of 10 per cent occurs when the amount of land that needs to be given over to nature conservation is discussed. It is, for instance, the rough area that the Forestry Commission is prepared to 'waste' (in the form of unplanted slopes, rides, wild edges and the like) in its plantations.[127] It is the proportion of the surface of Britain that the NCC recommends should be managed with conservation as a primary consideration.[128]

A tenth, or 'tithe', was of course the proportion of land or its produce which, in much of the ancient world, was given up as an offering to ensure the fertility of the soil and later appropriated as an institutionalized religious or political tribute. We could perhaps look on the devotion of land to nature conservation as a modern tithe. Its inspiration is similar, originating in a desire to ensure the continuance of life. And the understandable retort of a landowner who is being asked to give up a part of his productive land for this purpose is often exactly the same as the challenge which finally spelt the end of the corrupt tithe system of the nineteenth century – 'Who says so?'

The most difficult problem in establishing a conservation policy is not so much why we should do it, or which particular pieces of land or styles of management are involved, but *how* these decisions are reached and implemented. Whose interests are legitimately involved, and what kind of political and economic machinery is needed for them to find expression?

This brings us back full circle to the central paradox of planning for 'naturalness'. Nothing seems less appropriate for the protection and maintenance of the complex, sensitive and highly localized natural communities we have been looking at in this book than the ponderous processes of conventional planning. Yet leaving them to the mercy of an unbridled *laissez faire* would be even worse. Land is a strictly finite resource, and there is a good ethical – and, as we have seen, legal – case for arguing that its natural 'produce' is a *common* asset. We have also seen the special relationship which natural communities have with time (see page 43). What happens to them today becomes part of what they are tomorrow. If it is a destructive experience, its effects, in most cases, cannot easily be undone.

At the very least then we need to begin with something like Aldo Leopold's 'land ethic' (above) which reflects these principles and the way that wildlife's fate is inextricably connected with our own. Nature conservation could conceivably be separated out as a restricted, specialized objective inside this larger goal. But this is neither a practicable approach, except over a limited area of land, nor, I believe, a responsible one. As Leopold suggests, the 'health of the land' is ultimately an indicator of the state of man.

Yet the paradox is that the practical expression of a land ethic often requires political muscle of a kind which seems quite alien to the realization of ecologically responsible policies. We would not, for instance, expect much sympathy for conservation from the monolithic structures of the European Economic Community. The EEC's Common Agricultural Policy (CAP), with its declared intention of raising productivity by increased mechanization, the amalgamation of small farm units and the taking into cultivation of marginal lands, combined with its policy of hoarding food products to maintain price levels and its frontal attack on the biological diversity of crop strains, is notorious for being incompatible not simply with the needs of nature conservation but with just about every principle on which a conservative land-use policy would be based.

The one non-governmental body whose views the EEC does officially take note of – the European Environmental Bureau (EEB), a federation of some forty national conservation organizations – has produced a most ambitious and coherent critique of modern European agriculture. In a seminar on CAP in September 1978 it drew up a list of objectives which could be taken as they stand as the foundation of a rural land-use policy. It emphasized two underlying concepts:

The first is the special responsibility of agriculture as the central activity through which the economy of very large areas can be kept alive and healthy. Secondly, expression should be given to agriculture's unique obligation to future generations – its obligation to prefer methods which will conserve the fertility and will respect the natural and cultural heritage of the land rather than those which will gradually impoverish and destroy them. These are questions of future viability, and thus of survival itself.[129]

From these two concepts, it argued out a list of specific, working objectives and urged the EEC to incorporate these into a revised agricultural strategy. They included a careful selection of appropriate uses for every area of land, a reduction in the dependence on non-renewable resources (especially artificial fertilizers) and, conversely, the encouragement of sustained-yield systems and the recycling of organic wastes, and in general the development of varied and stable agricultural ecologies. An integral part of this objective would be the protection and enhancement of the rural environment (including its human communities) and the conservation of wildlife habitats and traditional landscapes – the conservation also, as a matter of urgency, of traditional rural skills and of the endangered gene pool of domesticated plants and animals. Finally, food policy should reflect these aims, seeking a high degree of local self-sufficiency, a reduction in additives and adulterants, and encouraging – for reasons both of health and of economy – a change in our dietary habits away from their current domination by intensively produced animal proteins and fats.

To the extent that some of these goals are matters 'of survival itself' they are beyond argument. Yet many are clearly subjective choices, and contentious ones at that, and it is not surprising that land-use policy in Britain shows little of the coherence of the EEB's manifesto. The irony is that we do have a token national commitment to many of the individual objectives. Since the Countryside Acts of 1967 and 1968, for instance, we have had a succession of enactments, directives and exhortations enjoining all government departments and public bodies to 'have regard to the desirability of conserving the natural beauty and amenity of the countryside'.[130] Yet in practice they have proved to be little more than vague good intentions. Although we now know, quite specifically, which kind of sites need to be protected and which land-management principles must be adopted if wildlife and 'natural beauty and amenity' are to be conserved, public bodies continue to act in apparent ignorance of this knowledge, to the extent of frequently following quite conflicting policies. The Water Authorities, for instance, subsidize drainage schemes on sites which the NCC has identified as needing to be kept wet. The Forestry Commission, in its statement of objectives (see page 66), talks of 'the forester's duty to respect our woodland inheritance' and of 'leaving options for future evolution', yet destroys part of this inheritance and closes off options irrevocably every time it replants an ancient wood with conifers. Even in the relationship between food policy and human health (which the EEB, quite properly, places on its schedule of the considerations which should guide agricultural policy) we have contradictory public policies. The MAFF continues to encourage farmers to increase their output of meat, sugar and dairy products – the very foods which the Health Education Council has urged us to cut down on. (Only in the field of energy, where the day of reckoning suddenly appears disturbingly close, has the need for a co-ordinated approach begun to be taken seriously with the formation, in 1978, of the Commission on Energy and the Environment.)

But it is not altogether surprising that there are such internal contradictions in our approach to land-use, for there are genuine conflicts of opinion and interest involved – most conspicuously between the interests of 'the public' and those of individual farmers and landowners. Yet if government has any kind of role in influencing the way our national land resources are used it must surely be in attempting to resolve these conflicts so that sectional interests do not take precedence over wider, communal interests.

I hope I have established by now that nature conservation is not the specialized interest it sometimes appears to be, but touches on the quality (and perhaps even the continuance) of all our lives. But, in the short term at least, it would be hard to argue that it should have priority over the production of adequate supplies of food. Certainly, if the public were asked to make a straight choice between a deterioration in our natural environment and an increase in food prices, there can be little doubt which way they would vote; and the assumption that this is the choice before us is what largely shapes public policy on land-use. But, as we have already seen, the real choices are nothing like as clear-cut or limited as this. Even inside the current pattern of farming there are areas of compromise where wildlife can be conserved without significant reductions in the output of food. In the planning of future agricultural policy the options are even wider. Although nature conservation choices are strictly limited (there are no alternative ways of 'growing' ancient woods or river systems – we can only maintain those we have at present) there are any number of ways in which our food could be produced. Professor Wibberley of Wye College, for example, has predicted that, by increasingly intensive and efficient use of high-quality land, we could by the year 2000 release 3 to 4 million acres of agricultural land for other purposes and still become self-sufficient in temperate foodstuffs.[131] Professor Watkin Williams, head of the Department of Agricultural Botany at Reading University, has produced a scenario which exposes the effects that arise from livestock holding a sacrosanct status in the mythology of modern western agriculture.[132] We currently feed *two-thirds* of our home-grown cereals to animals, which not only makes animals competitors with humans for food but destroys their traditionally efficient role in the agricultural cycle – that of 'holding' grain surpluses during the winter, manuring arable fields, etc. Professor Williams has estimated that, if we were to produce the 1 million tonnes of protein that we need to be self-sufficient directly from vegetable crops (particularly protein-rich leguminous plants) we would need no more than 10 million acres (4 million hectares) of land, and 36 million acres (14 million hectares) which are currently in agricultural use would become surplus to requirements. Then there is the even more heretical proposal of Richard Fordham, of the Department of Land Economy at Cambridge University, who has produced a model for a kind of suburban multiple-use of agricultural land, in which low-density development (based on a combination of dwellings with large productive gardens and pockets of amenity parkland) would be encouraged in areas that are currently devoted to high-intensity agriculture.[133]

Beyond these are more strictly technological possibilities: single-cell protein synthesis, the harvesting of a much wider range of sea foods and, above all, a concentration on increasing output by the breeding of high-yield and disease-resistant crop strains rather than by the use of artificial fertilizers and pesticides.

I am not suggesting that any one of these approaches is either preferable or acceptable as an alternative to our current food policy. Each one would have a different impact on our landscapes and wildlife, and would demand a drastic reorientation of the ways of life of those who live on the land. But they clearly *are* alternatives and, in contrast to the policies we currently follow, are in almost complete agreement on two fundamental points. First, they put a high premium on the other needs we have of our land. Secondly, they suggest that the harmonization of these needs with the development of a comparatively self-sufficient agriculture can be best achieved by a *reduction* of farming pressures – either by a more intensive use of less land or by change in the cropping patterns on the land currently under cultivation.

Our national food policy, as outlined in the two recent White Papers *Food from our own resources* (1975) and *Farming and the nation* (1979), shows neither the social and ecological awareness nor the imagination of these proposals.[134] Its central goal is a movement towards comparative self-sufficiency in temperate foodstuffs (we currently produce about two-thirds at home), which is commendable but hardly adventurous. With the escalating price of fuel likely to make transport and processing costs an ever increasing proportion of food prices, it would be irresponsible for *any* national government (and any region, for that matter) not to aim for local self-sufficiency. But the route the government has chosen to reach this goal (chiefly by encouraging outputs of beef, dairy products and sugar beet) is guided almost exclusively by narrow fiscal and political considerations. The White Papers do not consider the radical options that are open to us as to *how* we produce our own food, and they make only token acknowledgement of the impact the implementation of their proposals might have on all the other functions of the land.

In effect then we *do* have a land-use policy, formed out of the interplay of the Common Agricultural Policy and the White Papers mentioned above, but one which ignores almost all considerations save the interests of the farming profession and the fickle and often short-lived pressures of international trade. Its implications, on the other hand, involve the long-term future of the whole landscape and the interests of the whole community.

PLANNING OR PERSUASION?

A more broadly-based land-use policy would *not* imply a system of heavy-handed and detailed centralized planning, but a statement of the principles and priorities which we need to take account of if we are to make the best use of our limited resources. This would provide a framework inside which the needs of different land-users could be harmonized. But it would still beg the question of how much this 'harmonization' would have to be backed up by legislation and statutory planning controls – a question which we have in any case to answer with our current piecemeal approach to land-use.

There is a widespread feeling amongst most individuals and organizations involved in the day-to-day management of the countryside against any extension of statutory planning control to cover the fine details of land management. The Countryside Review Committee, for instance, (a forum for various government departments and agencies with an interest in and impact on the countryside) has expressed the view that:

a wholesale extension of the apparatus of development control would be unlikely to make any worthwhile contribution to the changing situation; and would in any case be administratively impractical.
Even the introduction of more limited new controls, covering the more sensitive changes such as hedge-removal, new fencing, or the ploughing up of footpaths, would be counter-productive. They would be costly; and there would be serious difficulties of definition and enforcement. Even more basic, such controls could well institutionalise the conflicts which they aimed to solve – and, essentially, would prove divisive. To avoid this the Committee believes there is a need for a consensus approach – seeking progress through the active co-operation of those directly concerned, whether landowners or local authorities, companies or rural communities. This means working with administrative, exploratory techniques – capable of sensitive and speedy readjustment in the light of changing circumstances . . . .[135]

The NCC acts in ways that suggest it is in broad agreement

with this view. Where it cannot purchase land, for instance, it prefers to use the various kinds of management agreement it is authorized to make with landowners, rather than seek stronger legislative powers.

This seems an eminently sensible way of approaching the problems of rural land-use. Yet it contrasts very strikingly with the more stringent controls which are exercised over urban and industrial development, and I think that we need to ask whether the preference for informal techniques which we, as the 'consuming' public, are being asked to accept is purely a matter of practicality or the expression of some more fundamental principle.

We should remember, at the outset, that there are already a number of statutory measures which broadly support nature conservation goals. Local authorities can impose Tree Preservation Orders, for instance, on whole groups of trees as well as individual specimens, so that they act as instruments of *woodland* conservation. (Ham Street Woods were saved initially by a Tree Preservation Order before they could be established as a National Nature Reserve.) They can also make Orders giving the public right of access over certain types of open country, which can have the effect of restricting drastic changes in the way it is managed. The NCC has the right to make Compulsory Purchase Orders for sites of outstanding importance, where these are under threat and where other means of safeguard have proved impossible. In fact the NCC has only ever used this power in two instances (both of which resulted from difficulties in tracing the owners of sites). But it was almost used again in 1979 over part of the Ribble Estuary, a case which demonstrated that it may be important to have a framework of legislative 'fail-safes' even when a 'consensus approach' is being followed.

The 5500 acres (2200 hectares) of saltmarsh and mudflats which form the heart of the Ribble Estuary are regarded as one of the most important sites in Europe for passage and wintering wading birds and wildfowl, and in addition support a nationally important breeding bird community. In 1978 this area was purchased by a private landowner who planned to drain it and convert the land to agricultural use. The NCC and other bodies fisrt attempted to acquire by ordinary negotiation. But the owner was unwilling to sell at this stage, and in January 1979 the NCC initiated its compulsory purchase procedure. Shortly afterwards the owner agreed to sell voluntarily, for a figure of £1.75 million. Contracts were exchanged by March of that year and the area has now been designated a National Nature Reserve. The NCC was understandably pleased that in the end it was able to secure the site by agreement. But it might not have been able to do so without the 'iron fist' of compulsory purchase in the background. Even with a land-use policy (under which, for instance, MAFF might be prevented from giving grants for drainage on sites of recognized conservation importance) it would still not be possible to restrain unco-operative landowners unless there were some ultimate resort to statutory control.

Yet the bulk of statutory controls which affect rural land-use are not concerned with changes of this kind, but only with those which *convert* countryside (farmed or otherwise) into urban or industrial land. The notification of Sites of Special Scientific Interest, for example, merely ensures that no permission is given to develop a site without the relevant planning authority considering the effect of the proposed development on its conservation importance. Permission does not even have to be *sought* for the kind of routine forestry and agricultural 'developments' that are responsible for most of the current destruction of our wildlife. Recent surveys by the NCC suggest that approximately 4 per cent of all scheduled sites are severely damaged each year, and in the majority of cases this is not a result of permission being given for conventional development but of changes in husbandry that are inimical to conservation.

Could a refined consensus approach really prevent this kind of erosion? Or is it in the public interest, despite the opposition of vested interests, vital to extend the apparatus of planning control to cover changes in agricultural and forestry practice? This is in many ways the heart of the problem, for in SSSIs we can see, in concentrated form, the conflict of interests which is occurring over the whole countryside. Most of them are privately owned areas of productive land. They are, by definition, of great interest to biological or geological scientists. And they are also part of the wider network of natural life in which we all have an interest.

The arguments in favour of extended development controls are clearest in the case of threatened, irreplaceable sites of national importance (like the Ribble Estuary) which need prompt and decisive protection of the kind that can only really be guaranteed by governmental agencies. With public spending now a contentious political issue, it is unlikely that the sums of money needed for outright purchase will be so readily available in future, in which case the only reliable safeguard may be a form of statutory control on changes in agricultural or forestry practice.

It is also hard to see what *essential* difference there is between, say, planting up a stretch of heathland with conifers and building a small factory on it, or for that matter between felling an ancient wood and demolishing a listed historic building. In each case irreparable changes are being made to the landscape, and interests far beyond those of the landowner are being threatened. And, although planning controls obviously do put restrictions on a potential developer's economic growth (and were also strongly opposed when they were first introduced), we could scarcely imagine living now without a measure of public control over the construction and destruction of buildings.

Ancient woods seem to me an instance where statutory planning controls could usefully be extended without greatly adding to the bureaucratic machinery or seriously restricting landowners' interests. Old woods are such fundamentally important features of the landscape and of such great natural and historical importance that there is a good case for treating them in exactly the same way as listed buildings (which cannot be demolished without the approval of the planning authority or, in the case of an appeal, the minister). It would not be difficult to draw up such a list. Most sizeable ancient woodlands are now known as a result of regional NCC surveys and, though they have never been totalled, I very much doubt if they would number more than 50,000 – as against the quarter of a million scheduled historic buildings. Such a scheduling would not imply that the wood would cease to have a commercial role but would simply ensure that it was not destroyed or coniferized.

Alternatively, the Forestry Commission (which, by the early 1980s, will have completed its own full survey of British woodlands) could honour its pledge to 'respect our woodland inheritance' by attaching much stricter conditions to the granting of felling licences. At present, a woodland owner is free to fell small trees and underwood as he wishes, and in addition up to 825 cubic feet (twenty-three cubic metres) of timber per three months for use on his own property (or much larger quantities if he has entered into a Dedication Scheme with the Commission and manages his woodland in accordance with an agreed Plan of Operations).[136] In most other circumstances he must obtain a felling licence. This is normally given as a matter of course once the wood has been inspected, though the Commission is empowered to impose replanting conditions. In the case of recognized ancient woods the Commission might apply these powers more rigorously and only grant a licence for felling timber if it was assured that the *wood* was not also to be cleared, and that subsequent management would follow at least some of the conservative principles we discussed in Part Two, Chapter 1.

Yet as soon as we begin to explore an area of potential legislation in detail like this, it becomes very clear what the differences are between 'urbanized' development and changes in husbandry practice. The very worst that can happen to a semi-natural habitat – its outright destruction – is very similar to the once-and-for-all changes that are involved in building or demolition. Yet, as conservationists, what we are looking for is usually more than just the avoidance of this final, irreversible act. We are looking for a *long-term commitment* to specific and often quite complex systems of management. We could hardly impose a coppice rotation on a wood by statutory planning controls, or legislate against the effects of windfall and disease in an ancient deer park.

It goes against the grain to think of intruding in the business of landowners and managers at this level. Even if we regard the land and its natural produce as a communal asset we must also consider the rights of individuals to work on it with some degree of personal freedom; and, even if it were practicable (which it is not), to direct landowners about what trees to promote in their hedgerows or how frequently to clear their ditches, this would entail crossing that invisible line between social accountability and institutional bullying. Men who work on the land for their livelihood have, I think, a relationship with their basic resource that is qualitatively different from that of other kinds of producers. It is an intimate, risky affiliation, at the mercy of factors which no agricultural technology can control, and often earning small and precarious financial rewards. At present, most small farmers may only be able to scrape a living by continuing to improve the productive capacity of their land, and, if we are to ask them to hold back for the good of the community, we must at the very least be prepared to make sure that they do not suffer financially. Yet financial incentives alone may not be enough. A farmer's relationship with the land is also backed by the profoundly ancient tradition of 'good husbandry'. He is committed, by what he is, to producing the best crops in the most skilful way he can. It reaches very deep, this law of the land, and most farmers find a weedless field full of fine wheat as aesthetically pleasing as a naturalist does a show of poppies in the corn.

For this reason I think that the idea of *compensation*, with its implicit suggestion that something is not being done which ought to be done, is too negative, and likely to be psychologically counter-productive in the long run. I believe that instead we should present the financial incentives to conservation as *rewards* and promote the idea that wildlife is itself a vital crop: that, far from being an abandonment of good husbandry, nature conservation also requires a great understanding of the land, and that combining it with the production of food or other material crops is the greatest challenge of all to a farmer's skills. Objectives of this kind could never be achieved by remote planning bodies or statutory controls. They require a more intimate and flexible relationship between all parties with an interest in the land, and a continuous and sympathetic exchange of ideas. It is, again, an *organic* approach, of the kind that Felix Paturi labelled – ironically, from this viewpoint – 'development' (see page 123).

LOCAL INITIATIVES

At the risk of over-simplifying what we are now beginning to see as a complex problem in social expectations and relationships, perhaps we could summarize what might be the minimum requirements of such an approach. It requires, first of all, *information*. Many landowners are simply not aware of the features of conservation importance on their property, or why and how these need to be maintained. It requires working *examples* of the way that conservation, forestry, agriculture and recreation can co-exist. It requires *finance*, to be given to landowners to fund constructive conservation and therefore needing to be generated somewhere in the economic system. And it needs an *organization* through which these various items can be discussed and transacted. The Strutt report, *Agriculture and the Countryside* (1978), possibly the most imaginative and positive official document on rural land-use to appear in recent years, suggests that the solution may lie in a network of locally-based consultative groups (backed perhaps by an inter-departmental body at national level).[137] These would involve representatives of all interested parties, including MAFF, the NCC, the National Farmers' Union, the Countryside Commission, the Forestry Commission, the tourist boards and, most important of all, the general public. Strutt recommends that the democratically-elected local authorities are in the best position to take the lead in organizing these regular local forums.

In fact there are already a number of schemes in existence at local authority level which could provide us with models. The Chilterns Standing Conference, for example, (formed to suggest general principles for the administration of the Chilterns AONB) was set up by Bedfordshire, Buckinghamshire, Hertfordshire and Oxfordshire County Councils, and includes representatives of most of the bodies listed above. Its policy statement, *A Plan for the Chilterns*, is not statutory, but is being followed by the bodies that helped draw it up and takes a very positive line on nature conservation.[138] It rates the land inside the AONB according to three categories. The first covers SSSIs and other sites of outstanding importance. The second, which covers almost half the AONB's 309 square miles (800 square kilometres), is concerned with larger 'zones' where conservation is not the primary land-use but which are still rich in natural interest and which should be managed in ways that take full account of this. In the third category, other interests, particularly farming, are pre-eminent, though the Conference expresses the hope that even here, 'wherever possible, provision should be made for wildlife conservation'. The plan also shows an encouraging sensitivity towards the need to conserve what is probably the outstanding natural feature of the Chilterns – the mantle of beechwoods that covers much of their central and southern reaches. Although the means the Conference suggests are biased towards forestry interests (and, drawn up in 1971, do not really recognize the ecological importance of natural regeneration), it is fully committed (with the support of the Forestry Commission) to the maintenance of a widespread beech 'presence' in the area.

In Hertfordshire we can see some of the ways in which these kind of suggestions are implemented at a local level. The County Council, for instance, has established a network of countryside managers, who liaise with the landowners in their territory on such matters as tree-planting, pond-digging and the management of woods and hedgerows. It also employs a number of ecologists, one of whom is investigating the economic possibilities of reviving coppice woodland management locally, and another the impact of the county's rapidly increasing population of horses on the survival and character of its permanent pastures.

Tree-planting has been a major activity with many local authorities. In Norfolk the County Council has followed up its survey of farmland trees (see page 127) with an impressive programme of replanting. In some cases it has financed this out of its own budget, but it has been principally concerned to help landowners make best use of the grants available for small-scale plantings from the Countryside Commission and the Forestry Commission.[139,140] In the first four years of the project, some 80,000 trees were planted annually in the county's agricultural landscape. One repentant prairie farmer in the arable heart of the county was assisted by the Council in planting up his land with more than 2000 specimens of seventeen native species, including an avenue of one of East Anglia's ancestral trees, the small-leaved lime. (The total cost of this scheme, incidentally, was less than £2000 – three-quarters of which was available as grant-aid.)

Essex County Council has also planted out small-leaved limes, particularly on roadsides. A good number of these came – in a pleasant example of across-the-boundaries co-operation – from Groton Wood, an ancient lime-coppice managed by the Suffolk Trust for Nature Conservation. And, in Suffolk itself, the Planning Department has embarked on a project to establish roadside and farmland trees by the promotion of saplings growing in the hedgerows (see page 126). With the assistance of the Countryside Commission and Burralls, the label manufacturer, it has devised a simple 'tree tie' which can be used to mark promising leading shoots in hedges and so help tractor-drivers avoid them when they are trimming hedges mechanically.

The management of waysides, which are already largely the responsibility of the local authorities, is an area very amenable to consultative and co-operative approaches. There are more than 200,000 hectares (500,000 acres) of roadside habitats (including hedges, ditches and scrub) in Britain, of which approximately half were managed as grassland up until 1975.

The preservation of our more colourful field weeds is one of the most intractable of all conservation problems. The scarcer species (like the field cow-wheat illustrated here) are virtually confined to arable farms, precisely where they are least wanted. A few species are being deliberately grown amongst ancient crops in farm museums, and there have been proposals for 'weed reserves' on waste patches in towns and by the sides of motorways. But in the wider countryside their survival depends very largely on the goodwill of farmers who are prepared to tolerate a small degree of inconvenience for the sake of some colour amongst the wheat.

One of the last colonies of field cow-wheat in Essex (in an area of rough grass between two arable fields) was preserved in just such a way, but its eventual extinction vividly demonstrates the difficulties involved in 'weed' conservation. The following account is taken from Stanley Jermyn's Flora of Essex (1974):

'Discovery of this site was purely by chance. In 1966, Miss E. V. Goodchild saw the flowers in a floral arrangement in the Essex Show and eventually their origin was traced back to this farm. The farmer stated that he had known Melampyrum there for at least a quarter of a century and preserved it on account of its beauty. It was later learned that the farm was to be sold and steps were taken to get the new owners to preserve the sites and the plants. In the spring of 1968 I was advised that most of the hedgerows and ditches were to go and the large triangular piece of rough grassland, where the main colony existed, was to be included in the larger field planned. The new owners offered to remove the plants, but being annual, this was not possible. By a careful search over one hundred seeds were found, and these, with soil from the site were transferred elsewhere. Despite these efforts the seeds did not germinate.'

The illustration, by Kenneth J. Adams, was drawn from field cow-wheat growing in another Essex site.

(Above) *Viper's-bugloss at Beckton gasworks, east London. These striking flowers have arrived here entirely of their own accord yet are growing in a virtually soil-less mixture of ash and tar. Urban wildlife is necessarily very resilient, and the most exciting sites in built-up areas are often those that have been left to develop naturally (see page 177).*

(Below) *By contrast, many purely natural communities, such as sand-dunes, are very fragile and need to be protected from erosion. Ynyslas Dunes, part of Dyfi NNR in central Wales, are a popular tourist area, but direct damage to the dune system has been avoided (and public access preserved) by a system of raised wooden walks (see page 175).*

(Above) *The village pond, often at the heart of the community and, properly taken care of, a haven for water-plants and animals, and a source of food and water for parish birds (see page 248).*

(Below) *Elms are vanishing from the rural landscape. Yet there are trees like the scarce native black poplar (a favourite of Constable's) which could make excellent replacements.*

Many of these verges have not been subject to the regular cultivation and chemical dressing that is now routine on agricultural leys, and cumulatively they represent a vital reserve for grassland plants and animals. But in 1975 the Department of the Environment advised local authorities to cut back on their roadside mowing programmes in order to save money, and the area of scrub and rank herbage has consequently increased considerably at the expense of grassland. This may be no bad thing in some places, as there was, prior to 1975, a tendency to over-manage verges. (Some were cut like lawns, half a dozen times a year.) But the pendulum may now have swung rather too far in the opposite direction, and in many places the dense unchecked growth is not only crowding out many traditional roadside herbs but becoming a threat to road safety. For once, the interests of economy and conservation are identical – the maintenance of stable roadside habitats with the minimum of management and expense. Many counties already have a number of roadside nature reserves, stretches of great natural interest that are managed according to programmes agreed by the Nature Conservation Trusts and the local authority's highways department. But what we are seeing now is an opportunity for much more intimate and widespread collaboration. Grassland ecologists and conservationists are well placed to advise local authorities on the most efficient *deployment* of their limited management resources. They can identify those lengths of verge that, because of, say, very attractive vegetation or peculiar soil conditions, are likely to need bespoke management; those that can be maintained as relatively short grassland by means of a single annual cut, and when this should be; and those that can safely be allowed to develop into scrub and be cut on a longer rotation. Michael Way, our leading authority on the conservation of roadside verges, hopes that it will not be long before all highways authorities have maps with their road verges graded in this way.[141]

In almost all the examples above we have seen a need for what we might call conservation impresarios – people who are in a position to act as advisers, agents, go-betweens, entrepreneurs;

Churchyards – a final resting place for many field-flowers and lichens, too.
Wylye, Wiltshire (see page 248).

who can spot ancient hedges, track down the cheapest contractors for digging ponds and put the farmer with a redundant ancient meadow in touch with the racehorse owner who has a penchant for herb-rich hay. Some such people are already employed by the more forward-looking local authorities. In a few selected experimental areas the Countryside Commission has also appointed project officers with a brief to play very much this kind of role. In others, working conservationists have taken the responsibility on their own initiative. In East Anglia, for instance, representatives of the NCC and the County Trusts have played a major role in reviving ancient coppice woodland. In Essex and Suffolk, by the middle of 1978, there were more than fifty woods being coppiced on a commercial basis. That the figure continues to rise has a good deal to do with the enterprise of the NCC's Deputy Regional Officer for Essex, Colin Ranson, who has produced guides (available to any interested woodland owner) on the management of coppices and on currently available markets. These make up a formidable and expanding list, covering furniture-makers, garden centres, sports goods manufacturers, pulpwood factories, and even River Authorities (who purchase bound faggots for shoring up river banks).

THE ALTERNATIVE RURAL ECONOMY

Nature conservation is at last discovering ways of becoming self-financing – or at least finding a modern economic relevance for traditional activities. There are an increasing number of examples of this, even on nature reserves. The RSPB has earned a very good income from the sale of gravel from pits on its reserve at Dungeness – not excavating it principally for its financial value but to restore the freshwater lagoons which had once been a feature of the shingle system before they were dried out by a drop in the water-table. In a similar operation the NCC has awarded contracts for peat-diggings in parts of Holme Fen National Nature Reserve in order to bring the level of the land *below* that of the water-table – as it was in a traditional fen. The peat is sold for horticultural purposes. And an increasing number of reed-marsh reserves are able to find markets for their cut reed with thatchers and handicraft suppliers, and thus provide an economic foundation for a necessary management practice.

But these commercial spin-offs are not, given present wage levels and land rents, sufficient to pay for the upkeep of reserves by themselves. The balance still has to be found. As for financing the network of rewards and administrative machinery that are needed for conservation in the wider countryside, there is no obvious, direct source of income. In the United States there are moves to generate money for these purposes by imposing excise taxes on such items as bird food, nest-boxes and binoculars. (97 per cent of state and federal wildlife funds are currently spent on game species largely because the hunting lobby is prepared to pay licence fees and special taxes on hunting and fishing gear.) Although some of these new taxes are supported by many American conservation organizations, including the influential National Audubon Society, I very much hope that nothing similar will ever be proposed in this country. Taxing the 'primary consumers' of wildlife, however indirectly, simply reinforces the damaging fallacy that conservation is nothing more than a specialized, minority interest. On the contrary, it is something which underpins the quality of all our lives, even when we are not aware of it, and this seems to me the clearest argument that it should, like hospital care, water supplies and other vital community services, be paid for by public funds. (A rate amounting to the price of a cup of coffee per head would double the NCC's annual grant from the government.)

Yet even if public spending were not the controversial issue that it currently is, there is no reason why every effort should not be made to find ways of making conservation *pay*. The most obvious source of money is countryside recreation, which, as we saw in Part Two, Chapter 3, is rapidly becoming the principle 'use' of our wildlife resources, and one that the public are clearly prepared to pay for, either directly or indirectly. In many of the less fertile areas of Britain recreation is already the most logical and potentially profitable agricultural 'crop', as Nan Fairbrother suggested in *New Lives, New Landscapes* (1970):

This controlled development of the uplands for lowland leisure might end for good the long struggle to live on the inadequate produce of their niggardly soils. . . . Such proposals, however, always bring moral objections about wasting farmland in a hungry world, and here the telling answer is an easy sum I worked out in round figures to help my poor calculation. The agricultural production of the uplands is 4 per cent of our whole. We grow half our food. Our human population is 50 million. Our dog population is estimated at 5 million (without counting an estimated 4 million cats and unknown numbers of horses). If four dogs eat as much as one man then by my reckoning our dogs eat the food production of the uplands (not reckoning the acres of good lowland pasture for horses and the large dairy herds for milk-drinking cats).

We may not relish the uplands as urban playgrounds but while we keep pets we can scarcely be moral about it. This is their logical development in our modern society; it is their true *industrial* use, and where the process is already established it has brought unmistakeable new life.[142]

I find this an unanswerable argument. Yet it is a good deal easier to state than to put into practice. The *fabric* of the traditional upland landscape (which the tourists come to enjoy) still needs to be maintained, and the interests of the 50,000 farmers who currently work its 16 million acres (6.5 million hectares) considered. They are the inheritors of ancient, hard-won skills, and would not take kindly to the prospect of being reduced to car-park attendants and small-time hoteliers. Yet I hope it is clear by now that authentically traditional skills are precisely what are needed if the natural habitats of the countryside are to be maintained. There is also ample room for the development of *progressive* farming skills in the marginal areas without in any way compromising their overriding social role as recreational centres. Upland farmers could, for instance, be encouraged to become involved more extensively with the raising of hardy, low-fat, ancient animal breeds, such as Soay sheep and White Park cattle. Again, the need for sensitive local consultative machinery is vital. Encouraging movements towards this are already under way in Snowdonia and the Lake District. The Upland Management Experiments were set up in 1969 by the Countryside Commission specifically to explore ways of encouraging farmers to improve landscape and recreational opportunities without prejudice to their own activities. At present they are chiefly concerned with advising on such matters as the improvement of footpaths and drystone walls and providing signposts and picnic sites. But with more financial backing from the tourist boards their responsibilities could be extended to cover the conservation of ancient meadows and small woodlands, both of which make such vital contributions to the scenic attractiveness of the areas.

Yet the most powerful initiatives are coming directly from the recreational public themselves who, through the voluntary bodies, is rescuing substantial areas of land from excessively intensive cultivation. We have touched already on the invaluable work of the Nature Conservation Trusts and the RSPB (which by the summer of 1979 had over 300,000 members, and reserve holdings of 80,000 acres (32,000 hectares). The role of the National Trust and National Trust for Scotland may be even more important. They have a combined membership of nearly 700,000 and estates nearing half a million acres (200,000 hectares). Most of their properties are of very high landscape and conservation value – including nearly 400 miles of the coastline of England and Wales – and 140 of them are included in NCR Grade 1 or 2 sites (see page 219).[143] One of the National Trust's properties in the Lake District provides a perfect example of self-financing all-round conservation: upland pastures grazed by a flock of Herdwick sheep that are the direct descendants of Beatrix Potter's own flock, and whose wool is woven into hats and sweaters for sale in the local National Trust shop.

The list grows. There is the Woodland Trust, whose aggressive purchasing strategy enabled it to acquire nearly 1000 acres (400 hectares) of woodland between its formation in 1972 and 1979; the Butser Iron Age Farm, where arable weeds are grown amongst ancient crops, and which is being used as a bulk source of seed for other 'weed reserves'. The potential number of organizations which, because of the interests of their members or financial supporters, could take an interest in the purchase or conservative management of land for recreation is almost limitless: angling clubs, Women's Institutes, breweries (the few on whose properties ancient meadows have been discovered have been immensely co-operative in ensuring their conservation), the Automobile Association (the largest organized voluntary body in the country, which in its annual handbook explicitly states: 'The Association stresses the vital importance of protecting the fabric of the countryside, with its flora and fauna. . . .'), camping and caravan clubs. . . . The private dream of one NCC warden I know is to buy and run a self-financing nature-reserve-cum-camping-site.

'Going to the countryside' is already the single most popular leisure activity in Britain, and it would be hard to over-estimate the scale on which the demand for recreation in natural surroundings is likely to increase in the future. Most forecasters estimate that, by 2000 A.D., 5 million people will be working a considerably contracted working week. And with the micro-electronic revolution likely to produce the emotional and sensory equivalent of old-time physical drudgery, it seems to me highly likely that more and more people will wish to spend their increased leisure in contact with living things. There is an understandable fear in some quarters that this will prove an impossible strain on a natural fabric already stretched to breaking point. But I believe that we should welcome and accommodate this revolution as the best chance we are likely to have this century for a renaissance of rural life, and as providing a role, at last, for a type of landscape that modern farming no longer has much use for. When the fourteenth-century poet William Langland fell asleep on the Malvern Hills (an area of outstanding natural beauty then, as now!) 'In a somer season whan soft was the sonne', he had a vision of the whole nation as 'A faire felde ful of folke . . . Of alle manner of men, the mene and the riche, Worching and wandryng as the world asketh' (*The Vision of Piers Plowman*). A countryside full of people 'worching and wandryng' is, I think, a happier prospect for the future than the empty monocultural desert dotted with barricaded nature reserves that seems to be the dream of many planners.

The movement back to the land is in fact already under way. For many people it is the turning into a way of life of what began as a recreation, a voluntary adoption of the low-intensity, marginal practices that were the traditional mediation between man and the natural world. In some parts of the country – in East Anglia, Dorset, Herefordshire, central Wales – the growing clusters of farm museums, craftsmen working with natural materials, ecologically-run communes, smallholdings returned to organic husbandry are already beginning to amount to an alternative rural economy. We could pick many examples, but I think it is the story of the rake factory in Whelnetham, Suffolk, that most graphically illustrates the way these new variations on ancient themes can influence the fortunes of the natural landscape.

For nearly a century this small village craft-shop manufactured mallets and scythe-handles and rakes from wood cut in the medieval coppices of Felsham Hall Wood (see page 74). By providing a market for the cut poles it ensured that the practice of coppicing continued in this wood long after it had disappeared from most of East Anglia. Then, in 1967, suddenly and unexpectedly, the bulldozers moved into the wood. Half of it had already been cleared before local residents realized what was happening. But they acted promptly and determinedly, and it was largely their dedication that prevented 800 years of history being destroyed at a stroke, and their generosity that helped the Society for the Promotion of Nature Reserves (now the SPNC) to purchase the remaining 125 acres (50 hectares) for the nation. At the same time a local doctor bought the factory and ensured the continuance of the ancient symbiosis between wood and workshop. A few years later the factory was purchased by another local benefactor, this time a public relations specialist with a private enthusiasm for ancient crafts and Victorian machinery. It continued to prosper, and the wood it bought from Felsham Hall Wood helped pay for a woodman to cut the coppice in winter.

But in 1976 the factory was faced with another crisis – this time, ironically, of entirely natural origins. Two summers of severe drought and disastrous grass crops had caused a slump in the demand for scythes and rakes, and the factory came close to shutting down. But, by a dogged application of his professional skills, the owner was able at the last minute to secure what must be the most improbable outlet ever found for coppice products. He won a contract for the manufacture of many thousands of ash milking-stools for use in a European-wide advertising campaign for a famous brand of jeans. The amount of wood needed was so large that he was able not only to guarantee a continuing market for ash poles from Felsham Hall Wood, but to import them from coppices as far afield as Dorset.

I have a feeling that John Clare, whose nostalgia for the lost spontaneity of his relationship with nature always fell short of piety, would have hugely enjoyed the nonsense of this. And such alliances between old practices and modern enterprise may prove an equally effective antidote to the more sickly of our own pastoral longings, as well as being one of the most promising ways forward for conservation. The natural landscape is a living record of our history, and we would be doing it a disservice if we did not try to contribute to it our contemporary gifts of invention, wit and opportunism. The capacity for such embodiments, as we have seen, is the unique and perennial magic of living communities.

THE HOME FRONT

Yet all this economic and administrative activity will be pointless – and quite likely fruitless – if it does not have the support and active involvement of the whole community. Conservation begins precisely where the pain and destruction of modern development are most keenly felt – in the parish, that 'indefinable territory to which we feel we belong, which we have the measure of'. I've often wondered (I hope with not too much scientific irreverence) whether it might be possible to draw up a list of 'community indicator species', an inventory of those plants and animals and natural features that people, wherever they live, find the greatest pleasure in sharing their lives with, and miss most when they disappear. I have a feeling that it would not be so very different from the catalogue of endangered features that I have drawn up in this book by the use of rather more detached lines of argument.

Certainly the parish 'key sites' – the boundary hedges and old tracks, the local common, the meeting-place trees and village ponds – are features with which we are already very familiar. They are also features which the local community is uniquely placed to protect, either formally, through parish organizations, or through the informal business of day-to-day living. Even features of wider interest often stand a better chance of being saved because of contacts between a landowner and his neighbours than because of any pressures from outside.

Parish councils already have responsibility for the management of village greens, and they could do much to enhance their natural attractiveness by arranging grazing or hay-cutting regimes. If the recommendations of the Royal Commission on Common Land are eventually ratified, they could also take an important role in managing local commons. They might even begin cutting wood from them again, or purchase (or plant up on waste ground) a 'community wood', along the lines of the communally-owned forests of Switzerland in which clear-felling has been prohibited for more than 100 years.[144] A ten-acre wood, cut on a coppice rotation of an acre a year, would produce an annual crop of more than ten tons of firewood for an indefinite period. In modern wood-burning stoves, this is more than enough to heat a village hall or school for the whole year.

The parish church can also play an important role. The churchyard often contains the last expanse of unimproved grassland in the community, and the walls and gravestones can carry fascinating and attractive communities of lichens. Even in the driest areas of East Anglia, most medieval churchyards hold between thirty and forty different species.

Yet it is the efforts which parishioners make on their own initiative that may have the most permanent and significant effects. There is the story of the Gospel Oak at Polstead in Suffolk, where the villagers planted out a new tree from the acorns of the mighty oak – probably the oldest in England when it finally collapsed early this century – under which the Saxon followers of St Cedd preached in the seventh century. A service is still held under the new tree on St Cedd's day. There was the local joiner in the Lincolnshire village of Gosberton who, one day in 1967, took it upon himself to restore the local pond. With the help of friends he turned what had become a rat-infested rubbish-tip into a community so rich that two years later the Lincolnshire Trust bought it as a nature reserve.[145] There is the village near my home that won a 'best-kept village' award in 1979 largely on the strength that it had *not* reduced its roadside verges to manicured lawns – an outcome which did credit to participants and judges alike. Next to it is the village which has set up what must be one of the very few wood-pastures created this century, by fencing their overgrown down-land common and installing a herd of Soay sheep. And perhaps most moving of all is the famous story of the three pairs of bee-eaters that nested in a Sussex sand-pit in the summer of 1955. It was the first time these brilliant, harlequin-plumaged Mediterranean birds had ever bred in Britain, and the local people took them into their hearts, tolerating with great concern and dignity the influx of sightseers who came to marvel at this benediction on a glorious summer. Years afterwards Garth Christian found that the memory of the visitation still lingered in the neighbourhood. Every time he visited a local school to lecture he would find children raising their hands to say, 'Please, sir, in the village where I live, we had bee-eaters.'[146]

John Fowles once described nature as 'the poetry of survival', and went on to say: 'The greatest reality is that the watcher has survived and the watched survives. . . . Nobody who has comprehended this can feel alone in nature, can ever feel the absolute hostility of time.'[146] In improbable encounters like those with the bee-eaters – privileged, unpredictable, yet in their moment profoundly meaningful – we can begin to see the wider cultural meaning that nature holds for us. Yet we can feel it in the ordinary day-to-day experiences, too, in the shared hardships of winter, and in the return of the swallows and swifts in the spring.

As I write these last pages I can see the swifts milling above our parish church, gathering for their departure. It is the saddest moment of the year for me and I know that next May I will be fretting over the empty sky, wondering if they will ever return. They nest in the church, which was built in 1222, and in the smaller Baptist chapel nearby, which dates from 1864. More live in the eccentric eaves of the Victorian terrace cottages which crowd along the railway and, with nice irony, in the roof of a 1930s insecticide factory by the canal. How good it would be if we also found room for them in our modern buildings (as they do in Amsterdam, where re-roofing is illegal unless access for swifts is retained).[11]

I cannot quite see them from where I am sitting, but just beyond the parish church there will be swallows hawking over the moats of our ruined Norman castle. They nest just 100 yards away, on the iron girders of a bridge that carries the main Birmingham to Euston railway line, and in their short journeys for food are bridging a thousand years of history. Such is the territorial loyalty of these birds that they are quite likely the descendants of the tribe that must have nested in the castle outbuildings in the eleventh century.

And just beyond the castle I can make out the crest of our common, the scene in 1866 of one of the most celebrated victories over enclosure. That was the year Lord Brownlow fenced off over 400 acres of Berkhamsted Common. The legality of the action was dubious, and the immorality quite clear and, in the early hours of 7 March, 130 London navvies hired by the commoners marched up from the station and tore down the three miles of iron railings. Part of the area they liberated was an ancient wood-pasture, whose extraordinary beech pollards still survive – the direct descendants of trees that were being cut by the Saxons long before the Normans christened them the 'foreign wood' . . . .

It is at this point, remembering how my own townspeople – men, women and children – flocked up to the common that March day 100 years ago, and picked their token sprigs of gorse to celebrate that the place was their own again, that, for me, the temporizing and compromise have to stop. I know that we will have to fight the battle for our common, and for much else, all over again, against forms of enclosure more insidious and less easily undone than Lord Brownlow's fences. The intricate fabric of our landscape is the result of a weaving together of human and natural life that spans five millennia. It has incorporated the growth of human settlement, foreign invasion, the building of castles and churches, even the coming of the railways and the canals, and still the thread has stayed intact. It will not be able to incorporate the irreversible changes threatening it today.

We cannot just casually replace one thing by another. A plantation will not 'do' for an ancient wood. A dandelion cannot stand in for a primrose. When the swifts return it is crucial that they are *swifts*, not starlings, and that they are *returning*. They become, for their brief stay, a symbolic reminder – as the whole natural world is, in a way – that the alternative to progress is not stagnation but *renewal*. This is. the revelation that Ted Hughes celebrated in his own tribute to the swifts' return:

> They've made it again,
> Which means the globe's still working, the Creation's
> Still waking refreshed, our summer's
> Still all to come –
> And here they are, here they are again. . . .

> From 'Swifts'[147]

Directory of Organizations

Compiled by Philip Oswald
and David Withrington

*Members of the public may join.

BOTANICAL SOCIETY OF THE BRITISH ISLES*

c/o Department of Botany, British Museum (Natural History), Cromwell Road, London SW7 5BD

The BSBI, the principal botanical society in Britain, is an association of amateur and professional botanists whose common interest lies in the study of British vascular plants (flowering plants, ferns and related groups). Besides publishing a journal, *Watsonia*, and other literature and arranging conferences, symposia and field meetings, it has been responsible for organizing the Distribution Maps Scheme (which culminated in the publication in 1962 of *Atlas of the British Flora*). It also campaigns for the conservation of the British flora, pressing for legislation, collaborating in surveys, and producing posters and leaflets with the financial support of the NCC and the WWF (British National Appeal).

BRITISH TRUST FOR CONSERVATION VOLUNTEERS LTD*

10–14 Duke Street, Reading, Berkshire RG1 4RU

The BTCV was established in 1970 to consolidate the work of the Conservation Corps founded by the Council for Nature in 1959. It now operates the National Conservation Corps and eight regional offices; some 115 local groups are affiliated. The Trust promotes and executes practical conservation work for wildlife and amenity undertaken by young volunteers over sixteen years of age. The work takes the form of residential and weekend tasks on nature reserves, historic sites, amenity areas and urban land. Instruction is given in various skills such as tree-planting, hedging, ditching and maintenance of tools.

COUNCIL FOR THE PROTECTION OF RURAL ENGLAND*

4 Hobart Place, London SW1W 0HY.

The CPRE was formed in 1926 (as the Council for the Preservation of Rural England) to improve, protect and preserve the rural scenery and amenities of the English countryside and its towns and villages. It provides advice and seeks to influence public opinion. It also investigates, and when necessary makes representations about, development proposals and schemes affecting the countryside. The CPRE has forty-two branches and county associations. The Association for the Protection of Rural Scotland and the Council for the Protection of Rural Wales fulfil similar functions.

COUNTRYSIDE COMMISSION

John Dower House, Crescent Place, Cheltenham, Gloucestershire GL50 3RA.

The Countryside Commission was established by the Countryside Act 1968, replacing the National Parks Commission. It is financed through the Department of the Environment. It keeps under review all matters relating to the conservation and enhancement of landscape beauty and amenity in England and Wales and to the provision and improvement of facilities for enjoyment of the countryside, including the need to secure access for open-air recreation. The Commission designates National Parks (of which there are ten in England and Wales) and Areas of Outstanding Natural Beauty, submits proposals for long-distance footpaths, gives grants for tree-planting and other projects, and encourages the provision of country parks and picnic sites. It also promotes the Country Code and provides an information service. Examples of the Commission's experimental projects are the Upland Management Experiments, the Demonstration Farms Project and the Urban Fringe Experiment.

COUNTRYSIDE COMMISSION FOR SCOTLAND

Battleby, Redgorton, Perth PH1 3EW

The Commission was set up to exercise functions conferred under the Countryside (Scotland) Act 1967 for the provision, development and improvement of facilities for enjoyment of the Scottish countryside and for the conservation and enhancement of its natural beauty and amenity.

COUNTRYSIDE REVIEW COMMITTEE

c/o Department of the Environment, Tollgate House, Houlton Street, Bristol BS2 9DJ

The CRC was established in 1974 and completed its work in 1979. It was chaired and serviced by the Department of the Environment. Its members, who served in a personal capacity, included officers of that Department, of the Ministry of Agriculture, Fisheries and Food, of the Department of Transport, of the Welsh Office and of the main public agencies concerned – the Countryside Commission, Nature Conservancy Council, Development Commission, Forestry Commission and Sports Council. The terms of reference of the Committee were (in summary) to review the state of the countryside in England and Wales and the pressures upon it; to examine existing policies; to consider whether changes of policy or practice were necessary to reconcile objectives such as agricultural production with the conservation of the countryside, the enhancement of its natural beauty and its enjoyment by the public; and to make recommendations. The Committee produced an introductory discussion paper, *The Countryside – Problems and Policies*, and four topic papers, the last of which was *Conservation and the Countryside Heritage*, published in September 1979. These are available from government bookshops.

DEPARTMENT OF AGRICULTURE AND FISHERIES
FOR SCOTLAND

Chesser House, 500 Gorgie Road, Edinburgh EH11 3AW

The DAFS is responsible for the promotion of agriculture and the fishing industry in Scotland. The Department administers the Deer (Scotland) Act 1959. As regards fisheries, its duties include participation in international arrangements for conservation and other aspects of fishing and in EEC negotiations on fisheries policy, financial support for the fishing industry, assistance for fishery harbours, scientific research and the protection of Scottish fisheries by the Department's fleet of fishery cruisers.

DEPARTMENT OF THE ENVIRONMENT

2 Marsham Street, London SW1P 3EB

The DoE has a wide range of responsibilities, all concerned with the physical environment. These include co-ordination of all government work on the prevention of environmental pollution (with special responsibility for clean air and the control of noise, wastes and water pollution) together with the protection of Ancient Monuments and Historic Buildings, and policy on urban conservation and the conservation and recreational use of the countryside. But the Department also has overall responsibility for other major policy areas such as housing, inner city renewal, new towns, the construction industry, the structure and function of local government, and the system of land-use planning.

In Scotland, Wales and Northern Ireland many of the Department's functions are carried out by the Scottish Development Department, the Welsh Office and the Department of the Environment for Northern Ireland respectively.

EUROPEAN ENVIRONMENTAL BUREAU

Vautierstraat 31, 1040 Brussels, Belgium

The EEB was established in 1975 and is a federation of over forty national non-governmental organizations concerned with environmental conservation in the member countries of the EEC. Its main function has been to lobby the EEC institutions and member governments on matters of environmental policy. The EEB aims to promote an equitable and sustainable lifestyle based upon the conservation of the environment and restoration and better use of human and natural resources. UK-based members include the Civic Trust, the Conservation Society, the Council for Environmental Conservation (CoEnCo), the Council for the Protection of Rural England, Friends of the Earth, the

International Institute for Environment and Development, and the Town and Country Planning Association.

FORESTRY COMMISSION

231 Corstorphine Road, Edinburgh EH12 7AT

The Forestry Commission was established in 1919 and, under legislation now consolidated in the Forestry Act 1967, is charged primarily with the production of timber for industry and, as secondary objectives, with the provision of recreational facilities, with wildlife management and with paying due regard to amenities of the countryside. As the forest Authority it is responsible for administering the grant scheme to private woodland owners, forestry research, the implementation of forestry legislation (mainly concerning plant health) and licensing the felling of growing trees. The Commission has a target rate of 3 per cent return on its own forestry operations. The ministers responsible for forestry policy are the Minister of Agriculture, Fisheries and Food, the Secretary of State for Scotland and the Secretary of State for Wales.

FRIENDS OF THE EARTH LTD*

9 Poland Street, London W1V 3DG

FOE was founded in the USA in 1969, and in 1970 opened an office in London. There are now member organizations in some twenty countries. In the UK there is a head office with over 150 local groups. FOE believes that human beings should live in harmony with, rather than at the expense of, the natural environment and that economic and social policies should be shaped with this in mind. The main accent in FOE has been on environmental action – from loft insulation and restoring derelict land to demonstrations against whale-hunting and campaigns for returnable bottles and better facilities for cyclists.

GREENPEACE LTD

Colombo Street, London SE1 8DP

Greenpeace was formed in 1971 to protest against nuclear tests in the Aleutian Islands. Its vessel *Greenpeace I* sailed into the testing site, and enough publicity was generated for the US Atomic Energy Commission to close down the site, making the entire island a bird sanctuary. Greenpeace's UK-based activities started in 1978 and have included intervention during the dumping of British radioactive waste in the Atlantic, confrontations with Spanish, Norwegian and Icelandic whaling fleets, and support for the campaign against grey seal culls in Orkney. Greenpeace does not have any formal membership but seeks public support for its activities. It is committed to non-violent direct action in defence of the environment.

INSTITUTE OF TERRESTRIAL ECOLOGY

68 Hills Road, Cambridge CB2 1LA

The ITE was established in 1973 (when the Nature Conservancy Council was set up) as an institute of the Natural Environment Research Council, its core being the research staff and stations of the former Nature Conservancy. The Institute's ecological research is partly fundamental (funded through the NERC from the Department of Education and Science) and partly commissioned by 'customer' organizations, including the NCC. Its Biological Records Centre at Monks Wood Experimental Station near Huntingdon originated in the Distribution Maps Scheme of the Botanical Society of the British Isles, but now covers a much wider field.

INTERNATIONAL UNION FOR CONSERVATION OF NATURE AND NATURAL RESOURCES*

Avenue du Mont Blanc, CH-1196 Gland, Switzerland

The IUCN was formed in 1948 as a union of sovereign states, government agencies and non-governmental organizations, and now has members in about a hundred countries. Individuals may become friends, associates or benefactors of the Union. The IUCN draws on the knowledge and experience of a global network of more than 700 scientists and professionals through six Commissions covering threatened species, protected areas, ecology, environmental education, environmental planning, and environmental policy, law and administration. It provides the secretariat for the Convention on International Trade in Endangered Species of Wild Fauna and Flora and the Convention on Wetlands of International Importance especially as Waterfowl Habitat. It works closely with the United Nations Environment Programme and other UN agencies. The IUCN has a special relationship with the WWF, originally set up as its fund-raising arm. It organizes programmes of action for the protection and rational use of the planet's living resources of plants and animals – particularly through the concept of 'eco-development', which forms the backbone of *A World Conservation Strategy*, published in March 1980. The 'lead' member of the IUCN in the UK is the NCC.

MAMMAL SOCIETY*

62 London Road, Reading, Berkshire, RG1 5AS

The Mammal Society was formed in 1954. It is concerned with the procurement of factual information on mammals rather than their protection and conservation. To this end it organizes field studies on distribution, behaviour and ecology of mammals. It has sub-groups, for example the Bat Group, for members with special interests.

MINISTRY OF AGRICULTURE, FISHERIES AND FOOD

Whitehall Place, London SW1A 2HH

The MAFF is responsible in England for administering government policy for agriculture, horticulture and fishing industries. In association with other bodies in the UK, it is responsible for the administration of the EEC Common Agricultural Policy and for various national support schemes. It also administers schemes for the control and eradication of animal and plant diseases and the improvement and drainage of agricultural land. Some of the MAFF's responsibilities for animal health extend to Scotland and Wales. Its Agricultural Development and Advisory Service (ADAS) gives advice to landowners, farmers and growers on a wide range of agricultural matters including available grants.

NATIONAL TRUST*

42 Queen Anne's Gate, London SW1H 9AS

The National Trust was founded in 1895 and works for the

preservation of places of historic interest and natural beauty in England, Wales and Northern Ireland. The Trust's 236 properties include nearly 100 large country houses, sixteen castles, sixty-eight gardens, forty-five nature reserves and fifteen country parks. In its estates of more than 400,000 acres (160,000 hectares) – making it the largest private landowner in Britain – there are nearly 400 miles of coastline and areas of downland, moorland, woodland, farmland and waterways. The Trust has over ninety local groups and runs Acorn Camps, where young people carry out practical conservation tasks. Its total membership is 600,000.

NATIONAL TRUST FOR SCOTLAND*

5 Charlotte Square, Edinburgh EH2 4DU

The NTS was founded in 1931 to promote the care of fine buildings, historic places and beautiful countryside in Scotland. The Trust's properties cover over 80,000 acres (32,000 hectares) and include castles and cottages, historic sites and beauty spots, mountains and islands (including Ben Lawers and St Kilda National Nature Reserves). The NTS has some 90,000 members.

NATURAL ENVIRONMENT RESEARCH COUNCIL

Polaris House, North Star Avenue, Swindon, Wiltshire SN2 1EU

The NERC was established by Royal Charter in 1965 under the Science and Technology Act and is financed through the Department of Education and Science. It encourages, plans and executes research in those sciences – physical, geological and biological – that relate to man's natural environment and its resources. The Council's component bodies include the ITE and the Sea Mammal Research Unit. Among the Council's duties is that of providing the Secretary of State with scientific advice on matters related to the management of seal populations.

NATURE CONSERVANCY COUNCIL

19-20 Belgrave Square, London SW1X 8PY

The NCC was established by Act of Parliament in 1973 'for the purposes of nature conservation and fostering the understanding thereof'. It is financed through the DoE. (Its predecessor, the Nature Conservancy, was set up in 1949 and was from 1965 to 1973 a component body of the NERC.) The Act defines nature conservation as 'the conservation of flora, fauna or geological or physiographical features'. The NCC's main functions are establishing and managing National Nature Reserves in Great Britain – of which there are nearly 170 at present, covering over 300,000 acres (120,000 hectares) – advising ministers and government departments, providing advice and disseminating knowledge about nature conservation, and commissioning or supporting relevant research. The NCC has a number of specific duties such as advising local authorities about establishing Local Nature Reserves, notifying Sites of Special Scientific Interest (SSSIs) to planning authorities, and granting or approving certain licences in connection with wildlife legislation. It has the power to make grants to local authorities, voluntary bodies and others towards the cost of projects it would itself have power to carry out, and to enter into management agreements over SSSIs (which may include a financial contribution). The NCC is governed by a Council whose members are appointed by the Secretary of State for the Environment. Its Great Britain headquarters are in London, and it also has headquarters for England, Scotland and Wales and fifteen Regional Offices.

NATURE CONSERVATION TRUSTS*

c/o Society for the Promotion of Nature Conservation, The Green, Nettleham, Lincoln LN2 2NR

The Trusts are independent incorporated bodies registered as charities. They aim to promote the conservation of the natural features of the countryside by all possible means – by the establishment and management of nature reserves, through co-operation with statutory bodies, landowners and other organizations and individuals, and through education and publicity. Thirty-eight Trusts (many of them called Naturalists' or Conservation Trusts) cover England and Wales on a county or regional basis, and the Scottish Wildlife Trust has branches throughout Scotland. There are also Trusts in Northern Ireland and the Isle of Man. The first of the Trusts, the Norfolk Naturalists' Trust, was established in 1926. Between them the Trusts administer about 1000 nature reserves and have 120,000 members.

ROYAL SOCIETY FOR THE PROTECTION OF BIRDS*

The Lodge, Sandy, Bedfordshire, SG19 2DL

Founded in 1889, the RSPB gained a Royal Charter in 1904. Its aim is to encourage conservation of wild birds by developing public interest in their beauty and place in nature. Its work includes scientific research, enforcement of protection laws, management of some eighty reserves, and educational work, including publishing and film production. It runs a Young Ornithologists' Club, with its own magazine. The RSPB has the largest membership of the UK's voluntary nature conservation bodies (over 300,000).

SOCIETY FOR THE PROMOTION OF NATURE CONSERVATION*

The Green, Nettleham, Lincoln LN2 2NR

The SPNC was founded in 1912 as the Society for the Promotion of Nature Reserves (SPNR) and incorporated by Royal Charter in 1916. A new Charter granted in 1976 broadened its objectives. It seeks to promote the conservation, study and appreciation of nature and the establishment and management of nature reserves. It is the national association of the Nature Conservation Trusts, each of which is a corporate member of the Society and appoints a member to its Council. The SPNC recently adopted the WATCH Club as its junior section.

WILDFOWL TRUST*

Slimbridge, Gloucestershire GL2 7BT

The Wildfowl Trust was founded by Sir Peter Scott in 1946 and now has five centres with collections of ducks, geese and swans on view to the public as well as refuges for wild birds in the Ouse Washes and the Solway Firth. The Trust is concerned with the scientific study of wildfowl in the wild state and in captivity, and related investigations; with the propagation of wildfowl in captivity, especially those species which are in danger of extinction; and with the education of the public by all available means to a greater appreciation of wildfowl in particular and of nature in general. Its research department co-ordinates the National Wildfowl Counts and houses the International Waterfowl Research Bureau.

WOODLAND TRUST*

Butterbrook, Harford, Ivybridge, Devon PL21 0JQ

The Woodland Trust was registered as a charity in 1972 to protect, by ownership, areas of broadleaved trees. It manages over twenty-five woodlands in a way that produces a valuable visual amenity and wildlife habitat. Where necessary, existing woods are restored to indigenous broadleaved trees and specially acquired areas are re-established by planting. A new tree is planted for every new member.

WORLD WILDLIFE FUND*

British National Appeal, 29–31 Greville Street, London EC1N 8AX

The WWF was founded in Switzerland in 1961 and has now established National Appeals in over thirty countries. It raises money for a programme of projects to protect endangered plants, animals and their habitats and to promote public awareness of wildlife conservation. The British National Appeal organizes a Wildlife Youth Service for young people between the ages of five and eighteen, particularly in school groups. Part of the money raised in the UK is sent to support international activities. Recent WWF campaigns include 'Operation Tiger', 'Tropical Rain Forest Campaign' and 'The Seas Must Live'. The WWF works closely with the IUCN, which provides much of the scientific advice for its activities.

WORLDWATCH INSTITUTE

1776 Massachusetts Avenue N.W., Washington D.C. 20036, USA

Worldwatch Institute is an independent, non-profit-making research organization created to analyse and to focus attention on global problems. The Institute started to publish Worldwatch Papers in 1975, and there are now more than thirty titles in this series, which is available on subscription. They include Eric Eckholm's *Disappearing Species – The Social Challenge*, published as Paper 22 in 1978.

References and Further Reading

1. John Clare, from *The Autobiography* (quoted in *Rainbows Fleas and Flowers*, ed. Geoffrey Grigson, John Baker, 1971).
2. *Sunday Times*, 11 June 1978.
3. NCC, *The Management of Grey Seals in Scotland*, internal document, 1979.
4. IUCN, *A World Conservation Strategy* (first draft), IUCN, 1978.
5. Eric Eckholm, *Disappearing Species – the Social Challenge*, Worldwatch Paper 22, Washington, 1978.
6. Lewis Thomas, 'Natural Man' in *The Lives of a Cell*, Viking, New York, 1974.
7. F. H. Perring and L. Farrell (eds.), British Red Data Books: I *Vascular Plants*, SPNC, 1977.
8. Annie Dillard, *Pilgrim at Tinker Creek*, Jonathan Cape, 1975.
9. John Parslow, *Breeding Birds of Britain and Ireland*, T. and A. D. Poyser, 1973.
10. Derek Ratcliffe, 'The Status of the Peregrine in Great Britain', *Bird Study*, 10, 1963.
11. For extensive surveys of the current status and distribution of British breeding birds, see: J. T. R. Sharrock, *The Atlas of Breeding Birds in Britain and Ireland*, British Trust for Ornithology/Irish Wildbird Conservancy, 1976.
12. See, for instance, Robert Hudson, *Threatened Birds of Europe*, Macmillan, 1975. (Based on a 1973 report to the Council of Europe by the International Council for Bird Preservation.)
13. Richard Mabey, Introduction to Gilbert White, *The Natural History of Selborne*, Penguin, 1977.
14. W. H. Hudson, *Nature in Downland*, London, 1923.
15. For a background of Henslow's life, see: Jean Russell-Gebbett, *Henslow of Hitcham*, Terence Dalton, 1977.

16. Alec Bull, 'A century of change', *Suffolk Natural History*, 17 (3) 1977.
17. Derek Ratcliffe, 'Thoughts towards a philosophy of nature conservation', *Biological Conservation*, 9(1), 1976.
18. Garth Christian, *Down the Long Wind*, George Newnes, 1961.
19. J. M. Fletcher, 'Annual rings in modern and medieval times', in M. G. Morris and F. H. Perring (eds.), *The British Oak*, published for the BSBI by E. W. Classey, 1974.
20. R. H. Richens, Studies on *Ulmus*, e.g. 1. 'The Range of Variation in East Anglian Elms', *Watsonia*, 3, 1955, etc. 'Essex elms', in *Forestry*, 40, 1969, gives a full list of the earlier papers.
21. Gerald Wilkinson, *Epitaph for the Elm*, Hutchinson, 1978.
22. B. Conrad and W. Poltz, *Report on Bird Protection in the EEC*, Möggingen, 1975.
23. NCC Press Office, file note, January 1979.
24. C. Bonsey, 'The Problems of Recreation on Sites of Archaeological and Ecological Interest', in *Old Grassland - Its Archaeological and Ecological Importance*, eds. J. Sheail and T. C. E. Wells, Nature Conservancy, 1969.
25. Roy Gregory, *The Price of Amenity*, Macmillan, 1971.
26. ICI eventually gave a £100,000 grant for a research project into the ecology of Upper Teesdale. The results are in: A. R. Clapham (ed.), *Upper Teesdale: The Area and its Natural History*, Collins, 1978.
27. House of Lords Debates (1966–7) 280, Cols. 801–65.
28. *Horizon*, BBC 2, 20 January, 1978.
29. D. L. Hawksworth, F. Rose and B. J. Coppins, 'Changes in the lichen flora of England and Wales attributable to pollution of the air by sulphur dioxide', in *Air Pollution and Lichens*, eds. B. W. Ferry, M. S. Baddeley and D. L. Hawksworth.
For general surveys of lichen ecology see the rest of the previous symposium, and: David Richardson, *The Vanishing Lichens*, David & Charles, 1975, and Oliver Gilbert, *Wildlife Conservation and Lichens*, Devon Trust for Nature Conservation Ltd, 1975.
30. Francis Rose, 'The epiphytes of oak', in M. G. Morris and F. H. Perring (eds.), *The British Oak*, published for the BSBI by E. W. Classey, 1974.
31. Stephen Potter and Laurens Sargent, *Pedigree: Words from Nature*, Collins, 1973.
32. Documents relating to the Inquiry over Dover District Coun-

cil Tree Preservation Orders Nos. 11/ 12/ and 14/1977. DoE File Nos. SE2/5275/146/10, 11, 13 and 14.

33. Oliver Rackham, *Trees and Woodland in the British Landscape*, Dent, 1977. The best introduction to the historical ecology of woodlands. See also *Ancient Woodlands: the Constant Spring*, Edward Arnold, 1980.

34. *The Forestry Commission's Objectives*, Forestry Commission, 1975.

35. Oliver Rackham, *Hayley Wood: Its History and Ecology*, Cambridgeshire and Isle of Ely Naturalists' Trust, 1975.

36. See, for instance, the works of H. C. Darby, particularly *Domesday England*, Cambridge University Press, 1977.

37. Phyllida Rixon, 'History and Former Woodland Management', in *Bedford Purlieus: its history, ecology and management* eds. G. F. Peterken and R. C. Welch, ITE, 1975.

38. G. M. L. Locke, *Census of Woodlands, 1965–67*, Forestry Commission, HMSO, 1970.

39. G. F. Peterken, 'Long-term changes in the woodlands of Rockingham Forest and other areas', *Journal of Ecology*, 64, March 1976.

40. George Peterken, along with Oliver Rackham, has been a major architect of modern woodland conservation theory. His ideas about 'developmental' factors are outlined in: G. F. Peterken, 'Developmental factors in the management of British woodlands', *Quarterly Journal of Forestry*, 68, 1974, and 'General principles for Nature Conservation in British woodlands', *Forestry*, 50, (1) 1977, and Habitat conservation priorities in British and European woodlands', *Biological Conservation*, 11, 1977.

41. G. F. Peterken, 'A method of assessing woodland flora for conservation using indicator species', *Biological Conservation*, 6 (4) 1974.

42. L. J. Mayes, *The History of Chairmaking in High Wycombe*, Routledge & Kegan Paul, 1960.

43. P. Stuttard and K. Williamson, 'Habitat requirements of the nightingale', *Bird Study*, 18 1971.

44. P. F. Garthwaite, *Policies, management and marketing of hardwoods in south-east England*. Report for the NCC, 1976.

45. M. G. Morris and F. H. Perring (eds.), *The British Oak*, published for the BSBI by E. W. Classey, 1974.

46. Francis Rose and Paul T. Harding, 'Pasture woodlands in lowland Britain, and their importance for the conservation of

the epiphytes and invertebrates associated with old trees'. Report for the NCC, 1978.

47. *Kilvert's Diary 1870–1879: Selections from the Diary of the Rev. Francis Kilvert,* edited by William Plomer, Cape, 1944.

48. R. C. Steele, *Wildlife Conservation in Woodlands,* Forestry Commission, HMSO, 1972. An excellent general survey of the conservation measures that can be taken *inside* woods.

49. I. Newton and D. Moss, 'Breeding birds of Scottish pinewoods', in *Native Pinewoods of Scotland,* eds. R. G. H. Bunce and J. N. R. Jeffers, ITE, 1977. See the remainder of this symposium for accounts of regeneration etc. in the Scottish pinewoods.

50. G. F. Peterken and C. R. Tubbs, 'Woodland regeneration in the New Forest, Hampshire, since 1650', *J. App. Ecol.,* 2, 1965.

51. E. J. Hobsbawm and George Rude, *Captain Swing,* Lawrence & Wishart, 1969.

52. *New Agricultural Landscapes,* Countryside Commission, 1974.

53. *New Agricultural Landscapes, a discussion paper.* CCP 76a, Countryside Commission, 1974.

54. NCC, *Nature Conservation and Agriculture,* 1977.

55. Katie Williams, 'Plague in the Wheat', *The Countryman,* Summer, 1979.

56. E. Pollard, M. D. Hooper and N. W. Moore, *Hedges,* Collins, 1974. The most comprehensive book on the history and ecology of hedgerows.

57. Felix Paturi, *Nature, Mother of Invention: the Engineering of Plant Life,* Thames & Hudson, 1976.

58. Max Hooper, 'The Botanical Importance of our Hedgerows', in *The Flora of a Changing Britain,* ed. F. H. Perring, published for the BSBI by E. W. Classey, 1970.

59. G. Else, J. Felton and A. Stubbs, *The Conservation of Bees and Wasps,* NCC, 1978.

60. *Hedgerow and Park Timber and Woods of under Five Acres 1951,* Forestry Commission, HMSO, 1953.

61. P. N. G. Hardy and J. R. Matthews, *Farmland Tree Survey of Norfolk,* Norfolk County Council, 1977.

62. E. Duffey *et al., Grassland Ecology and Wildlife Management,* Chapman & Hall, 1974. (The introductory chapters provide an excellent account of the history of grassland.)

63. Royal Commission on Environmental Pollution, *Agriculture and Pollution,* HMSO, 1979.

64. J. W. Blackwood and C. R. Tubbs, 'A quantitative study of chalk grassland in England', *Biological Conservation*, 3 (1) October 1970.
65. A. Carys Jones, *The Conservation of Chalk Downland in Dorset*, Dorset County Council, 1973.
66. *A Study of Exmoor*, HMSO, 1978.
67. R. G. Stapledon, *The Plough-up Policy and Ley Farming*, Faber, 1939.
68. C. H. Gimingham, *Ecology of Heathlands*, Chapman & Hall, 1972.
69. D. N. McVean and J. Lockie, *Ecology and Land Use in Upland Scotland*, Edinburgh, 1969.
70. NCC, *Second report covering the period 1 April 1975–31 March 1976*, HMSO, 1976.
71. Graham Harvey, 'Grassland production and "bag nitrogen" ', *New Scientist*, 15 February 1979.
72. C. Newbold, 'Wetlands and agriculture', in *Conservation and Agriculture*, eds. J. Davidson and R. Lloyd, Wiley, 1977.
73. For a good case study of the problems raised by estuarine conservation see: Dee Estuary Conservation Group, *The Dee Estuary: a surviving wilderness*, DECG, 1976.
74. NCC South-West Region, *The Somerset Wetlands Project – A Consultation Paper*, 1977, and *Summary of Responses*, 1978.
75. Bryan Sage, 'The Rook in Britain', *New Scientist*, 29 June 1978.
76. J. Sheail and T. C. E. Wells, 'Old Grassland – its Archaeological and Ecological Importance', *Monks Wood Experimental Station, Symposium No. 5*, Nature Conservancy 1969.
77. NCC, West Midlands Region, *Lowland Meadow Sites in the South-West Midlands*, First Report 1973, Second Report 1975
78. William Cobbett, on the proposed enclosure of Horton Heath, Dorset (*circa* 1830). Quoted in W. G. Hoskins and L. Dudley Stamp, *The Common Lands of England and Wales*, Collins, 1963. Horton Heath remained unenclosed and is now a Site of Special Scientific Interest.
79. C. E. M. Joad, 'The People's Claim', in *Britain and the Beast*, ed. Clough Williams Ellis, Readers' Union, 1938.
80. George Waterson, *Ospreys in Speyside*, RSPB, 1966.
81. Colin Tubbs, 'Poor substitute for wilderness', *Birds*, Summer 1979.

82. D. Lowenthal and H. C. Prime, *Geographical Review*, 55, 1965.
For different perspectives on the rights and preferences of the recreational public in the countryside, see, for instance: Marion Shoard, 'Recreation: the key to the survival of England's countryside', in *Future Landscapes*, ed. Malcolm MacEwan, published for the CPRE by Chatto & Windus, 1976; Chris Smith, *National Parks: a strategy for survival*, Fabian Tract 456, 1978; W. E. S. Mutch, *Public recreation in National Forests: a factual survey*, Forestry Commission, HMSO, 1968.
83. Countryside Commission, *Areas of Outstanding Natural Beauty: a discussion paper*, CCP 116, 1978.
84. W. G. Hoskins and L. Dudley Stamp, *The Common Lands of England and Wales*, Collins, 1963. The best account of the workings and history of the commons.
See also: D. R. Denman, R. A. Roberts and H. J. F. Smith, *Commons and Village Greens*, Leonard Hill, 1977; and Commons, Open Spaces and Footpaths Preservation Society, *Our Common Heritage*, 1978. Lord Eversley, *Commons, Forests and Footpaths*, 1910.
85. David Corke (ed.), *Epping Forest – the natural aspect*, Essex Field Club, 1978.
86. R. H. Gretton, 'Lot-meadow customs at Yarnton, Oxon.', *Economic Journal*, March 1910; and 'Historical notes on the lot-meadow customs at Yarnton, Oxon', *Economic Journal*, March 1912.
87. Eric Duffey, *Nature Reserves and Wildlife*, Heinemann, 1974.
88. Colin Tubbs, *The New Forest: an ecological history*, David & Charles, 1968.
See also: New Forest Joint Steering Committee, *Conservation of the New Forest*, 1971.
89. Royal Commission on Common Land, 1955–1958, *Report*, Cmnd 462, HMSO, 1958.
90. Duncan Mackay, 'Cliffe Marshes de-registration', *Journal of the Commons, Open Spaces and Footpaths Preservation Society*, Summer 1979.
91. J. E. Lowday and T. C. E. Wells, *The Management of Grasslands and Heathland in Country Parks*. A Report to the Countryside Commission prepared by the ITE, CCP 105, 1977.
92. A. D. Bradshaw, 'Conservation problems in the future', *Proceedings of the Royal Society of London*, B. 197, 1977.

93. W. G. Teagle, *The Endless Village*, NCC, West Midlands Region, 1978.
94. Lyndis Cole, *Nature Conservation in Urban Areas*, Report for the NCC, 1978.
95. Richard Mabey, *The Unofficial Countryside*, Collins, 1973.
96. E. F. Greenwood and R. P. Gemmell, 'Derelict industrial land as a habitat for rare plants in S. Lancs' (v.c. 59) and '. . . in W. Lancs' (v.c. 60), *Watsonia*, 12, 1978.
97. P. J. W. Langley and D. W. Yalden, 'The decline of the rarer carnivores in Great Britain during the nineteenth century', *Mammal Review*, 7 (3 & 4) 1977.
98. Leslie Brown, *British Birds of Prey*, Collins, 1976. Gives histories of all our breeding species.
99. Donald Watson, *The Hen Harrier*, T. and A. D. Poyser, 1977.
100. J. Sheail, *Nature in Trust, The History of Nature Conservation in Britain*, Blackie, 1976.
See also: David Elliston Allen, *The Naturalist in Britain: a social history*, Allen Lane, 1976.
101. *Protection of Birds Act 1954*, HMSO.
102. *Protection of Birds Act 1967*, HMSO.
103. *Badgers Act 1973*, HMSO.
104. Peter Hardy, *A Lifetime of Badgers*, David & Charles, 1975.
105. MAFF, *Bovine Tuberculosis in Badgers*, First Report, 1976, Second Report, 1977, Memorandum, 1977.
106. See, for instance: Dr N. P. W. Littler, 'Badgers: how the men from the ministry may be wrong', *The Times*, 13 March 1978; and David Coffey, 'Death to Badgers?', *New Scientist*, 17 November 1977.
107. *Conservation of Wild Creatures and Wild Plants Act 1975*, HMSO.
108. Rodney B. West, 'The Suffolk Otter Survey', *Suffolk Natural History*, 16 (6) 1975.
109. S. Macdonald and C. F. Mason, 'The status of the otter (*Lutra lutra*) in Norfolk', *Biological Conservation*, 9, 1976.
110. *Otters 1977*, Joint Otter Group, NCC/SPNC, 1977.
111. P. R. F. Chanin and D. J. Jefferies, 'The decline of the otter *Lutra lutra* in Britain: an analysis of hunting records and discussion of causes.' *Biological Journal of the Linnean Society*, 10, (3), September 1978.
112. Angela King, John Ottaway and Angela Potter, *The Declining Otter. A Guide to its Conservation*, Friends of the Earth, 1976.

113. *The Endangered Species Act*, 1973 (Public Law, 93 205; 87 Stat. 884), US Department of the Interior, 1973.

114. John Fowles, 'The Blinded Eye', *Animals*, January 1971.

115. Bert Axell, *Minsmere: Portrait of a Bird Reserve*, Hutchinson, 1977.

For a contrasting 'biography' of a National Nature Reserve, see Richard Williamson, *The Great Yew Forest: Kingley Vale – a National Nature Reserve*, Macmillan, 1978.

For theoretical discussions of the concept of nature reserves, see: V. Westhoff, 'New Criteria for Nature Reserves', *New Scientist*, 16 April 1970; and Eric Duffey, *Nature Reserves and Wildlife*, Heinemann, 1974.

116. Mary Gilham, 'Canal Corridors for Wildlife', in *Everyman's Nature Reserve*, ed. Eve Dennis, David and Charles, 1972.

117. C. Easton, 'Nature Reserves Programme of the Trusts/ SPNC' (paper presented to the SPNC conference on nature reserves, April 1978). The information in the rest of this paragraph is based on other papers given at this conference, including:

118. John Crudass, 'The RSPB and its reserves'.

119. John Fowles (ed.), *Steep Holm: a case history in the study of evolution*, published for the Kenneth Allsop Memorial Trust by the Dorset Publishing Co., 1978.

120. *Conservation of Nature in England and Wales*, Cmd 7122, HMSO, 1947.

121. *National Parks and Access to the Countryside Act 1949*, HMSO.

122. Derek Ratcliffe (ed.), *A Nature Conservation Review: The selection of biological sites of national importance to nature conservation in Britain*, 2 vols., Cambridge University Press, 1977.

123. *Nature Conservancy Council Act 1973*, HMSO.

124. *Countryside Act 1968*, HMSO.

125. A. G. Tansley, 'The conservation of British vegetation and species', in *The Changing Flora of Britain*, ed. J. E. Lousley, a 1952 symposium of the BSBI, proceedings published in 1963.

126. Aldo Leopold, *A Sand County Almanac*, Oxford University Press, 1949.

127. R. Larsen, 'Compatibility of forestry with conservation of the environment', 1978, (paper presented to the SPNC conference on natures reserves, April 1978).

128. Norman Moore, 'Nature Reserves – NCC viewpoint and policy', 1978, (paper presented to the SPNC conference on nature reserves, April 1978).

129. EEB, *Common Agricultural Policy: conclusions drawn by the EEB from a seminar on the Common Agricultural Policy*, September 1978.
130. See, for example *Nature Conservation and Planning*, Circular 108/77 (DoE) 150/77 (Welsh Office), HMSO, 1977.
131. A. M. Edwards and G. P. Wibberley, *An Agricultural Land Budget for Britain*, University of London, 1971.
132. Watkin Williams, 'UK food production: resources and alternatives', *New Scientist*, 8 December 1977.
133. Richard Fordham, 'Turning our farms into gardens', *New Society*, 8 July 1971.
134. MAFF, *Food from our own resources*, HMSO, 1975, and *Farming and the nation*, HMSO, 1979.
135. CRC, *The countryside – problems and policies. A discussion paper*, DoE, HMSO, 1976.
136. *Forestry Act 1967*, HMSO.
137. *Agriculture and the countryside*, Advisory Council for Agriculture and Horticulture in England and Wales, 1978.
138. Chilterns Standing Conference, *A Plan for the Chilterns*, 1971.
139. Forestry Commission, *Advice for woodland owners*, HMSO, 1977.
140. Countryside Commission, *Local authority tree planting programmes in the countryside*, Advisory Series 1, HMSO, 1977.
141. J. M. Way, 'Roadside verges and conservation in Britain: a review', *Biological Conservation*, 12, 1977.
142. N. Fairbrother, *New lives, new landscapes*, Architectural Press, 1970.
143. J. H. Hemsley, 'The National Trust and nature reserves', (paper presented to the SPNC conference on nature reserves, April 1978).
144. Garth Christian, *Tomorrow's Countryside*, Murray, 1966.
145. John Dyson, *Save the village pond*, Ford Motor Company for the Save the Village Pond Campaign, 1974.
146. Garth Christian, 'The Bee-eaters' in *Down the Long Wind*, George Newnes, 1961.
147. Ted Hughes, 'Swifts' in *Season Songs*, Faber, 1976.
For this last chapter see also: Peter Burns (ed.), *Do-it-yourself nature conservation*, Avon Community Council, Bristol, 1977; and W. G. Hoskins, *The making of the English landscape*, Hodder & Stoughton, 1955.

Index